Measures of Spirituality/Religiosity—Description of Concepts and Validation of Instruments

Measures of Spirituality/Religiosity—Description of Concepts and Validation of Instruments

Special Issue Editor

Arndt Büssing

MDPI • Basel • Beijing • Wuhan • Barcelona • Belgrade

Special Issue Editor
Arndt Büssing
Witten/Herdecke University
Germany

Editorial Office
MDPI
St. Alban-Anlage 66
4052 Basel, Switzerland

This is a reprint of articles from the Special Issue published online in the open access journal *Religions* (ISSN 2077-1444) from 2015 to 2017 (available at: https://www.mdpi.com/journal/religions/special_issues/measures-of-spirituality-religiosity)

For citation purposes, cite each article independently as indicated on the article page online and as indicated below:

LastName, A.A.; LastName, B.B.; LastName, C.C. Article Title. *Journal Name* **Year**, *Article Number, Page Range.*

ISBN 978-3-03897-758-2 (Pbk)
ISBN 978-3-03897-759-9 (PDF)

Cover image courtesy of unsplash.com user Yan Berthemy.

Contents

About the Special Issue Editor

Arndt Büssing (*1962) is a medical doctor and since 2010 full professor for "Quality of Life, Spirituality and Coping" at the Witten/Herdecke University (Germany). His research interests are (1) empirical studies on quality of life, spirituality and coping (i.e., spirituality as a resource to cope; spiritual needs; spiritual dryness), (2) non-pharmacological integrative medicine interventions to treat patients with chronic diseases (i.e., meditation, yoga), and (3) questionnaire development specifically in the field of spirituality and coping.

Editorial

Measures of Spirituality/Religiosity—Description of Concepts and Validation of Instruments

Arndt Büssing

Institute for Integrative Medicine, Faculty of Health, Witten/Herdecke University, Gerhard-Kienle-Weg 4, 58313 Herdecke, Germany; Arndt.Buessing@uni-wh.de

Academic Editor: Klaus Baumann
Received: 10 January 2017; Accepted: 10 January 2017; Published: 16 January 2017

Why do we need some more questionnaires to measure aspects of spirituality/religiosity when we already have so many well-tried instruments in use?

One answer is that research in this field is growing and that new research questions continuously do arise. Several of these new questions cannot be easily answered with the instruments designed for previous questions. The field is expanding and, consequently, the research topics.

A further answer is that several of the already established and conceptually very clear instruments are rather 'exclusive' as they are specific for distinct groups with circumscribed views and religious orientations. The disadvantage is that they are not inclusive enough to be used for persons with distinct spiritual views or even secular perspectives. To overcome this problem, multidimensional instruments were developed which cover existential, prosocial, religious and non-religious forms of spirituality, hope, peace and trust—and several more. The disadvantage of these 'inclusive' instruments is the fact that some are conceptually broad and rather unspecific, but they might be suited quite well for culturally and spiritually diverse populations when the intention is to compare such diverse groups. On the other hand, some of the instruments may be 'contaminated' with personality traits and dimensions of mental health and wellbeing, and thus the results might be 'false positive' because they do not measure specific aspects of spirituality (with the multiple attempts made so far to define it).

In fact, there is a multitude of definitions, ranging from 'exclusive' to 'inclusive' definitions. Two statements may exemplify this:

- Spirituality means "the succession of Christ (...) in a life enwrought by the Holy Spirit, which also includes the experience of the world and responsibility for the world" [1].
- Spirituality is "a search for the sacred" [2] and "has to do with the paths people take in their efforts to find, conserve, and transform the sacred in their lives." [3]

For research it might be unsatisfactory that researchers cannot rely on one consented definition. However, when the points of view are so heterogeneous, we may talk about different spiritualities (plural) which might be relevant for persons (either religious or non-religious). This approach opens the field of research and makes it even more attractive.

Further, we need conceptually plausible instruments for research, but also for practical use in various settings. Maybe there is not one perfect instrument to measure a multifaceted dimension such as spirituality, but several instruments, to cover: (1) the behavioral components of spirituality; (2) the attitude components; and (3) the 'background' (the numinous) which is often difficult enough to operationalize and to measure. We also need instruments to measure spiritual coping strategies and spiritual needs on the one hand, and spiritual wellbeing on the other hand, as independent and additional measures. We also need sensitive and intelligent cultural adaptations of established questionnaires in order to acquire data from different societies and cultures. However, we should retain the original items, structure and scaling in order to compare such findings later on.

This is the reason why more research on new instruments is needed as can be found in this Special Issue, and to stimulate a critical debate about their pros and cons.

Conflicts of Interest: The author declares no conflict of interest.

References

1. Jaspert, Bernd. *Spiritualität oder Frömmigkeit. Beiträge zur Begriffsklärung*. Nordhausen: Verlag Traugott Bautz, 2013.
2. Pargament, Kenneth I. *The Psychology of Religion and Coping*. New York: Guilford Press, 1997.
3. Zinnbauer, Brian J., Kenneth I. Pargament, and Allie B. Scott. "The Emerging Meanings of Religiousness and Spirituality: Problems and Prospects." *Journal of Personality* 67 (1999): 889–919. [CrossRef]

 *religions*

Article

Children's Spiritual Lives: The Development of a Children's Spirituality Measure

Kelsey Moore [1,*], Carlos Gomez-Garibello [2], Sandra Bosacki [3] and Victoria Talwar [1]

1   Department of Educational and Counseling Psychology, Faculty of Education, McGill University, Montréal, QC H3A 1Y2, Canada; victoria.talwar@mcgill.ca
2   Centre for Medical Education, Faculty of Medicine, McGill University, Montréal, QC H3A 1H3, Canada; carlos.gomez-garibello@mcgill.ca
3   Faculty of Education, Brock University, Catharines, ON L2S 3A1, Canada; sbosacki@brocku.ca
*   Correspondence: kelsey.moore@mail.mcgill.ca

Academic Editor: Arndt Büssing
Received: 7 March 2016; Accepted: 14 July 2016; Published: 25 July 2016

Abstract: Previous researchers who have studied children's spirituality have often used narrow measures that do not account for the rich spiritual experiences of children within a multi-faith context. In the current study, we describe the initial stages of development of a children's spirituality measure, in which items were derived from children's spiritual narratives. An exploratory factor analysis of the items revealed three main factors, including Comfort (Factor 1), Omnipresence (Factor 2), and Duality (Factor 3). As rated by their parents, children from families that were more spiritual and religious had higher scores on the newly-developed measure. Limitations and future directions are discussed.

Keywords: spirituality; children; measures

---

1. Introduction

Researchers exploring children's spirituality have tended to use narrow quantitative measures and questionnaires (e.g., frequency of religious service attendance) that do not account for the rich spiritual and religious experiences of children in a multi-faith context [1]. Despite increases in religious and spiritual diversity, and the interactions of faith groups in pluralistic contexts, most measures of spirituality used in North America are often derived from Christian-based ideologies [2]. This finding is especially germane to Canada, which is very heterogeneous with respect to spiritual and religious practices. In Canada, Christianity is the predominant religion with approximately 22 million adherents from various denominations. There are over one million adherents to Islam. Sikhism and Hinduism each have approximately half a million followers, whereas Judaism and Buddhism each have approximately 400,000 observers [3].

Existing measures often inadequately reflect the variety of religious and spiritual identities that are present in North American society [4]. Researchers such as Cotton, Larkin, Hoopes, Cromer, and Rosenthal [5], challenge the research community to extend its investigation beyond religious service attendance to include broader spiritual concepts, such as the personal relationship with a higher being. In response, the purpose of the current study was to develop a spirituality measure for children from diverse faith backgrounds in order to capture dimensions of children's spiritual lives common to many faith traditions.

Given that the objective of this research was to examine spirituality in the lives of children living within a pluralistic context, ubiquitous spiritual notions (e.g., relationship with a higher power, purpose and meaning in life, spirit-body dualism) [6] that transcend cultures and creeds were of particular relevance. Our intention was not to oversimplify the complexity of spirituality, but to explore spiritual experiences that appear across religious groups. In particular, children's personal relationship with the sacred was of special importance, as it is often deemed a robust protective factor against negative psychological outcomes (e.g., [7,8]), and thus may play an important role in their lives.

1.1. Children's Spiritualty

In psychology, the conceptualization of spirituality dates back to the very beginning of the discipline with the work of William James [9]. James advanced the notion of connecting religion to the experiential dimensions of spirituality rather than the institutional aspect, observing that different religions often use similar concepts, such as *divinity* and *transcendence*. Given that the main objective of the current study is to better understand children's spiritual lives, it is germane to understand the evolution of theories concerning children's spiritual development.

James Fowler [10] developed a faith development theory based on the notion of discontinuous stages of spiritual development. This theory is presented in relation to Jean Piaget's theory of cognitive development, Erik Erikson's theory of psychosocial development, and Laurence Kohlberg's theory of moral development. In each of these models, children are acknowledged as having the capacity to progress from concrete to abstract thinking as they mature. Fowler situates the stages of spiritual development within these developmental models, suggesting that, as children mature, they have an increased ability to become more aware and engaged with their spirituality.

In a move away from Fowler's spiritual developmental framework, proponents of the "spiritual child movement" ([11], p. 968) distanced themselves from traditional stage-structural cognitive-based theories. For instance, Hart [12] proposed that the stages of spiritual development are more fluid than were once understood, as children often have the ability to understand complex issues, but may struggle to express themselves. Although children are often perceived at large as egocentric or unable to take another's perspective, Hart emphasized children's seemingly innate ability to recognize complex issues, such as injustice, suffering, and compassion. Based on his anthropological studies and interviews with hundreds of individuals about their spiritual experiences, Hart argued that children often ask existential questions and have the ability for "deep metaphysical reflection" ([12], p. 9).

To date, the study of children's spiritual development continues to challenge researchers [13]. According to Hart ([12], p. 8), defining spirituality is like "trying to hold water in our hands", and so it is not surprising that trying to understand its developmental trajectory is perplexing. However, the field is moving towards clearer definitions of spirituality and conceptualizations of its development [14]. For instance, a social-ecology model has been put forward as means to better understand children's varied contexts and how these factors shape their religious and spiritual development [14]. Boyatzis [13] contends that "children are spiritual beings first and then are acculturated (or not) in a religious tradition that channels intuitive spirituality into particular expressions (rituals, creeds, etc.) that have been passed through the faith tradition" ([13], p. 153). Drawing on Bronfenbrenner's ecological model of microsystems (e.g., school, religious group) and macrosystems (e.g., cultural landscape and ideology), he suggests that children's relationship with the divine emerges prior to "religious socialization" ([13], p. 153) and is subsequently shaped by the way in which it is cultivated in their environment. Through this framework, children are seen as very much capable of understanding the relation between themselves and a divine entity from a very early age [15]. In the same vein, Hart (2003) argues that spirituality is accessible throughout development, but it is often erroneously considered at the "top of the developmental ladder" ([12], p. 9) and, therefore, out of reach for children.

1.2. Measuring Spirituality

In general, researchers have developed measures mainly oriented to members of Judeo-Christian traditions [2]. Hill [16] proposes that most spirituality measures have been developed in the United States and are often deliberately, or unintentionally, rooted in Christian traditions. As summarized by Hill, experts in the area of measuring development have discussed both the strengths and limitations of developing overarching broad measures of spirituality versus more focused measures of specific religious traditions. The main challenge, as outlined by Hill, is to then use these measures in studies with appropriate populations to achieve validity and reliability. Sustained research and longitudinal data are necessary to better understand the strengths and weaknesses of both types of spirituality measures (i.e., concepts specific to a religious group versus broad concepts that transcend religious groups).

Underwood and Teresi [17] found that when they used a spirituality measure with adult participants, the term *God* was the most easily understood across religious and spiritual groups. They suggested: "those outside the Judeo-Christian orientation, including Muslims, people from indigenous religious perspectives, and agnostics, were generally comfortable with the word, being able to translate it into their concept of the divine" ([17], p. 24). They reported that questions, in which the term God was used, were not problematic in their factor analysis, which led them to conclude that this term may be appropriate to use across religious groups. Evidently, in recent years, researchers have begun to invest in the development of spirituality measures and have discussed the nuances of item development. However, researchers have tended to place more focus on the development of these measures for adult populations (e.g., [1,18]).

1.3. Children's Spirituality Measures

Despite a recent proliferation of spirituality measures, most of these measures are oriented towards adults [19]. In the early 2000s, Fisher [20] reported finding only one measure designed specifically for children, which was in an unpublished doctoral dissertation. As a result, Fisher developed a children's spirituality measure (i.e., Feeling Good Living Life questionnaire) to provide educators with a tool to efficiently assess the role of spirituality in the lives of children in school. More recently, Fisher [21] reviewed all known spiritualty measures for children and adolescents. In his review of approximately 30 multi-item measures, he identified very few published measures that were specifically developed for school-aged children (7–11 years). The Multidimensional Life Satisfaction Scale for Children (primary school age; [22]), Feeling Good Living Life Spiritual Well Being Questionnaire (5–12 years; [20]), Spiritual and Religious Thriving in Adolescents (9–15 years; [23]), and the Benefit Finding Scale for Children (7–18 years; [24]) are all published scales that have been subjected to factor analysis with child populations.

Since Fisher's [21] review, there have been a small number of newly-developed children's spirituality measures (e.g., [25,26]). For instance, Stoyles et al. [25] developed the Children's Sensitivity Scale for Children, which is centered on children's ability to reflect about themselves and the world but does not include any questions pertaining to a child's relationship with the transcendent. Sifers et al. [26] used a diverse sample to develop and validate a Youth Spirituality Scale for children (7–14 years). The measure was piloted and showed signs of validity and reliability, but is still in the stages of requiring further validation. To date, there are no known spirituality measures that have been developed for school-aged children from a diversity of religious and spiritual backgrounds in Canada. Furthermore, no known measures use Canadian children's multi-faith spiritual narratives as the basis of measure item development.

Notably, Fisher's [20] spiritual measure is the only aforementioned scale that includes items pertaining to children's relationship with the transcendent. Specifically, this measure draws on four domains entitled personal, communal, environmental, and transcendental spiritual wellbeing [20,27]. This measure has been used to examine young children's spirituality in relation to variables, such as children's happiness (e.g., [28]). More recently, Fisher [7] demonstrated that the transcendental domain on his scale had the strongest relation to overall wellbeing. He states that his research "present[s] good evidence for claiming that relating with God is the most important factor for spiritual well-being (from the four factors studied)". Similar to items captured in Fisher's [20] transcendental domain, an objective of the current study is to gain a more nuanced understanding of the qualities that comprise the relationship between children and the transcendent; thus, the Children's Spiritual Lives measure was developed.

1.4. Children's Spiritual Lives

Based on the evolving theories of children's spirituality discussed in recent literature (e.g., [12,13]), researchers should be cautious not to underestimate children's ability to engage with their spirituality; items that comprise quantitative measures should be more sensitive to children's sophisticated spiritual perspectives. Certainly, children's answers on a Likert scale will not capture the complexities and intricacies of spirituality, but can serve as a research tool to quickly gain a better understanding of children's spiritual lives. Indeed, a future objective, for which this study is a stepping-stone, is to refine and validate this measure so that it may eventually be used to better understand the relation between spirituality and psychological health in the lives of children. A quantitative measure, such as this one, can be used to quickly assess the role of spirituality in relation to psychological health in children in both clinical and research settings.

As previously mentioned, items on this newly-developed measure were derived from a qualitative study in which children's rich spiritual narratives were elicited in semi-structured interviews [29]. In this qualitative study, sixty-four children from diverse religious and cultural backgrounds were asked about their thoughts and feelings related to spiritual concepts. Semi-structured interviews were used to better understand the breadth and depth of children's spiritual perspectives; these interviews were coded into salient themes, which were subsequently used to guide item development. Thus, this newly-developed measure was derived from children's narratives and developed in the context of literature supporting the notion that children may have a more sophisticated understanding of spirituality than was once perceived.

2. Methods

2.1. Participants

A total of 368 Canadian children (7–11 years, 54% female; $M = 9.2$ years, $SD = 18.44$) from diverse faith and cultural backgrounds participated in the study (see Table 1). In an effort to recruit a diverse sample, participants were recruited through community centers, local newspapers, and public places; on several occasions, a researcher went to these public places and set up a booth to advertise the study and those who were interested participated. Participants were also recruited through a research lab located in a multicultural Canadian city. At the lab, parents and children who were participating in non-related studies in the lab's waiting room were asked if they would like to hear more about an opportunity to participate in a study on children's spirituality. Those that expressed interest participated. As a result of this recruitment strategy, an accurate response rate cannot be reported. Three hundred is the recommended number of participants for conducting factor analysis [30].

Table 1. Parent-reported demographics and religious and spiritual information.

Variable	Response Choices	Frequency (%)
How Religious	Not Religious	77 (20.9)
	Somewhat Religious	190 (51.6)
	Very Religious	90 (24.5)
	Not Identified	11 (3.0)
How Spiritual	Not Spiritual	51 (13.9)
	Somewhat Spiritual	216 (58.7)
	Very Spiritual	83 (22.6)
	Not Identified	18 (4.9)
Place of Worship	Not at all	90 (24.5)
	Once a week	111 (30.2)
	Once a month	58 (15.8)
	3–4 times a year	69 (18.8)
	Once a year	35 (9.5)
	Not Identified	5 (1.4)

Table 1. *Cont.*

Variable	Response Choices	Frequency (%)
Religious Affiliation *	Catholic	138 (37.5)
	No Religion	52 (14.1)
	Muslim	48 (13.0)
	Jewish	48 (13.0)
	Hindu	23 (6.2)
	Christian (no denomination)	14 (3.8)
	Eastern Orthodox	12 (3.3)
	Protestant	11 (3.0)
	Anglican	11 (3.0)
	United	11 (3.0)
	Baptist	5 (1.4)
	Presbyterian	9 (2.4)
	Greek Orthodox	6 (1.6)
	Baha'i	4 (1.1)
	Wiccan	1 (0.3)
	Sikh	1 (0.3)
	Buddhism	1 (0.03)
	Evangelical	1(0.03)
	Pentecostal	1 (0.03)
	Lutheran	1 (0.03)
Cultural Group **	North American	146 (39.7)
	South American	16 (4.4)
	European	245 (66.6)
	Oceanian	0 (0.0)
	African	14 (3.8)
	Asian	88 (24.0)
Languages Spoken	One	110 (29.9)
	Two	144 (39.1)
	Three or more	114 (31.0)

Note: * Approximately 10 percent of parents reported more than one religious affiliation. For example, one parent reported that their family was Catholic and Muslim; ** Approximately 60 percent of parents reported more than one affiliated cultural group. For example, one parent reported that their family was Filipino, Canadian, and Irish. Reported groups included: French, Scottish, Greek, Korean, Irish, Polish, English, Canadian, German, Dutch, Italian, Jewish, Romanian, Chinese, Mexican, Belgium, Cherokee Indian, Welsh, American, South Asian, Ukrainian, Indian, African American, Afghani, Lebanese, Swedish, Danish, Portuguese, South African, Finnish, Pakistani, Arabic, Egyptian, Persian, Czech, Spanish, French-Canadian, Filipino, and English.

2.2. Materials and Procedure

Parents signed a consent form and completed a brief demographic questionnaire with questions pertaining to their cultural background, socio-economic status, and religious affiliation. In addition, on the demographic questionnaire, parents rated the level of religiosity and spirituality in their family (i.e., very religious/spiritual, somewhat religious/spiritual, not at all religious/spiritual). Parents also reported how often they go to a place of worship (i.e., not at all, once a year, 3–4 times per year, once a month, once a week).

Children's assent was obtained before the completion of the Children's Spiritual Lives measure. Children completed the questionnaire by answering questions relating to spirituality on a five-point Likert scale, ranging from *strongly disagree* to *strongly agree*. The researcher read the questionnaire aloud to children who then answered the question by indicating their response on the measure. In some cases, children who could read verbalized that they wanted to complete the items independently and were permitted to do so. Consistent with Ubani and Tirri [31] and Cotton et al. [5], the term *God* was used in the measure's items, but children were encouraged to use their preferred term for a higher power. To respect certain faith orientations and traditions that do not use the word *God*, this term was presented as *G-d* on this spirituality measure. Children received a small toy for their participation.

3. Analyses and Results

3.1. Initial Item Development

In the initial stage of this measure's development, a pool of items related to children's spirituality was created. This pool consisted of 64 items that were largely based on themes that emerged in a qualitative study in which children's diverse ideas of spirituality were explored (i.e., for more detail regarding the themes in which the questions were rooted, please see [29]). Items were developed in the context of existing research and theory in the field of children's spirituality. Following item development, these items were reviewed and edited for clarity and theoretical relevance by expert researchers in developmental and educational psychology, both of whom have an expertise in children's spiritual and moral development.

3.2. Exploratory Factor Analysis

A factor analysis is typically used to examine the inter-correlations between large numbers of items and to reduce the items into smaller groups known as factors [32]. In the current factor analysis, the reported factors contain correlated variables that measure similar underlying dimensions in the data that are interpretable in a theoretical sense. Given the fact that some participants did not answer all 64 items (11% of the total number of observations), the pattern for the missing values was examined using the multiple imputation option in SPSS version 20 (Armonk, NY: IBM Corp). The results suggested that the missing values did not follow a pattern; thus, missing data fell into the Missing Completely at Random (MCAR) category. In order to address the problem of missing observations, multiple imputations were computed. The Mersenne Twister generator was used as the option that fits best to impute MCAR. This process yielded five datasets with no missing values.

Examination of these five datasets suggested that there were no differences across them; for that reason, the first imputation was used for the current factor analysis. A principal component analysis was run with Varimax extraction and Kaiser normalizations. Factor solutions were considered in the rotated matrix based on the following criteria: (a) Eigenvalues of 1.0 or greater; and (b) factor loadings greater than 0.3 [33]. The rotated solution included 12 factors. Items and loadings on three factors are presented in Table 2. Thirty-three items were eliminated, as they did not load onto these factors.

Table 2. Factor loadings for exploratory factor analysis with Varimax rotation.

Factor 1 (Comfort)	Factor Loadings
I pray to G-d or talk to G-d when I feel sad	0.84
When I want to feel better, I talk or pray to G-d	0.81
I ask G-d for help	0.76
When I pray to G-d or talk to G-d I feel better about things	0.76
G-d helps me by making me feel strong	0.75
G-d helps me by making me think of new ideas	0.74
I pray to G-d or talk to G-d when I feel sad or worried about something	0.73
G-d helps me by giving me advice	0.72
I pray to G-d because I want to thank G-d for all of the good things in my life	0.71
When I think about G-d, I feel happy	0.71
G-d can make people feel better	0.69
I pray to G-d or talk to G-d when someone is sick or when someone dies	0.69
G-d keeps people company when they feel sad and lonely	0.63
G-d listens to my thoughts and wishes	0.68
I make wishes to G-d and the wishes come true	0.58
% Variance	220.70
Eigenvalues	140.52
Cronbach's Alpha	0.96
Skewness	0.78
Kurtosis	−0.04

Table 2. *Cont.*

Factor 2 (Omnipresence)	Factor Loadings
G-d always knows how I feel, even without talking	0.45
G-d is everywhere in the world and watches over everybody	0.50
G-d created all the people in the world and knows all of them	0.46
I think G-d listens to everyone	0.50
It is impossible for G-d to watch over everybody (reversed item)	0.63
There are too many in the world for G-d to know all of them (reversed item)	0.62
There are too many people in the world for G-d to listen to (reversed item)	0.68
G-d will never know what I am thinking to myself (reversed item)	0.57
% Variance	80.66
Eigenvalues	50.54
Cronbach's Alpha	0.91
Skewness	0.79
Kurtosis	−0.05
Factor 3 (Duality)	
Every person has a body and something inside them, like a soul or spirit	0.78
People do not have a soul or a spirit (reversed item)	0.66
Everyone has a body, but having a soul or a spirit is fake (reversed item)	0.66
I think that people have something like a soul or a spirit that lives inside them	0.64
% Variance	50.62
Eigenvalues	30.60
Cronbach's Alpha	0.81
Skewness	1.06
Kurtosis	1.24

3.3. Description of Factors

Although 12 factors emerged, three factors that showed the strongest factor loadings and that could be interpreted in a theoretical sense were chosen. Factor 1 (i.e., Comfort) includes 15 items that focus on God as a key source of support and comfort. Items range from seeking help or new ideas from God to talking or praying to God to feel happy or comforted. Factor 2 (i.e., Omnipresence) includes eight items that concern the ubiquity of God. These items are centered on themes of God being able to hear and see everyone as an omnipresent being and creator of the world. Factor 3 (i.e., Duality) includes four items and encompasses the notion of dualism, that is, having a soul or a spirit apart from the body (see Table 2). A fourth factor was initially included on the measure (i.e., four items), but was later eliminated, as it was not interpretable in a theoretical sense.

3.4. ANOVAS and Post-Hoc Analyses

There were significant differences between parents' reports of their families' religiosity (not religious, somewhat religious, very religious) and children's scores on Factor 1 (Comfort) $F = (2,356)$, 71.86, $p < 0.001$, Factor 2 (Omnipresence) $F = (2,356)$, 53.97, $p < 0.001$, and Factor 3 (Duality) $F = (2,356)$, 20.04, $p < 0.001$. Post hoc analyses revealed that there were significant differences ($p < 0.05$) between all three levels of religiosity on all factors. In sum, the more religious parents rated their families, the higher their children's scores on the factors. There was one exception; there was no significant difference between very religious and somewhat religious groups and children's scores on Factor 3 (see Table 3).

Table 3. Means and standard deviations by group (parent reported levels of religiosity and spirituality) on children's factor composite scores.

Factors	Level of Religiosity/Spirituality	M (SD)
Factor 1 (Comfort)	Not Religious	42.79 (14.65)
	Somewhat Religious	57.96 (11.91)
	Very Religious	63.76 (7.56)
	Not Spiritual	42.33 (14.48)
	Somewhat Spiritual	55.97 (13.18)
	Very Spiritual	63.15 (8.69)
Factor 2 (Omnipresence)	Not Religious	24.99 (8.54)
	Somewhat Religious	32.56 (6.46)
	Very Religious	35.15 (4.78)
	Not Spiritual	24.55 (8.93)
	Somewhat Spiritual	31.75 (7.08)
	Very Spiritual	34.80 (5.30)
Factor 3 (Duality)	Not Religious	15.01 (3.68)
	Somewhat Religious	16.95 (2.79)
	Very Religious	17.79 (2.33)
	Not Spiritual	14.65 (3.85)
	Somewhat Spiritual	16.77 (2.79)
	Very Spiritual	17.88 (2.50)

There were significant differences between parents' reports of their families' spirituality (not spiritual, somewhat spiritual, very spiritual) and children's scores on Factor 1 (Comfort) $F = (2,350)$, 43.01, $p < 0.001$, Factor 2 (Omnipresence) $F = (2,350)$, 33.73, $p < 0.001$, and Factor 3 (Duality) $F = (2,350)$, 19.20, $p < 0.001$. Post-hoc analyses revealed that there were significant differences ($p < 0.05$) between all three levels of spirituality on all factors (see Table 3). In sum, the more spiritual parents rated their families, the higher their children's scores on the factors.

4. Discussion

The Children's Spiritual Lives measure was developed specifically for Canadian school-aged children and grounded in their narratives. An exploratory factor analysis revealed items that clustered together to create three interpretable factors (i.e., Comfort, Omnipresence, Duality). As expected, children of parents who rated their families as very religious or very spiritual had higher scores on the Children's Spiritual Lives measure. This is consistent with Boyatzis' [13] conceptualization of spiritual development. Although spirituality may be deeply intrinsic, it is fostered and channeled by one's environment. Thus, it can be conjectured that children who have more opportunities to interact in highly religious and spiritual contexts, may have a spiritual life that is being more intentionally nurtured and supported.

Indeed, these emergent factors suggest that children have the ability to think about abstract spiritual concepts in a very personal manner, such as seeking comfort from a higher power. Children were also able to engage with concepts of the divine being omnipresent. That is, they perceived the transcendent as having supernatural qualities that go beyond time and space. They were also able to respond to items on the measure, which were related to the idea of having a body that is separate from a spirit or a soul. This suggests that children have some degree of understanding concepts related to duality and may draw distinctions between human and divine properties. Consistent with the underpinnings of the spiritual child movement [11] children may be more inclined to connect with their spirituality than was once thought and, thus, their ability for spiritual engagement should not be overlooked. This measure makes a valuable contribution by offering a more elaborate and nuanced depiction of the relationship between children and the transcendent through its identification of three common factors. These factors give insight into the ways children view and relate to the transcendent.

5. Limitations and Future Directions

This newly-developed measure has not yet been validated by a confirmatory factor analysis; thus, continued exploration of the scale's strengths and weaknesses is warranted to ensure that it is appropriate to use with children from diverse faith and cultural backgrounds living in a pluralistic society. As recommended by Hill [16], this measure should be further validated with a population similar to the one for which it was developed. The diversity in this sample is reflective of the religious landscape found in Canada [3]. Nonetheless, it should be noted that a large percentage of the sample, albeit from various denominations, is Christian. Continued efforts should continue to be made to recruit a diverse sample to better understand how these factors are perceived across cultures and creeds. In future iterations of this measure's development, participant response rates will also be collected to better understand the sample; this was a limitation of the current study.

In future research concerning this measure's development and refinement, items will be reviewed by expert researchers and clinicians in the field of children's spirituality and spiritual development. Focus groups and interviews with children considered to be "spiritual exemplars" [34] from diverse traditions could also provide deeper insight into the applicability of these items across religious and spiritual groups. Alternate styles of response-choices will also be considered. For instance, allowing the opportunity for children to add qualitative comments after responding to a Likert question may yield richer responses (e.g., mixed methods design) and a deeper understanding of children's spiritual perspectives. Once the scale has reliable and valid psychometrics, convergent validity with existing measures, such as the transcendental subscale of the Feeling Good Living Life questionnaire [20] and the religious well-being subscale on the Spiritual Well Being Scale [35], should be explored. Taken together, the present study provides an examination of the initial stage of measure development in a sample of diverse school age Canadian children.

Acknowledgments: Social Sciences and Humanities Research Council Seed Grant 820-2008-1011.

Author Contributions: With the guidance and support of Victoria Talwar and Sandra Bosacki, Kelsey Moore conceptualized and designed the study. Kelsey Moore wrote the manuscript and Sandra Bosacki and Victoria Talwar provided feedback and editing for content and clarity. Carlos Gomez-Garibello assisted in the analyses of the data set and with the interpretation of the results. All authors approved the final manuscript.

Conflicts of Interest: The authors declare no conflict of interest.

References

1. Houskamp, Beth, Lynne Fisher, and Margaret Stuber. "Spirituality in Children and Adolescents: Research Findings and Implications for Clinicians and Researchers." *Child and Adolescent Psychiatric Clinics of North America* 13 (2004): 221–30. [CrossRef]
2. Roehlkepartain, Eugene, Peter Benson, Pamela Ebstyne King, and Linda Wagener. "Spiritual development in childhood and adolescence: Moving to the scientific mainstream." In *The Handbook of Spiritual Development in Childhood and Adolescence*. Edited by Eugene Roehlkepartain, Pamela Ebstyne King, Linda Wagener and Peter Benson. Thousand Oaks: Sage Publications, 2006, pp. 1–15.
3. Canada, Statistics. *2013 Census of Canada Special Interest Table: Religions in Canada*. Ottawa: Statistics Canada, 2013.
4. Moberg, David. "Assessing and Measuring Spirituality: Confronting Dilemmas of Universal and Particular Evaluative Criteria." *Journal of Adult Development* 9 (2002): 47–60. [CrossRef]
5. Cotton, Sian, Elizabeth Larkin, Andrea Hoopes, Barbara Cromer, and Susan Rosenthal. "The Impact of Adolescent Spirituality on Depressive Symptoms and Health Risk Behaviors." *Journal of Adolescent Health* 36 (2005): 529. [CrossRef] [PubMed]
6. Barrett, Justin. *Born Believers: The Science of Children's Religious Belief*. New York: Free Press, 2012.
7. Fisher, John. "The importance of relating with God for spiritual well-being." In *Spirituality: New Reflections on Theory, Praxis & Pedagogy*. Edited by Martin Fowler, Michael Weiss and John Hochheimer. Oxford: Inter-Disciplinary Press, 2012, pp. 147–61.
8. Miller, Lisa. "Spiritual Awakening and Depression in Adolescents: A Unified Pathway or 'two Sides of the Same Coin'." *Bulletin of the Menninger Clinic* 77 (2013): 332–48. [CrossRef] [PubMed]

9. James, William. *The Varieties of Religious Experience: A Study in Human Nature*. London: Collier-Macmillan, 1961.
10. Fowler, James. *Stages of Faith: The Psychology of Human Development and the Quest for Meaning*. San Francisco: Harper & Row, 1981.
11. Oser, Fritz, George Scarlett, and Anton Bucher. "Religious and spiritual development throughout the lifespan." In *Handbook of Child Psychology. Vol. 1: Theoretical Models of Human Development*. Edited by William Damon and Richard Lerner. Hoboken: John Wiley and Sons, 2006, pp. 942–98.
12. Hart, Tobin. *The Secret Spiritual World of Children*. Novato: New World Library, 2003.
13. Boyatzis, Chris. "Spiritual development during childhood and adolescence." In *The Oxford Handbook of Psychology and Spirituality*. Edited by Lisa Miller. New York: Oxford University Press, 2012, pp. 151–64.
14. King, Pamela Ebstune, and Chris J. Boyatzis. "Religious and spiritual development in childhood and adolescence." In *The Handbook of Child Psychology and Developmental Science*, 7th ed. Edited by Michael Lamb, Cynthia Coll and Richard Lerner. Hoboken: Wiley, 2015, pp. 975–1021.
15. King, Pamela Ebstyne, and Chris J. Boyatzis. "Exploring adolescent spiritual and religious development: Current and future theoretical and empirical perspectives." *Applied Developmental Science* 8 (2004): 2–6. [CrossRef]
16. Hill, Peter. "Measurement assessment and issues in the psychology of religion and spirituality." In *Handbook of the Psychology of Religion and Spirituality*. Edited by Raymond Paloutzian and Crystal Park. New York: Guilford Press, 2013, pp. 48–74.
17. Underwood, Lynn, and Jeanne Teresi. "The Daily Spiritual Experience Scale: Development, Theoretical Description, Reliability, Exploratory Factor Analysis, and Preliminary Construct Validity Using Health-related Data." *Annals of Behavioral Medicine* 24 (2002): 22–33. [CrossRef] [PubMed]
18. Cotton, Sian, Meghan E. McGrady, and Susan L. Rosenthal. "Measurement of religiosity/spirituality in adolescent health outcomes research: Trends and recommendations." *Journal of Religion and Health* 49 (2010): 414–44. [CrossRef] [PubMed]
19. Monod, Stéfanie, Mark Brennan, Etienne Rochat, Estelle Martin, Stéphane Rochat, and Christophe J. Büla. "Instruments Measuring Spirituality in Clinical Research: A Systematic Review." *Journal of General Internal Medicine* 26 (2011): 1345–57. [CrossRef] [PubMed]
20. Fisher, John. "Feeling Good, Living Life: A Spiritual Health Measure for Young Children." *Journal of Beliefs & Values* 25 (2004): 307–15.
21. Fisher, John. "Getting the Balance: Assessing Spirituality and Well-being among Children and Youth." *International Journal of Children's Spirituality* 14 (2009): 273–88. [CrossRef]
22. Huebner, Scott. "Preliminary Development and Validation of a Multidimensional Life Satisfaction Scale for Children." *Psychological Assessment* 6 (1994): 149–58. [CrossRef]
23. Dowling, Elizabeth, Steinunn Gestsdottir, Pamela Anderson, Alexander Von Eye, Jason Almerigi, and Richard Lerner. "Structural Relations Among Spirituality, Religiosity, and Thriving in Adolescence." *Applied Developmental Science* 8 (2004): 7–16. [CrossRef]
24. Phipps, Sean, Alanna Long, and Johanna Ogden. "Benefit Finding Scale for Children: Preliminary Findings from a Childhood Cancer Population." *Journal of Pediatric Psychology* 32 (2007): 1264–71. [CrossRef] [PubMed]
25. Stoyles, Gerard John, Bonnie Stanford, Peter Caputi, Alysha-Leigh Keating, and Brendan Hyde. "A Measure of Spiritual Sensitivity for Children." *International Journal of Children's Spirituality* 17 (2012): 203–15. [CrossRef]
26. Sifers, Sarah, Jared Warren, and Yo Jackson. "Measuring spirituality in children." *Journal of Psychology and Christianity* 31 (2012): 205–14.
27. Gomez, Rapson, and John W. Fisher. "Domains of spiritual well-being and development and validation of the Spiritual Well-Being Questionnaire." *Personality and Individual Differences* 35 (2003): 1975–91. [CrossRef]
28. Holder, Mark D., Ben Coleman, and Judi M. Wallace. "Spirituality, religiousness, and happiness in children aged 8–12 years." *Journal of Happiness Studies* 11 (2010): 131–50. [CrossRef]
29. Moore, Kelsey, Victoria Talwar, and Sandra Bosacki. "Canadian Children's Perceptions of Spirituality: Diverse Voices." *International Journal of Children's Spirituality* 17 (2012): 217–34. [CrossRef]
30. DeVellis, Robert F. *Scale Development: Theory and Applications*. Thousand Oaks: Sage, 1991.
31. Ubani, Martin, and Kirsi Tirri. "How Do Finnish Pre-adolescents Perceive Religion and Spirituality?" *International Journal of Children's Spirituality* 11 (2006): 357–70. [CrossRef]

32. Tabachnick, Barbara, and Linda Fidell. *Using Multivariate Statistics*. Boston: Pearson Education, 2013.
33. Comrey, Andrew, and Howard Lee. *A First Course in Factor Analysis*. New York: Oxford University Press, 1992.
34. King, Pamela Ebstyne, Casey E. Clardy, and Jenel Sánchez Ramos. "Adolescent spiritual exemplars: Exploring spirituality in the lives of diverse youth." *Journal of Adolescent Research* 29 (2013): 186–212. [CrossRef]
35. Paloutzian, Raymond F., and Craig W. Ellison. "Loneliness, spiritual well-being, and quality of life." In *Loneliness: A Sourcebook of Current Theory, Research and Therapy*. Edited by Letitia Anne Peplau and Daniel Perlman. New York: Wiley, 1982.

Article

Selecting the Best Version of SHALOM to Assess Spiritual Well-Being

John Fisher [1,2]

1   Faculty of Education & Arts, Federation University Australia, Ballarat, Victoria 3350, Australia;
    j.fisher@federation.edu.au; Tel.: +61-438-395-915
2   Department of Rural Health, Faculty of Medicine, Dentistry & Health Sciences, University of Melbourne,
    Victoria 3010, Australia; jwfisher@unimelb.edu.au

Academic Editor: Arndt Büssing
Received: 1 March 2016; Accepted: 27 April 2016; Published: 30 April 2016

Abstract: This paper extends the reporting of contemporary use of the Spiritual Health and Life-Orientation Measure (SHALOM), which provides flexibility to researchers, enabling them to choose the version of the instrument that best suits the cohort under investigation. SHALOM was built on a solid theoretical foundation, provided by the Four Domains Model of Spiritual Health/Well-Being. It comprises 20 items that assess spiritual well-being, as reflected in the quality of relationships that each person has with themselves, others, the environment, and/or with God. Summary results are reported from 30 recent studies. SHALOM provides a unique form of assessment that is statistically stronger than just assessing lived experiences, in that spiritual harmony/dissonance is studied by comparing each person's "lived experiences" with her/his "ideals" for spiritual well-being. SHALOM has been sought for use with hundreds of studies in 29 languages, in education, healthcare and wider community. A generic form of SHALOM was developed to expand the Transcendental domain to include more than God. However, recent studies have shown that relating with God is most important for spiritual well-being. The best version of SHALOM to assess spiritual well-being depends on the needs of the clients/participants and the project goals of the researcher. This will involve a selection between the original form of Spiritual Well-Being Questionnaire-SHALOM for comparison with other measures and investigation of characteristics influencing spiritual well-being; or the dissonance method for spiritual care; and either the original or the generic version of SHALOM for use with non-religious/secular participants.

Keywords: spiritual well-being; assess; SHALOM; God

---

1. Introduction

Many, if not most, papers about it say that, "Spirituality is hard, if not impossible, to define." It is difficult to declare the exact meaning or scope of spirituality. However, that is also the case for concepts such as "love" and "beauty", but people still use these terms as if they agree on what they mean. With spirituality, people have attempted to describe its properties in various ways, including outlining the historical contexts in which the term has been used [1], epistemologically [2,3], or by type [4].

When the positive psychological construct of well-being is added to spiritual aspects of humanity, there is potential for greater confusion. However, the National Interfaith Coalition on Aging's (NICA) framework definition of spiritual well-being (SWB), as "the affirmation of life in a relationship with God, self, community and environment that nurtures and celebrates wholeness" [5], was supported by an intensive qualitative study, which provided an expanded description of spiritual health as:

A, if not *the*, fundamental dimension of people's overall health and well-being, permeating and integrating all the other dimensions of health (*i.e.*, physical, mental, emotional, social and vocational).

Spiritual health is a dynamic state of being, shown by the extent to which people live in harmony within relationships in up to four domains of spiritual well-being:

Personal domain—wherein one intra-relates with oneself with regards to meaning, purpose and values in life.

Communal domain—as shown in the quality and depth of interpersonal relationships, relating to morality, culture and religion.

Environmental domain—beyond care and nurture for the physical and biological, to a sense of awe and wonder, for some, the notion of unity, with the environment.

Transcendental domain—relationship of self with some-Thing or some-One beyond the human level (*i.e.*, ultimate concern, cosmic force, transcendent reality, or God) [6].

This description of SWB in four domains encompasses the vast majority of components of SWB mentioned in contemporary literature, which has expanded exponentially over the last two decades [7].

It is one thing to describe spirituality, but another to measure it. Moberg [8], and Koenig [9], have raised concerns about measuring spirituality in research projects. Judicious selection of an appropriate instrument is needed. With the increasing interest in spirituality and well-being, especially over the last 30 years, numerous quantitative surveys have been developed to investigate this area [10–13]. Quantitative survey is an accepted and sound research method to be employed in this area [14–18].

Expanding on a previous report of spirituality measures [19], the Four Domains Model of SWB provided a theoretical foundation to critique 260 available measures of spirituality and well-being [20]. This compendium of multi-item measures is organised by year of development within three types of spirituality measures, namely (i) spiritual health/well-being measures; (ii) spirituality measures; and (iii) related/partial spirituality measures, for four sections of studies (i) of a General nature; (ii) in University only; (iii) in Schools (with youth); and (iv) Health settings. The advice of Zwingmann *et al.* needs to be heeded in selecting instruments for studies in spirituality. As well as "measurement intentions and item wording . . . psychometric properties, length of the instruments, and the possibility for comparisons with prior studies" need to be considered [21]. The 260 instruments mentioned were described by composition of items within the four domains of spirituality, plus religious items and "others". Comment was made regarding the status of each instrument with respect to Factor Analysis. The number and type of people in each study were reported together with place (country) in which each study was performed. The first author was named to readily access the reference list, with the final column providing information regarding the source through which to retrieve a copy of each instrument.

Of available measures used to assess spirituality, recent comments have reported that the Spiritual Well-Being Questionnaire (SWBQ)-SHALOM (Spiritual Health and Life-Orientation Measure) is well-accepted ([22,23]; [24], p. 41). The survey design, content, style of responses and statistical analysis employed in SWBQ-SHALOM are consistent with standard quantitative research methodology. National and international studies have shown the suitability of SHALOM for research in SWB in a variety of settings and languages [25]. A summary of this research has spawned considerable interest, being downloaded 10,069 times from the time of its publication in December 2010 to March 2016.

2. Development of SHALOM (the Spiritual Health and Life-Orientation Measure)

The history of the development of SHALOM has been detailed previously [25–27]. The 20-item SHALOM comprises five items in each of four factors that investigate the quality of relationships that people have with themselves, with others, with the environment, and/or with a Transcendent Other (most often called God). The items chosen for the personal SWB were "a sense of identity, self-awareness, joy in life, inner peace and meaning in life"; those for the Communal SWB were "love of other people, forgiveness toward others, trust between individuals, respect for others, kindness toward other people"; Environmental SWB investigated "connection with nature, awe at a breathtaking view, oneness with nature, harmony with the environment, sense of 'magic' in the environment"; Transcendental SWB inspected "personal relationship with the Divine/God, worship of the Creator, oneness with God, peace with God, prayer life." Responses are given on a 5-point Likert scale from 1 = very low to 5 = very high. Exploratory factor analyses strongly supported the four domains of SWB, which also cohered into a single higher-order factor labelled spiritual well-being [27].

SHALOM is actually two instruments in one. Two responses per item were gleaned for the Spiritual Health measure (which assesses "lived experience") And the Life-Orientation Measure (which assesses "ideals" for spiritual well-being). The difference between the ideals and lived experience scores was used to investigate the level of spiritual harmony/dissonance, as a basis for pastoral care.

Before SHALOM was developed, all but one of reported quantitative SWB studies had been undertaken with adults and older youth, who were mainly in universities. Apart from the desire to produce a spiritual health/well-being measure for use with young people, it was asserted that development of a measure that had language that was meaningful to young people should also be useful for a wide range of adults. Subsequent studies with secondary school students, together with university students and church attenders were used to show that the SWBQ, the lived experience sector of SHALOM, had good reliability, with Cronbach's alpha, composite reliability and variance extracted. The SWBQ also has good construct, concurrent, discriminant and predictive validity, and also shows factorial independence from personality [27]. Further analyses revealed "general support for the psychometric properties of the SWBQ from an Item Response Theory (IRT) perspective" [28], making this instrument the first of only three spiritual well-being questionnaires to report IRT [29,30]. "Multi-group factor analysis also [showed] gender equivalencies for the SWBQ" [31].

3. Applications of the SWBQ—SHALOM

Since its development in 1999, the SWBQ-SHALOM has been sought for use in hundreds of studies in 29 languages. However, only a minority of those requests have so far resulted in publications from completed projects, many of which are still in the planning and data-gathering stages. The best of intentions can also be way-laid for a variety of reasons, including changes in priorities or employment during the project; lack of funding or other support for the project; inclement health by researcher or family member; political influence such as "separation of church and state" in the USA; search for culturally-specific content. Using such specific measures has disadvantages in that the results cannot be compared with those in other groups. Moberg has emphasised the need to "combine particularistic and universal strategies for clinical assessments and scientific research in SWB" [14].

The SWBQ—SHALOM is a measure that has shown its general applicability in a wide range of settings. Summary findings have previously been reported from 28 projects, which employed the original 20-item form of SHALOM, and from another three that used variations on the original. Several studies were mentioned there in which only total scores for SWB, not the individual factor scores, were used [25]. Findings from another 30 recent studies using the complete measure are listed in Table 1.

Table 1. Spiritual well-being (SWB) levels from recent studies using the Spiritual Well-Being Questionnaire–Spiritual Health and Life-Orientation Measure (SWBQ–SHALOM).

				Four Domains of SWB							
	Schools			PER		COM		ENV		TRA	
Ref	Sample	Country	n	x	SD	x	SD	x	SD	x	SD
	students										
[32]	Sec Anglican Female	UK	228	4.00	0.86	4.24	0.72	3.19	0.97	2.73	1.26
[33]	Secondary	Spain	114	3.75	0.80	3.82	0.69	3.18	0.92	2.65	1.17
[34]	Sec nonreligious	Hong Kong	305	3.53	0.80	3.59	0.78	3.00	0.85	2.51	1.05
	Religious school1		341	3.73	0.65	3.75	0.63	3.25	0.75	3.09	1.01
	Religious school2		409	3.57	0.71	3.66	0.67	3.18	0.71	2.72	1.06
[35]	Secondary	Hong Kong	14828	3.54	0.78	3.64	0.76	3.10	0.85	2.71	1.03
[36]	Secondary	Australia	114	3.86	0.68	4.12	0.56	3.54	0.85	3.14	0.97

Table 1. Cont.

| | | | | Four Domains of SWB | | | | | | | |
| | UNIVERSITY | | | PER | | COM | | ENV | | TRA | |
Ref	Sample	Country	n	x	SD	x	SD	x	SD	x	SD
[37]	AOG Liberal Arts	USA	375	3.94	0.54	4.08	0.66	3.06	0.91	3.82	0.91
[38]	Nurse education	Indonesia	105	4.09	0.67	4.04	0.73	3.92	0.78	4.20	0.73
[39]	Teacher ed. students	Hong Kong	573	3.95	0.64	4.05	0.60	3.46	0.71	2.95	1.11
		Australia	557	4.06	0.67	4.28	0.60	3.26	0.83	2.56	1.12
[40]	RE students	Turkey	137	4.22	0.77	4.31	0.62	4.07	0.81	4.43	0.75
	Divinity students		122	4.03	0.79	4.05	0.72	3.88	0.76	4.22	0.77
[33]	Ed Psych students	Spain	151	4.29	0.61	4.21	0.56	3.51	0.89	2.26	1.15
[41]	Psych students	UK	101	3.75	0.81	3.87	0.71	3.01	1.02	2.35	1.30

| | | | | Four Domains of SWB | | | | | | | |
| | Health | | | PER | | COM | | ENV | | TRA | |
Ref	Sample	Country	n	x	SD	x	SD	x	SD	x	SD
[42]	Nurses of dementia pts	Australia	21	4.51	0.60	4.60	0.52	4.01	0.86	3.44	1.21
	Family		23	3.69	0.77	4.25	0.66	3.64	0.95	3.62	0.89
[43]	Nurses	USA	33	3.98		3.95		3.15		4.03	
[44]	Cancer patients	Portugal	169	3.10	0.84	3.47	0.57	3.25	0.97	3.66	0.92
[45]	Renal patients	UK	72	2.43	1.16	2.37	1.08	2.39	1.10	2.40	1.18
[46]	Organ donor	Israel	312	3.92	0.63	3.99	0.58	3.43	0.86	1.99	1.11
[47]	Nurses	Israel	260 *	4.06		4.04		2.84		3.38	
[48]	Medical sciences	Iran	157	4.43	0.73	4.31	0.69	4.17	0.76	4.58	0.73

	Church										
[49]	Chinese immigrants	Ireland	68	3.65	0.63	3.80	0.72	3.33	0.67	3.66	0.69
[50]	Religious sisters	Indonesia	186	4.14	0.52	4.13	0.44	4.10	0.48	4.46	0.44
[51]	Buddhist chaplains	USA	48	3.16	0.82	3.66	0.65	3.41	0.91	2.58	1.27
[52]	Religious sisters	Vietnam	271	3.89	0.58	3.72	0.57	3.59	0.65	4.12	0.64

	Business										
[53]	Home economists	International	66	4.03	0.85	4.05	0.75	3.50	1.04	2.93	1.25
[54]	Public Corporation	Puerto Rico	265	4.58	0.66	4.36	0.74	3.92	0.95	4.33	0.96

	Community										
[55]	Community	Portugal	439	3.77	0.58	3.72	0.54	3.56	0.74	2.90	0.96
[56]	Physical Activity	Portugal	342	3.80	0.62	3.82	0.57	3.67	0.74	3.12	0.87
[57]	Elderly	Portugal	52	2.99	1.11	3.44	0.84	3.62	0.84	3.19	0.99
[58]	Consumers	Australia	1011	3.54	0.79	3.64	0.73	3.15	0.87	2.65	1.26
[59]	Public	UK	43 *	3.53		3.83		3.17		1.61	
[60]	Public	Portugal	320	3.60	0.66	3.71	0.58	3.41	0.74	2.71	1.01

Notes: (Some studies did not provide SD data); * = estimated values extracted from results; PER = Personal domain of SWB; COM = Communal domain of SWB; ENV = Environmental domain of SWB; TRA = Transcendental domain of SWB.

A cursory inspection of means between the two batches of results using SHALOM showed:

For School students—comparable values for each domain across the two samples, with variations on Transcendental SWB by religious affiliation, but students' scores were lower than those reported by school staff.

For University students—the more religious students in the second batch scored higher on Environmental and Transcendental SWB.

In Health settings, providers scored higher than patients on each domain.

In Churches—it was not surprising to note that those in religious orders scored higher on Transcendental SWB than church attenders.

In Business—there appears to be a marked cultural variation, with people from Puerto Rico outscoring others on each domain of SWB.

In Community—domestic violence victims from South Africa reported a stronger relationship with God (Transcendental SWB) than did others.

Alternative Versions of the SWBQ

SHALOM was built on the four domains model of spiritual health/well-being from which twelve items were selected to represent each domain, being reduced to the five items with highest item-total correlation. No instrument can give an absolute measure of SWB. However, in order to check the consistency, or otherwise, of responses using different items, a second set of five items per domain were extracted from the same cohort as for the original SHALOM to form another psychometrically sound measure called SWBQ2 [61]. As their items varied, it was not surprising to find that the factor scores varied between SHALOM and SWBQ2 for Personal, Communal and Environmental SWB, but not the Transcendental domain, due to positive and negative variations between schools cancelling each other on this factor (see Table 2).

An additional alternative version of the SWBQ—SHALOM employed a scale score from 1 to 6 [24]. Two further researchers only used selected items from the total 20-item instrument [62,63] and one more used the total score instead of factor scores [64].

Table 2. Alternate versions of the SWBQ-SHALOM used to assess SWB.

ALTERNATE										Four Domains of SWB				
SWBQS		cf SHALOM			PER		COM		ENV		TRA			
Ref	Sample	Country	n	x	SD	x	SD	x	SD	x	SD			
[24]	Mental health	USA^	4667	3.44	0.89	3.70	0.82	3.00	1.13	0.85	1.38			
[61]	SWBQ2	Aust-	460	3.67	0.75	3.59	0.67	3.36	0.79	3.20	0.98			
[61]	SHALOM	ralia	460	3.75	0.79	3.93	0.69	3.18	0.95	3.17	1.16			
Generic Version				PER		COM		ENV		TRA#				
[65]	Web survey: Theistic T	I'nat	453	4.02	0.74	4.04	0.70	3.38	0.96	3.41	1.20			
			262	4.08	0.70	4.08	0.68	3.36	0.94	3.94	1.87			
	other religious T		84	4.06	0.71	4.03	0.75	3.62	0.91	3.15	1.08			
	Non-religious T		70	3.88	0.75	3.91	0.64	3.45	0.82	2.79	1.11			
	Non-belief		37	3.75	0.90	4.05	0.81	2.83	1.18	1.45	0.87			

Note: ^ scale scores 1–6, instead of normal 1–5; PER = Personal domain of SWB; COM = Communal domain of SWB; ENV = Environmental domain of SWB; TRA = Transcendental domain of SWB; I'nat = International; T = Transcendent; # the generic version used the word "Transcendent" instead of theistic words.

The above results show that using different scale scores or adding, subtracting, or modifying any of the five items in each of the four domains of SHALOM yields different instruments, results from which cannot be compared with other studies using the original SHALOM, with its 20 items and 5-point Likert scale. They should therefore be given different names.

4. Generic Version of SHALOM

At conferences, three people made comments that SHALOM was too God-oriented, even though the word was only mentioned in three of the twenty items in SHALOM, in contrast to, for example, the ten times in the 20 items in the Spiritual Well Being Survey [66]. It appears that what these people were really saying is that they would only be happy with no reference to God, in accord with their world-view. This limited view of the world does not fit with most Western civilisations, where census data show that a majority of the populace claim adherence to God-based religions [67]. Traditional Western views of spirituality arose from religious studies, especially in the Catholic Church [68].

Many authors concur with Seaward's view, "Although spirituality and religion are separate but related concepts that often overlap, it is inconceivable to separate the concept of spirituality from the divine aspect of the universe" ([69], p. 77). That notwithstanding, in light of the claim of theistic bias levelled at the existing SHALOM, four of the five original Transcendental factor items had the words "God", "Divine" and "Creator" replaced by the word "Transcendent". In the revised version, respondents were presented with the statement, "When people believe their lives are influenced by SomeOne or SomeThing beyond the human and natural worlds, they use different words". To effect the instruction for participants to *"Please choose one of the following to show what best describes the supernatural influence in your life"*, eighteen alternatives were provided, namely "Allah, Angel/s, Buddha, Deceased person, Deity/deities, Divine, Fate, Father God, Gaia, God, Heaven, Higher power, Higher self, Mystery, Otherness, Presence, Something there, Universe/universal spirit," or respondents could indicate "Not an area in which I believe" (see results in Table 2). The "Tao" was inadvertently omitted from the list, although no respondents in that study indicated Taoism as their preferred religion/world-view from 26 alternatives provided. Tao has now been added to the generic version of SHALOM.

Confirmatory factor analyses revealed that the modified, generic form of SHALOM showed acceptable model fit, comprising four clearly delineated domains of spiritual well-being. Of particular interest was the finding that the modified Transcendental domain of spiritual well-being holds together well statistically and provides the greatest explanation of variance in spiritual well-being overall [65,70], as has been shown with the original version of SHALOM [61,71,72] and in a junior spiritual well-being questionnaire called "Feeling Good, Living Life" [73]. Those respondents who indicated relating with God as their Transcendent revealed that this relationship enhances relationships with themselves and other people more strongly than that done by alternative religious or non-religious Transcendents, or none [65]. This study and others have shown that relating with God is most important for spiritual well-being [61,71,72]. Thus, it appears that NICA correctly listed God first in their description of SWB [5]. It is also interesting to note that ninety per cent of 260 available multi-item measures of spirituality/well-being reported items assessing relationship with God [20]. It is important to note that removal of God from any study would leave only humanistic, existential well-being. For example, this would be the case if the ten items on Religious well-being (querying relationship with God) were removed from the Spiritual Well-Being Survey then only ten items on Existential well-being would remain [66]. It is valid then to question whether any study that deletes God is truly a measure of *spiritual* well-being.

Although some words have been changed in it (see Section 3 above), the modified SHALOM can be employed in future studies as a generic measure of spiritual well-being across a variety of worldviews, because the inherent structure of the instrument remains intact. However, the nature of the cohort under investigation should determine which version of SHALOM is used, not the world-view of the investigators.

5. Spiritual Harmony/Dissonance

Almost all available spirituality/well-being measures [20] only seek a single response to indicate respondents' level of lived experience on items/factors investigated by the nominated scales. Instruments developed by Fisher [26,65,74] use a novel technique, in that they compare each person's "lived experience" with their "ideals" for spiritual well-being. In other words, each person becomes the standard against which they are measured, rather than being compared or grouped by using some arbitrary norm. The difference between the "ideals" and "lived experience" score indicates the level of harmony or dissonance in each domain. This is a fairer approach of assessing spiritual well-being because each person is allowed to view each term in light of their own understanding of it, rather than having their view compared with someone else's.

Analyses have shown that using dissonance scores for each of the 20 items in SHALOM actually provides a statistically stronger instrument than just using the "lived experience" scores, as is done in other spirituality measures [61]. The dissonance technique thus provides a better measure of quality of relationships in the four domains, which reflect spiritual well-being. An application of this technique, in a recent web survey using SHALOM, revealed that "spiritual harmony shared the strongest relationship with mental health when compared to any other variable used in this study" ([24], p. 84). This finding applied equally well to the religious and secular participants in that study. Dissonance, referred to as "spiritual incongruence", was found to be a significant predictor of burnout among Buddhist chaplains [51].

Dissonance scores generated using SHALOM can provide carers with insight into their clients' spiritual well-being in the four domains assessed. For example, secondary school students with large dissonance scored lower on the Oxford Happiness Inventory, higher on psychoticism (assessed using the Junior Eysenck Personality Questionnaire-Revised), and reported less help from God, parents and self for developing spiritual well-being. As teachers and religious leaders were not implicated in the lower levels of help, they need to be aware of the supporters who are, in order to aid the holistic development of their students [75]. Such insights can be invaluable to carers such as teachers, chaplains and those in aged and palliative care. However, these spiritual nurturers need appropriate training and experience in this area to become aware of their clients' needs and to adequately help their clients, as previous studies have shown that carers' lived experience influences how well they provide spiritual care [76,77].

6. Truncated Version of SHALOM?

A few researchers are looking for quick and easy ways to assess spiritual health/well-being. Considerable effort has recently been expended investigating 26 studies that have employed the full 20-item version of SHALOM, with a total of 30,514 participants, to see if SHALOM could be reduced in size, whilst maintaining its integrity.

Item-total correlations were inspected for the five items in each of the four domains comprising SHALOM. At the outset, it needs to be noted that each of the items showed large (> 0.5) correlational values in each factor, within the 26 studies for which full data were available.

In the Personal domain, the two items which consistently showed highest item-total correlational values were "inner peace" and "joy in life" followed closely by "meaning in life". Although "a sense of identity" and "self-awareness" trailed the field equally, they were still statistically strong items in this domain. Theoretically, according to the Four Domains model of SH/SWB, these latter two items are key elements of relationship with oneself.

In the Communal domain, the two items that consistently showed highest correlational values were "kindness towards other people" and "respect for others", with "trust between individuals" a close third, followed by "forgiveness towards others" and "a love of other people". All were still statistically strong items in this domain. Forgiveness and love are also strong features, which theoretically reflect quality of relationships with other people.

In the Environmental domain, the three items with highest correlational values were "oneness with nature", "connection with nature" and "harmony with the environment", followed by "a sense of 'magic' in the environment" and "awe at a breathtaking view". Once again, all were still statistically strong items in this domain. The wording of the first three items was sufficiently similar to yield strong correlations. The last two items reflected different aspects of relationship with the environment.

In the Transcendental domain, the three items with highest correlational values were "oneness with God", "peace with God" and "worship of the Creator", followed closely by "personal relationship with the Divine/God" and "prayer life". All were remarkably strong statistically, with average item-total correlation values exceeding 0.9. The last two items are theoretically paramount in terms of relationship with God.

Exploratory factor analyses were performed to test the underlying structure of each of the four factors, beginning with the 5-item sets, reducing to 3, then 2. The Kaiser-Meyer-Olkin (KMO) test of sampling adequacy requires 0.6 as a minimum for good factor analysis [78]. The 5-item factors showed highest KMO values, all at 0.80 and above (shown in bold in Table 3), whereas the 3-item factors were weaker, especially in the Personal and Communal factors, with KMO values less than 0.7 (see Table 3). The 2-item "factors" were completely inadequate with KMO values of only 0.5.

Table 3. Sampling adequacy for 5- and 3-item versions of SHALOM.

SHALOM	PER		COM		ENV		TRA	
	KMO	%var	KMO	%var	KMO	%var	KMO	%var
5-item	0.80	58	0.83	60	0.83	63	0.89	80
3-item	0.69	68	0.68	70	0.72	75	0.74	83

Note: KMO = Kaiser-Meyer-Olkin values of sampling adequacy; %var = % variance explained.

Retention of the three items with highest item-total correlations for each factor yielded an improved percentage of variance explained, which would be expected. More importantly, however, lower KMO values, indicating less favourable measures, resulted from deletion of two items per factor. The significant loss in perspective regarding spiritual health/well-being that would be attained does not warrant removal of any of these items. In effect, saving approximately two to three minutes in completion of the questionnaire would markedly reduce the depth of understanding revealed by respondents' perspectives and life experiences related to spiritual well-being. Conclusion, "Take the extra time. It is definitely worth it!" Justice cannot be done to a complex construct such as SH/WB by attempting to assess it with a few, or even a handful of, items [20].

7. Limitations

While many of the studies provided results of exploratory factor analyses and some alpha values for factors, only a small number reported confirmatory factor analyses [35,37,56,61]. It would be beneficial if each study that used SHALOM provided results of confirmatory factor analyses to further validate this instrument in the wide range of settings and countries in which it is being used. This would provide additional confidence for other researchers comparing results from their studies with those reported here and previously [25].

8. Conclusions

Spiritual well-being is a complex issue which cannot be adequately addressed in a few words, nor can it be adequately assessed using instruments with only a few items. This paper has reviewed the contemporary use of a 20-item spiritual well-being questionnaire called SHALOM. Although it must be stressed that 20 items cannot provide an exhaustive assessment of spiritual well-being, this instrument has been shown to be a sound statistical measure within a variety of age groups in a good range of nations.

The "lived experience" component of SHALOM can be favourably compared with other standard measures of spirituality/well-being, although SHALOM differs from them in that it uses the same number of items in each of its four domains, thus not privileging any one domain over the others. As a growing number of studies are reporting their findings using SHALOM, it is becoming increasingly useful as a database upon which to compare other studies using a single-response technique.

However, SHALOM uses the unique double-response technique of comparing each person's "lived experience" with their "ideals" for SWB. This a fairer approach to assessing spiritual well-being as it has been shown that the difference in scores between the "ideals" and "lived experiences", called "spiritual harmony/dissonance", provides a statistically stronger measure than using only "lived experience", which is what other measures employ. This dissonance technique is very useful for spiritual carers to gain insight into their clients' spiritual needs.

As each person is compared with themselves, in each domain, if they score low on both ideals and lived experience in any domain, they do not reveal any spiritual dissonance therein. This notion of spiritual harmony (statistical opposite of dissonance) applied equally well to religious and secular participants in a study employing the original version of SHALOM [24]. Nevertheless, a few non-religious people objected to the use of "God"-words in the Transcendental domain items. These words have been modified to provide a generic version of SHALOM, which is not quite as statistically robust as the original form. The question was also raised as to whether studies deleting God could be considered "spiritual".

In keeping with the title of this paper, the best version of SHALOM to assess spiritual well-being depends on the needs of the clients/participants and the project goals of the researcher. This will involve a selection between the original form of SWBQ–SHALOM for comparison with other measures and investigation of characteristics influencing SWB; or the dissonance method for spiritual care; and either the original or the generic version of SHALOM for use with non-religious/secular participants.

Conflicts of Interest: The author declares no conflict of interest.

Abbreviations

The following abbreviations are used in this manuscript:

NICA	National Interfaith Coalition on Aging
SHALOM	Spiritual Health And Life-Orientation Measure
SH/WB	Spiritual Health/Well-Being
SWBQ	Spiritual Well-Being Questionnaire

References

1. Walter Principe. "Toward defining Spirituality." *Studies in Religion* 12 (1983): 127–41.
2. Heather M. Boynton. "Children's spirituality: Epistemology and theory from various helping professions." *International Journal of Children's Spirituality* 16 (2011): 109–27. [CrossRef]
3. John Swinton, and Stephen Pattison. "Moving beyond clarity: Towards thin, vague, and useful understanding of spirituality in nursing care." *Nursing Philosophy* 11 (2010): 226–37. [CrossRef] [PubMed]
4. David O. Moberg. "Expanding Horizons for Spirituality Research." 2011. Available online: http://hirr. hartsem.edu/sociology/spirituality-research.html (accessed on 15 October 2013).
5. National Interfaith Coalition on Aging. *Spiritual Well-Being: A Definition.* Athens: National Interfaith Coalition on Aging, 1975.
6. John W. Fisher. "Spiritual Health: Its Nature and Place in the School Curriculum." Ph.D. Thesis, University of Melbourne, Parkville, Australia, 1998.
7. Sergei A. Kharitonov. "Religious and Spiritual Biomarkers in both Health and Disease." *Religions* 3 (2012): 467–97. [CrossRef]
8. David O. Moberg. "Spirituality research: Measuring the immeasurable." *Perspectives on Science and Christian Faith* 62 (2010): 99–114.
9. Harold G. Koenig. "Concerns about measuring 'spirituality' in research." *Journal of Nervous & Mental Diseases* 196 (2008): 349–55. [CrossRef] [PubMed]
10. Peter C. Hill, and Ralph W. Hood, eds. *Measures of Religiosity.* Birmingham: Religious Education Press, 1999.
11. Douglas A. MacDonald, Jeffrey G. Kuentzel, and Harris L. Friedman. "A survey of measures of transpersonal constructs. Part II—Additional instruments." *Journal of Transpersonal Psychology* 31 (1999): 155–77.
12. Harold G. Koenig, Michael E. McCullough, and David B. Larson, eds. *Handbook of Religion and Health.* Oxford: Oxford University Press, 2001.
13. Bella Vivat. "Measures of spiritual issues for palliative care patients: A literature review." *Palliative Medicine* 22 (2008): 859–68. [CrossRef] [PubMed]

14. David O. Moberg. "Assessing and measuring spirituality: Confronting dilemmas of universal and particular evaluative criteria." *Journal of Adult Development* 9 (2002): 47–60. [CrossRef]
15. David O. Moberg. "Research in spirituality, religion, and aging." *Journal of Gerontological Social Work* 45 (2005): 11–40. [CrossRef] [PubMed]
16. Sian Cotton, Meghan O'Grady, and Susan Rosenthal. "Measurement of religiosity/spirituality in adolescent health outcomes: Trends and recommendations." *Journal of Religion & Health* 49 (2010): 414–44. [CrossRef] [PubMed]
17. Harold G. Koenig. *Spirituality & Health Research: Methods, Measurement, Statistics and Resources.* West Conshohocken: Templeton Press, 2011.
18. Nan Park, Beom Lee, Fei Sun, David Klemmack, Lucinda Roff, and Harold Koenig. "Typologies of religiousness/spirituality: Implications for health and well-being." *Journal of Religion & Health* 52 (2013): 828–39. [CrossRef] [PubMed]
19. John Fisher. "The Four Domains Model: Connecting spirituality, health and well-being." *Religions* 2 (2011): 17–28. [CrossRef]
20. John W. Fisher. "A critique of quantitative measures for assessing spirituality and spiritual well-being." In *Spirituality, Global Practices, Societal Attitudes and Effects on Health.* Edited by Edith C. Roberts. New York: Nova Science Publishers Inc., 2015, pp. 91–131.
21. Christian Zwingmann, Constantin Klein, and Arndt Büssing. "Measuring Religiosity/Spirituality: Theoretical Differentiations and Categorization of Instruments." *Religions* 2 (2011): 345–57. [CrossRef]
22. Trevor Moodley. "The Relationship between Coping and Spiritual Well-Being during Adolescence." Ph.D. Thesis, Department of Psychology, University of the Free State, Bloemfontein, South Africa, 2008.
23. Eltica Jager Meezenbroek, Bert Garssen, Machteld Berg, Dirk Dierendonck, Adriaan Visser, and Wilmar Schaufeli. "Measuring spirituality as a universal human experience: A review of spirituality questionnaires." *Journal of Religion & Health* 51 (2012): 336–54. [CrossRef] [PubMed]
24. Jonathan T. Moore. "Dogmatism, coping, and spirituality: Predicting mental health among the religious and the secular." Ph.D. Thesis, University of Louisville, Louisville, KY, USA, 2013.
25. John Fisher. "Development and application of a Spiritual Well-Being Questionnaire called SHALOM." *Religions* 1 (2010): 105–21. [CrossRef]
26. John W. Fisher. "Developing a Spiritual Health and Life-Orientation Measure for secondary school students." In *Research with a Regional/Rural Focus: Proceedings of the University of Ballarat Inaugural Annual Research Conference.* Edited by Janette Ryan, Vivienne Wittwer and Peter Baird. Ballarat: University of Ballarat, Research and Graduate Studies Office, 1999, pp. 57–63.
27. Rapson Gomez, and John W. Fisher. "Domains of spiritual well-being and development and validation of the Spiritual Well-Being Questionnaire." *Personality & Individual Differences* 35 (2003): 1975–91. [CrossRef]
28. Rapson Gomez, and John W. Fisher. "Item Response Theory analysis of the Spiritual Well-Being Questionnaire." *Personality & Individual Differences* 38 (2005): 1107–21. [CrossRef]
29. Todd W. Hall, Steven P. Reise, and Mark G. Haviland. "An Item response Theory Analysis of the Spiritual Assessment Inventory." *The International Journal for the Psychology of Religion* 17 (2007): 157–78. [CrossRef]
30. Olfa Mandhouj, Jean-François Etter, Delphine Courvoisier, and Henri-Jean Aubin. "French-language version of the World Health Organization quality of life, spirituality, religiousness and personal beliefs instrument." *Health and Quality of Life Outcomes.* 2012, 10, pp. 39–50. Available online: http://www.hqlo.com/content/10/1/39 (accessed on 26 February 2015).
31. Rapson Gomez, and John W. Fisher. "The Spiritual Well-Being Questionnaire: Testing for model applicability, measurement and structural equivalencies and latent mean differences across gender." *Personality & Individual Differences* 39 (2005): 1383–93. [CrossRef]
32. Mary Hostler, e-mail text "Anglican Girls' School Spiritual Survey" to author, 7 June 2013.
33. Antonio Muñoz-García, and Maria J. Aviles-Herrera. "Effects of academic dishonesty on dimensions of spiritual well-being and satisfaction: A comparative study of secondary school and university students." *Assessment & Evaluation in Higher Education* 39 (2014): 349–63. [CrossRef]
34. Irene Mok. "A Study of the Spiritual Health of Adolescents in Three Hong Kong Secondary Schools." Ph.D Thesis, Hong Kong Institute of Education, Hong Kong, China, 2013.

35. Celeste Y. M. Yuen. "Gender differences in life satisfaction and spiritual health among the junior immigrant and local Hong Kong secondary students." *International Journal of Children's Spirituality* 20 (2015): 139–54. [CrossRef]
36. Rebecca Norwood. "Adolescent Spiritual Well-Being as a Determinant of Physical Health and Well-Being." Master's Thesis, University of Wollongong, Wollongong, Australia, 2013.
37. Patrick Malaret and Vanguard University of Southern California, e-mail text "Spiritual Well-Being of Students in a Liberal Arts College" to author, 27 March 2013.
38. Andi Sugianto. *Factors Correlated with the Provision of Spiritual Care by Nursing Students*. BSc Nursing Research Project; Tangerang: Universitas Pelita Harapan, 2013.
39. John W. Fisher, and Ping Ho Wong. "Comparing levels of spiritual well-being and support among pre-service teachers in Hong Kong and Australia." *Religious Education Journal of Australia* 29 (2013): 33–40.
40. John W. Fisher, and M. Kamil Coskun. "Investigating spiritual well-being among Divinity and Religious Education students in Turkey." *Religious Education Journal of Australia* 29 (2013): 21–28.
41. Emma Donohue. "Investigating the relationship between spirituality, happiness and professional psychological help-seeking behaviour." Bachelor's Thesis, University of Bolton, UK, 10 October 2015.
42. John W. Fisher. "Staff's and family members' spiritual well-being in relation to help for residents with dementia." *Journal of Nursing Education & Practice* 2 (2012): 1–9. [CrossRef]
43. Carol Sykes. *Spiritual Health in Nurses Practising in End-of-Life Care*. Jackson: Union University, forthcoming.
44. Silvia Caldeira, Emilia G. de Carvalho, and Margarida Vieira. "Between spiritual well-being and spiritual distress: Possible related factors in elderly patients with cancer." *Revista Latino-Americana de Enfermagem* 22 (2014): 28–34. [CrossRef] [PubMed]
45. Ali Ashraifeen. "Influence of Spirituality on Health Outcomes and General Well-Being in Patients with End-Stage Renal Disease." Ph.D. Thesis, University of Stirling, Stirling, UK, 2015.
46. Anat P. Bortz, Tamar Ashkenazi, and Semyon Melnikov. "Spirituality as a predictive factor for signing an Organ Donor card." *Journal of Nursing Scholarship* 47 (2015): 25–33. [CrossRef] [PubMed]
47. Miri Faster, Israel, e-mail text "Investigation of How Nurses' Spiritual Well-Being Relates to Their Work" to author, 25 July 2014.
48. Marzieh Nojomi, Iran University of Medical Sciences, e-mail text "Spiritual aspects of quality of life" to author, 15 April 2015.
49. Xuefei (Gabrielle) Jin. *Exploring Motivations for Conversion to Christianity among Irish Chinese Immigrants and the Relationship between Religiosity and Spiritual Well-Being*. Bain Theology & Psychology Research Project; Dublin: All Hallows College, 2015.
50. Rita T. Silalahi. "Emotional Intelligence and Personality Traits on the Spiritual Well-Being of the Junior Religious Sisters in a Community." Master's Thesis, Graduate School, University of Santo Tomas, Manila, Philippines, 2014.
51. Lynette M. Monteiro. "Burnout and Spiritual Incongruence: An Evidence-Based Counselling Model for Buddhist Chaplains." Bachelor's Thesis, Upaya Zen Institute, Santa Fe, NM, USA, 2011.
52. Nguyen Bao Uyen. "Exploring the Relationship between Spiritual Well-Being and Psychological Well-Being among Religious Sisters in Vietnam." Ph.D. Thesis, De La Salle University, Manila, Philippines, 28 February 2016.
53. Jay R. Deagon. "Cross-Cultural Views and Perceptions of Spiritual Health and Well-Being in Home Economics Sites: Public Expressions and Social Enactments." Ph.D. Thesis, Griffith University, Queensland, Australia, 2014.
54. Brenda I. Sanchez. "The Perception of the SWB and Its Relationship with Optimism, Autoefficacy and Organizational Citizenship Behavior in a Workplace Sample from a Public Corporation of Puerto Rico." Ph.D. Thesis, Carlos Albizu University, San Juan, Puerto Rico, 2012.
55. Maria J. Gouveia, Marta Marques and José L. Pais Ribeiro. "Versã Portuguesa do questionário de Bem-Estar Espiritual (SWBQ): Análise confirmatória da sua estrutura factorial." *Psicologia, Saúde & Doenças* 10 (2009): 285–93.
56. Maria J. Gouveia, José L. Pais Ribeiro, and Marta Marques. "Estudo da invariaçia do Questionário de Bem-estar spiritual (SWBQ) em praticantes de Atividades Fisicas de Inspiração Oriental." *Psychology, Community & Health* 1 (2012): 140–50. [CrossRef]

57. António M. F. Veiga. "Análise Crítica da Adaptação do Instrument Shalom, a Uma Amostra de Idosos." Master's Thesis, Instituto Universitário Ciéncias Psicológicas, Sociais e da Vida, Lisbon, Portugal, 2014. Available online: http://www.rcaap.pt/detail.jsp?id=oai:repositirio.ispa.pt:10400.12/3076 (accessed on 22 February 2016).

58. Rafi Chowdhury, and Mario Fernando. "The role of spiritual well-being and materialism in determining consumers' ethical beliefs: An empirical study with Australian consumers." *Journal of Business Ethics* 13 (2013): 61–79. [CrossRef]

59. Eluned Mulligan, Bath, UK, e-mail text "Assessing the Concurrent Validity of the WHOQOL-SPRB Bref: A New Measure of Spiritual Quality of Life" to author, 9 May 2012.

60. Inês N. de Brito. "Relação entre o bem-estar spiritual e sintomas psicopatológicas na população adulta Portuguesa." Master's Thesis, Instituto Universitário, ISPA, Lisboa, Portugal, 2014.

61. John W. Fisher. "Assessing spiritual well-being: Relating with God explains greatest variance in spiritual well-being among Australian youth." *International Journal of Children's Spirituality* 18 (2013): 306–17. [CrossRef]

62. Sangaroon Jaiwongpab. "Spiritual Health among Relatives of Critically Ill Patients." Master's Thesis, Chiang Mai University, Chiang Mai, Thailand, 2016.

63. Mahdi Esfahani, Ghazali Musa, and Selins Khoo. "The influence of spirituality and physical activity on responsible behaviour and mountaineering satisfaction on Mount Kinabalu, Borneo." *Current Issues in Tourism*. Published electronically 3 December 2014. [CrossRef]

64. Philé Swanepoel, Karel G.F Esterhuyse, Roelf Beukes, and Nico Nortjé. "Die rol van coping in die verband tussen geestelike welstand en depressive by predikante." *HTS Teologiese Studies/Theological Studies*. 2012. Available online: http://dx.doi.org/10.4102/hts.v68i1.1071 (accessed on 13 May 2015).

65. John W. Fisher. "Comparing the influence of God and other Transcendents on spiritual well-being." *Religious Education Journal of Australia* 30 (2014): 9–15.

66. Craig Ellison. "Spiritual well-being: Conceptualization and measurement." *Journal of Psychology & Theology* 11 (1983): 330–40.

67. Central Intelligence Agency. "World Fact Book—Religions." 2010. Available online: https://www.cia.gov/library/publications/the-world-fact-book/religions (accessed on 26 January 2014).

68. Richard H. Schmidt. *God Seekers: Twenty Centuries of Christian Spiritualities*. Grand Rapids: Wm Eerdmans Publishing Co., 2008.

69. Brian L. Seaward. *Health of the Human Spirit: Spiritual Dimensions for Personal Health*. Boston: Allyn & Bacon, 2001.

70. John W. Fisher. "You can't beat relating with God for spiritual well-being: Comparing a generic version with the original spiritual well-being questionnaire called SHALOM." *Religions* 4 (2013): 325–35. [CrossRef]

71. John Fisher. "Investigating the importance of relating with God for school students' spiritual well-being." *Journal of Beliefs & Values* 31 (2010): 325–34. [CrossRef]

72. John W. Fisher. "The importance of relating with God for spiritual well-being." In *Spirituality: New Reflections on Theory, Praxis & Pedagogy*. Edited by Michael Weiss and Martin Fowler. Oxford: InterDisciplinary Press, 2012, pp. 147–61.

73. John W. Fisher. "God counts for children's spiritual well-being." *International Journal of Children's Spirituality* 20 (2015): 191–203. [CrossRef]

74. John Fisher. "Feeling Good, Living Life: A spiritual health measure for young children." *Journal of Beliefs & Values* 25 (2004): 307–15. [CrossRef]

75. John Fisher. "Impacting teachers' and students' spiritual well-being." *Journal of Beliefs & Values* 29 (2008): 252–61. [CrossRef]

76. John W. Fisher, and David J. Brumley. "Nurses' and carers' spiritual well-being in the workplace." *Australian Journal of Advanced Nursing* 25 (2008): 49–57.

77. John W. Fisher, and David J. Brumley. "Palliative care doctors need help with spiritual well-being." *Journal for the Study of Spirituality* 2 (2012): 49–60. [CrossRef]
78. Barbara G. Tabachnick, and Linda S. Fidell. *Using Multivariate Statistics*, 5th ed. Chicago: University of Chicago Press, 2007.

 *religions*

Brief Report

The Inventory of Complicated Spiritual Grief: Assessing Spiritual Crisis Following Loss

Laurie A. Burke * and Robert A. Neimeyer

Department of Psychology, University of Memphis, Memphis, 400 Innovation Drive, TN 38152, USA; neimeyer@memphis.edu
* Correspondence: laburke@memphis.edu; Tel.: +1-503-673-1848

Academic Editor: Arndt Büssing
Received: 12 February 2016; Accepted: 28 May 2016; Published: 4 June 2016

Abstract: Following the death of a loved one, many grievers endorse spirituality as a source of both solace and strain. Studies show that some grievers struggle significantly with both their relationship with God and their faith community, a condition known as complicated spiritual grief (CSG). However, researchers have lacked a simple, multidimensional, well-validated, grief-specific measure of CSG. In this brief report, we reviewed the psychometric validation process and clinical utility of a measure called the Inventory of Complicated Spiritual Grief (ICSG), which was tested with 304 Christian grievers. The 18-item ICSG was shown to have strong internal consistency, high test–retest reliability, and convergent and incremental validity and supported a two-factor model, measuring one's insecurity with God and the disruption in one's religious practice.

Keywords: complicated spiritual grief; spiritual struggle; spiritual crisis; bereavement; complicated grief; meaning making

1. Introduction

Contemporary research has revealed that the death of a loved one can elicit a variety of responses in survivors. Psychologically, many bereaved individuals are able to bounce back relatively quickly after the death [1]. Some grievers experience symptoms of grief-related distress (e.g., anguish, sorrow) for a year or more before they are able to incorporate the loss into their lives [2]. Still other bereaved people struggle tremendously in coming to terms with the death or in making a life for themselves without their treasured loved one. This chronic condition, known as complicated grief (CG) [3], prolonged grief disorder [4], or persistent complex bereavement disorder [5], is a protracted, debilitating, sometimes life-threatening grief response. CG is characterized by a state of persistent grieving, wherein the mourner experiences profound separation distress, psychologically disturbing and intrusive thoughts of the deceased, and a sense that life is empty and meaningless [6,7].

Mounting research also suggests that for a subset of mourners who are spiritually inclined, bereavement can usher in a crisis of faith—a distinct time when their spiritual ways of experiencing and understanding life and their long-held religious beliefs are called into question. In the context of bereavement, prolonged and debilitating spiritual distress of this sort, which includes the collapse or erosion of the griever's sense of relationship to God and/or their faith community, has been termed complicated spiritual grief (CSG) [8,9] and has shown an empirically consistent association with CG [7,10–13].

For spiritual leaders, clinicians, and researchers who seek to create, apply, and assess psycho-spiritual treatments for spiritually inclined mourners who struggle with their faith following loss, this link between CG and CSG is critical. Until recently, however, in terms of measuring levels and aspects of spiritual distress experienced by grievers, there has been a paucity of bereavement-specific instruments to do so. This meant that those serving grievers were limited to the use of generic measures of spiritual struggle. Thus, Burke, Neimeyer, Holland *et al.* developed, tested, and validated a new measure of spiritual distress called the Inventory of Complicated Spiritual Grief (ICSG; see Appendix) [14] to bridge this critical gap. In terms of evaluating a griever's level of spiritual distress in the context of bereavement, to our knowledge, the ICSG is the only validated instrument in the field.

2. The Need for a Bereavement-Specific Measure of Spiritual Distress

Historically, researchers have measured spiritual struggle by accessing negative emotions, behaviors, and attitudes that an individual experiences in relation to God and, in some cases, to his/her spiritual network of believers. Specifically, studies have been conducted that examine spiritual distress using a single item (e.g., [15,16]), others use factor analysis to derive subscales [17], and still others investigate this construct using event-specific scales (e.g., [16]). Pargament *et al.*'s [18] Brief RCOPE includes two subscales, with one designed to capture signs of supportive spirituality (e.g., positive religious coping (PRC) and the other to capture signs of spiritual distress (e.g., negative religious coping (NRC); see also the Spiritual Assessment Inventory (SAI) [19]; Attitudes Toward God Scale-9 (ATGS-9); [20]). Although useful, these instruments assess spiritual struggle using only a few items. Some researchers support the parsing of such subscales into specific items (e.g., [21]), finding that this informs their exploration of aspects of spiritual struggle, such as anger and disappointment with God.

Now, however, the development and validation of a psychometrically sound measure designed specifically to capture signs of spiritual distress in bereavement (*i.e.*, ICSG) can advance grief research in new ways. Specifically, a more nuanced understanding of spiritual aspects of bereavement processes is now possible with the development of a measure of distinctive aspects of spiritual struggle, such as doubt and resentment toward God, dissatisfaction with religious activities and fellowship, and substantial changes in the griever's spiritual beliefs and behaviors following the loved one's death (see also [11]).

Compared to the more generic assessment of spiritual struggle found in such scales as the SAI (e.g., *There are times when I feel betrayed by God*; [19]), the Brief RCOPE (e.g., *Felt abandoned by God*; [18]), and the ATGS-9; (e.g., *Felt angry at God*; [20]), the ICSG provides a more fine-grained inquiry of spiritual crisis (e.g., *I don't feel very much like joining in fellowship to praise God or to glorify Him*; or *I sense the absence of God more than I do the presence of God*). Thus, CSG can be more comprehensively evaluated using the ICSG with its wide array of candidate items bearing on spiritually imbued responses reflective of the grief associated with the loss of a loved one. Currently available scales, such as the SAI [19], the Brief RCOPE [18], and the ATGS-9; [20], all of which were validated with non-bereaved adult samples experiencing a wide assortment of life stressors, may fail to measure spiritual crisis in the specific context of bereavement. Therefore, in an effort to help grievers reestablish a loving and close relationship with God "during times of frightening vulnerability" ([8], p. 304) and derive meaning from the deceased's life and death [22], Burke and her colleagues' [14] goal was to shed additional light on mourners' spiritually inflected struggles by testing their grief-specific scale with two diverse samples of bereaved adults.

2.1. Development

The original 28 items on the ICSG (see Appendix A) were derived from the results of several studies where data were collected from written self-reports and focus group participants, all of whom endorsed a Christian religious framework [9,11] and from ongoing collaboration with church pastors who routinely serve bereaved congregants. The original construct of CSG and interest in testing it arose from a study conducted by Shear and her colleagues [9]. Pastors at a large, well-established, Protestant church requested that Shear's research team develop and test a two-session, faith-oriented treatment for bereaved parishioners. To ascertain the affects of the loss on their faith, the researchers evaluated the grief experiences of a sample of African American congregants ($N = 31$). With response options ranging from "faith stronger than ever" to "faith seriously shaken," 19% of participants endorsed feeling as if their faith had been negatively altered by the death. This type of "spiritual grief" ([9], p. 7), as Shear's group referred to it, reflects a form of spiritually permeated anguish that arises when survivors protest the loss as being ostensibly untimely or unfair. Similarly, when believers, who view life events as being mediated by the hand of God, sense that the death of their cherished loved one came as a direct result of that same hand, this scenario can destabilize the griever's spiritual sense-making, as all of life's well-established assumptions are now likewise called into question.

Many researchers view grief reactions as falling on a continuum of highly resilient to severely complicated responses. For Shear and her colleagues [9], CSG occurs similarly. Grief that is expressed in spiritual terms is similar to grief that is experienced psychologically, where CSG characterizes the most problematic spiritual responses of all.

2.2. Validation

To more fully evaluate the psycho-spiritual construct of CSG, Burke, Neimeyer, Holland *et al.* [14] developed and validated the ICSG. First, in one sample, exploratory factor analysis (EFA) was used to test the scale's factor structure. In another sample, confirmatory factor analysis (CFA) was used. Second, associated constructs were examined to test convergent validity. Third, with scores from a general-purpose measure of spiritual struggle held constant, items that were correlated with complicated grief symptoms were used to test incremental validity. Finally, the ICSG was evaluated for test–retest reliability and internal consistency. Burke and her colleagues hypothesized that scales of complicated grief and NRC would reveal a positive association with ICSG, and a negative association with scales of meaning making and PRC.

The ICSG was tested using data from two samples [14]. One, the *community sample*, was made up of 152 adult grievers. The second, the *college student sample*, was made up of 152 bereaved University of Memphis psychology undergraduates. Psychometrically, an 18-item scale with two subscales emerged—*Insecurity with God* and *Disruption in Religious Practice*. An exploratory factor analysis that was conducted using data from the community sample supported this two-factor model. This model's generalizability was evidenced through use of confirmatory factor analysis, which was conducted using the student sample data. Consistent with initial hypotheses, the ICSG performed satisfactorily in providing a stable and coherent measure of spiritual distress in bereavement, which was evident in the high test–retest reliability and internal consistency of the ICSG total scores and both subscales.

Burke and her team [14] used the scale's item content to show that *Insecurity with God*, which was the first seven-item factor, measured the level to which the bereaved person struggled with confusion in relation to God, questioned His protective nature, and felt angry at God during bereavement. *Disruption in Religious Practice* emerged as an 11-item factor that evaluated the extent to which the death interfered with the mourner's religious practices, ability to worship, and relationship with his/her spiritual community. The sum of all items equals the ICSG's total score.

Subscale scores and total scores were correlated with representative scales in expected directions, indicating convergent and discriminant validity. In terms of convergent validity, for example, the following measures were statistically significantly associated with ICSG total scores in both the community and college student samples, respectively: the Inventory of Complicated Grief-Revised (ICG-R; [7]; $r = 0.34$, $r = 0.49$), the NRC subscale of the Brief RCOPE ([18]; $r = 0.43$, $r = 0.50$), and subscales of the Religious Coping Activities Scale (RCA; [23]), including Discontent ($r = 0.53$, $r = 0.57$) and Plead ($r = 0.31$, $r = 0.23$). In relation to discriminant validity, ICSG total scores showed a statistically significant negative association in both samples, respectively, with the following measures: the PRC subscale of the Brief RCOPE ($r = -0.36$, $r = -0.50$), subscales of the RCA, including Spiritual Based Coping ($r = -0.49$, $r = -0.63$), Good Deeds ($r = -0.32$, $r = -0.45$), Interpersonal Religious Support ($r = -0.15$ n.s., $r = -0.31$), and Religious Avoidance ($r = -0.27$, $r = -0.42$), and meaning making as assessed using the Integration of Stressful Life Experiences Scale (ISLES; [24]; $r = -0.28$, $r = -0.48$). Thus, on the one hand, higher ICSG total scores were related to elevated levels of complicated grief, negative religious coping, religious discontent, and religious pleading. On the other hand, higher ICSG total scores were related to lower levels of positive religious and spiritual coping, religious good deeds, interpersonal religious support, religious avoidance, and meaning made of loss.

Even after controlling for scores on the NRC subscale of the Brief RCOPE (a non-grief-specific measure of spiritual crisis), elevated levels of complicated grief were correlated with high levels of ICSG total scores in tests of incremental validity. This held true for both the college student samples ($\beta = 0.36$, $p < 0.001$) and the community samples ($\beta = 0.22$, $p = 0.009$).

Good internal consistency was found for both subscales (*Insecurity with God*, $\alpha = 0.89$ and 0.87; *Disruption in Religious Practice*, $\alpha = 0.93$ and 0.96) and for the 18-item ICSG as a whole ($\alpha = 0.92$ and 0.95) in the community and college student samples, respectively.

Evidence of the ICSG's long-term stability was documented in the form of high test–retest correlations for both subscales (*Insecurity with God*, $r = 0.96$, $p < 0.001$; *Disruption in Religious Practice*, $r = 0.95$, $p < 0.001$) and ICSG total scores ($r = 0.97$, $p < 0.001$) through use of follow-up data (3–4 weeks after the initial evaluation) from a subset of the college-aged grievers ($n = 31$).

3. Clinical Applications

The ICSG is clinically useful in evaluating the spiritually inclined griever's faith journey during bereavement. Additionally, it can help determine specifically which religious/spiritual issues might come up for a given believer while engaged in therapy. Because both mental health professionals and their spiritually distressed clients often feel unsure about how to broach the topic of spiritual discord following a death, use of an additional tool such as the ICSG is sometimes warranted. For example, in some cases, it may be that a therapist approaches discussions of a spiritual kind with hesitation and cautiousness. In other cases, it may be that a bereaved client feels a sense of self-disappointment and shame in expressing his/her honest sentiments toward God. Whatever the scenario, introducing conversations centered on such things as the survivor's confusion about how to make spiritual sense of the death, feelings of abandonment by fellow congregants, disappointment with God, or other complicated and emotive topics, thoughts, and responses can be challenging for many mourners.

Prior to its empirical validation, Burke and her team [14] recruited spiritually inclined grieving adults from a pool of eligible participants to partake in a focus group designed to refine the ICSG's content to better reflect the experience of spiritually inclined mourners. Five grievers participated in the focus group based on their endorsement of high levels of distress in terms of CSG, assessed using quantitative scales (e.g., the NRC subscale of the Brief RCOPE [18] or the Discontent subscale of the RCA [23]), or whose narrative responses to four open-ended questions (related to their thoughts and feelings about their relationship with both God and their spiritual community following the loss and about the ways in which the loss strengthened or challenged those relationships) suggested present, or past, spiritual distress (*i.e.*, earlier in the bereavement period). Focus group members were diverse in terms of age, race, time since loss, and cause of death and are briefly described here: Elaine,[1] a 65-year-old African American woman who lost her 24-year-old son, Bronson, to homicide 6.6 years prior; Latisha, a 36-year-old African American woman who lost her 69-year-old grandmother, Mabel, to natural, anticipated causes 9.4 months prior; Rhonda, a 23-year-old Caucasian woman who lost her 55-year-old mother, Norma, to natural, sudden causes 8.1 months prior; Caroline, a 59-year-old African American widow who lost her 55-year-old husband, Ronald, to homicide 3.5 years prior; and Suzanne, a 19-year-old Caucasian woman who lost her 68-year-old grandmother, Nell, to accidental causes 7.3 years prior.

The focus group participants were asked 15 questions derived from the results of prior narrative analyses. Members' responses were coded using directed content analysis to develop an *a priori* coding scheme. Completed analyses were followed up with member-checking and triangulation of the data.

---

[1]   Pseudonyms are used for focus group members, clients, and patients throughout manuscript.

Thus, conclusions drawn upon to inform the ICSG stemmed from the results of three sets of data (*i.e.*, the quantitative measures, the open-ended questionnaire, and the focus group sessions).

The responses of focus group members and other research participants who contributed written narratives revealed an overarching story of resentment and doubt toward God, dissatisfaction with the spiritual support received, and substantial changes in their spiritual beliefs and behaviors following the death. For instance, with regard to God, one participant's narrative spoke volumes about the source of clinically significant distress that highlighted how her assumptions about life and God had been shattered [25], compromising her ability to make spiritual sense of the death. Selena, a 29-year-old Caucasian woman who was grieving the loss of her 60-year-old father who died suddenly of natural causes, exclaimed, "I was very angry at God. I didn't want to pray or read my Bible. I was confused because of how I thought God was supposed to be. I knew in my heart that I could never turn my back on God because there is nowhere else worth turning, but I felt very betrayed by him."

To further illustrate Selena's sense of betrayal, we highlight below how items on the ICSG helped to identify the spiritual struggle of one severely distraught mother in her spiritual quest for meaning and purpose. Cassandra is a 34-year-old African American mother who was grieving the loss of her 2-year-old son following a tragic accident. She told us, "The first thought was 'What did I do wrong to cause my son to die?' I thought that maybe I hadn't been 'good' enough or had committed some sin that I wasn't aware of. I longed for the presence of God, to feel him near. By presence I mean a strong sense of peace." Whether Cassandra's expectations of God are valid is irrelevant. What her testimony tells us is that many believers have a well-developed perception of how God should interact with them, especially in times of dire need, and when those expectations are violated by subsequent events, in their eyes, God has failed them.

In relation to her would-be spiritual supporters, Cassandra added, "I felt that I was wronged by those in my spiritual community, because I was told to 'live right' and God would bless me. I knew that struggles would happen but not something as senseless as my baby dying. I felt a struggle between my faith and my feelings of anger, sadness, and terror. In fact, I lost confidence. At one time, I reverenced those in my spiritual community who I thought had the answers to the 'spiritual life' that one should lead. Most that I was in contact with before the loss seemed to have all the answers, but, after my son's death, they had none. But instead of saying that, they just abandoned me and my family. We were left alone with our grief. Eventually, we left that particular place of worship and found a new place." Here, Cassandra's narrative highlights how CSG is not primarily about disgruntled, disillusioned believers walking away from God. Rather, it appears to be primarily about spiritually hurting individuals who are desperately searching and seeking to make spiritual sense of their loss and are coming up short. Her experience confirms the surprising finding that a spiritual crisis does not necessarily indicate immature or weak faith [11]. Rather, when facing life without a treasured attachment figure, even people with a firm faith in God can unexpectedly falter under the burden of grief. Even when grievers walk away from God and/or their faith network, it does not rule out their return to either at a later date, especially once their grief symptoms subside.

Thus, by simply asking clients to complete the ICSG between or before sessions, counselors could find the scale useful as a therapeutic conversational catalyst for healing. The therapist might suggest that the patient "Start anywhere...Which of these items that you marked are important for you today? Are there one or two that really set you off when you think about God or your church?" As the clinician invites deep probing of the client's pain in order to craft and utilize treatment techniques precisely suited for the situation, discussions can ensue in which the spiritually distressed griever can finally speak the unspeakable. Often, up until that point, the person has held back a world of hurt, disappointment, discontentment, and resentment toward God, sensing that to directly target God or a fellow believer is somehow incongruous with being a "good Christian." Thus, a troubling loss can elicit confusing and complex emotions that well up inside a spiritually inclined griever but with no clear place to direct them.

Such was the case for Clarina, a 68-year old Caucasian client, who consulted a therapist (LAB) and endorsed high levels of spiritual distress on the ICSG seven years after the death of her husband following a lengthy battle with cancer. Follow-up conversations revealed a palpable reluctance to expound on any of her endorsed responses, stemming from what she referred to as the "fear-based faith" tradition in which she was raised. In fact, she was afraid to be angry with God, though she clearly was. She was timid about questioning his judgment, though everything within her screamed to do just that. Completing the ICSG, with its descriptive statements indicative of spiritual conflict, opened Clarina up spiritually, creating a willingness to explore her disgust, distrust, and disappointment with God in ways that felt safer than engaging in a verbal protest. Thus, introducing the ICSG items on paper gave Clarina an avenue with which to express her long-held pain and resentment. She subsequently took the therapist's suggestion to read a book on the same theme [26], which then became a weekly therapy topic that she initiated rather than avoided. Interestingly, similar methods also have been used successfully with mourners who are angry with God but who have long ago denounced their faith or who claim to never have espoused faith in the first place. For still other bereaved Christian clients who are open and willing, the provider can facilitate healing through a chairing experience [27–29], for example, where the survivor holds an imaginal conversation with God (or a fellow parishioner), allowing for a full expression of anger, anguish, and sorrow in a safe, supportive setting.

4. Limitations

Even though the ICSG has been tested with both African American and Caucasian samples, it remains to be seen whether the scale can be meaningfully used with bereaved individuals in other faith traditions, especially given that the items originated with Christian participants. For example, the ICSG likely would not be suitable for most non-monotheistic faith traditions (*i.e.*, ones that are not variations of Christianity, Judaism, or Islam), especially given its focus on a personal relationship with God, church attendance, and frequent fellowship with a like-minded community of believers. For this reason, other measures should be developed to better assess unique spiritual struggles that are expressed by grievers from other traditions of faith or belief (e.g., Buddhism, Hinduism, or less theistic spiritual or secular world views) using non-Christian terms and references.

5. Conclusions

The ICSG is an easy-to-use, multidimensional scale of spiritual crisis during bereavement that can be used in a variety of clinical settings and with a range of research samples. Our review of this scale leads us to hope that the ICSG will be widely used by providers of psycho-spiritual care and researchers as they evaluate and treat the phenomenon of spiritual struggle as it pertains specifically to grief rather than in the form of NRC or general spirituality. Moreover, the ICSG enables clinicians to distinguish between types of spiritual struggle—in terms of one's relationship with God or with their community of spiritual practice. Going forward, as this work proceeds beyond that of Christian or Abrahamic traditions, researchers should empirically test whether loss-related spiritual struggle is experienced by spiritually inclined individuals regardless of their faith tradition or lack of one. We also foresee that having a tool to measure the construct of CSG might make a valuable contribution to both research and practice in a way that ultimately promotes better grief outcomes. For example, future research that explores possible links between CSG and post-traumatic growth, or that develops and tests therapeutic interventions designed to ameliorate spiritual distress and promote resilience and meaning making among mourners could advance the field in terms of clinical understanding and by fostering positive outcomes in bereavement. Thus, we consider the ICSG to be useful in conceptualizing, appraising, and reporting grief-specific spiritual crises in response to a wide variety of applied disciplines, whether pastoral, clinical, or empirical.

Acknowledgments: The authors gratefully acknowledge the grant support from the Tennessee Board of Regents for the project *African Americans in Bereavement II: Assessment and Treatment of Complicated Spiritual Grief following Traumatic Loss* and Jamison Bottomley for his assistance with manuscript formatting.

Author Contributions: Laurie A. Burke spearheaded the research program on which this article is based, and took the lead in writing most of the text of the current manuscript. She continues to pursue research in spiritual adaptation to loss, both in the context of bereavement and in end-of-life care, such as response to a loved one's palliative care experience. The assessment of spiritual struggle remains a focus of her research, and she currently is refining measures of this construct. Robert A. Neimeyer served in a supportive role in many of the studies reported in this article, and shared responsibility for its composition, particularly in sections concerned with meaning making and the clinical implications of this research. He and his colleagues are actively pursuing research on predictors of complicated grief and are devising and validating interventions that focus on the search for significance in the wake of loss.

Conflicts of Interest: The authors declare no conflict of interest.

Abbreviations

The following abbreviations are used in this manuscript:

CG	complicated grief
CSG	complicated spiritual grief
ICSG	Inventory of Complicated Spiritual Grief
PGD	prolonged grief disorder
PCBD	persistent complex bereavement disorder
Brief RCOPE	Brief Religious Coping Scale
PRC	positive religious coping
NRC	negative religious coping
SAI	Spiritual Assessment Inventory-9
ATGS-9	Attitudes Toward God Scale-9
EFA	exploratory factor analysis
CFA	confirmatory factor analysis
RCA	Religious Coping Activities Scale
ISLES	Integration of Stressful Life Experiences Scale

Appendix A

Inventory of Complicated Spiritual Grief (ICSG)
Original 28-Item Version

1.   I don't understand why God has made it so hard for me.
2.   I no longer feel safe and protected by God.
3.   I struggle with accepting how a good God allows bad things to happen.
4.   I can't help feeling angry with God.
5.   I'm confused as to why God would let this happen.
6.   My trust in God has been shaken.
7.   I have withdrawn from my fellowship with other believers.
8.   I go out of my way to avoid spiritual/religious activities (e.g., prayer, worship, Bible reading).
9.   I find that spiritual/religious activities are not very fulfilling (e.g., prayer, worship, Bible reading).
10.   I have lost my desire to pray.
11.   I find it impossible to pray.
12.   I feel God is not listening when I pray.
13.   I feel my loss is unfair.
14.   I feel others who have not lost someone close are especially blessed.
15.   I feel others who have not lost someone close cannot understand me.
16.   I find it difficult to surrender my life to God.
17.   I feel like God has forsaken me, or like He has forgotten or passed over me.
18.   I don't feel as comforted by church fellowship as I used to.
19.   I don't feel very much like joining in fellowship to praise God or to glorify Him.
20.   The strong guiding light of my faith has grown dim and I feel lost.
21.   My faith has been shaken.

22. I am a faithful believer, so I don't understand why God did not protect me.
23. My focus is more on my loss than on the will of God.
24. I have lost my desire to worship.
25. I find it impossible to worship.
26. I sense the absence of God more than I do the presence of God.
27. The tragedy of my loss has made me question whether God truly exists.
28. I have concerns about my loved one's eternal welfare.

Appendix B

Inventory of Complicated Spiritual Grief (ICSG)

Please think about your loss of _____, and then read each statement carefully. Choose the answer that best describes how you have been feeling during the past 2 weeks including today. Please answer these based on how you *actually* feel, rather than what you *believe* you should feel.

Items	Not at all true	A little true	Some what true	Mostly true	Very definitely true
1) I don't understand why God has made it so hard for me.	0	1	2	3	4
2) I have withdrawn from my fellowship with other believers.	0	1	2	3	4
3) I go out of my way to avoid spiritual/ religious activities (e.g., prayer, worship, Bible reading).	0	1	2	3	4
4) I no longer feel safe and protected by God.	0	1	2	3	4
5) I find that spiritual/religious activities are not very fulfilling (e.g., prayer, worship, Bible reading)	0	1	2	3	4
6) I find it impossible to pray.	0	1	2	3	4
7) I struggle with accepting how a good God allows bad things to happen.	0	1	2	3	4
8) I find it difficult to surrender my life to God.	0	1	2	3	4
9) I don't feel as comforted by church fellowship as I used to.	0	1	2	3	4
10) I can't help feeling angry with God.	0	1	2	3	4
11) I don't feel very much like joining in fellowship to praise God or to glorify Him.	0	1	2	3	4
12) The strong guiding light of my faith has grown dim and I feel lost.	0	1	2	3	4
13) I'm confused as to why God would let this happen.	0	1	2	3	4
14) I have lost my desire to worship.	0	1	2	3	4
15) I find it impossible to worship.	0	1	2	3	4
16) I feel my loss is unfair.	0	1	2	3	4
17) I sense the absence of God more than I do the presence of God.	0	1	2	3	4
18) I am a faithful believer, so I don't understand why God did not protect me.	0	1	2	3	4

Notes: A sum of all items can be taken to compute an ICSG total score. Likewise, items 1, 4, 7, 10, 13, 16, and 18 can be summed to compute the Insecurity with God subscale, and items 2, 3, 5, 6, 8, 9, 11, 12, 14, 15, and 17 can be summed to compute the Disruption in Religious Practice subscale.

This scale is published in the public domain to encourage its use by interested clinicians and researchers. No formal permission is required for its duplication and use beyond citation of its source and authorship.

References

1. George A. Bonanno, and Stacey Kaltman. "The Varieties of Grief Experience." *Clinical Psychology Review* 21 (2001): 705–34. [CrossRef]
2. George A. Bonanno, and Anthony D. Mancini. "Bereavement-related Depression and PTSD: Evaluating Interventions." In *Psychological Interventions in Times of Crisis.* Edited by Laura Barbanel and Robert J. Sternberg. New York: Springer, 2006, pp. 37–55.
3. Holly G. Prigerson, Ellen Frank, Stanislav V. Kasl, Charles F. Reynolds, Barbara Anderson, George S. Zubenko, Patricia R. Houck, Charles J. George, and David J. Kupfer. "Complicated Grief and Bereavement Related Depression as Distinct Disorders: Preliminary Empirical Validation in Elderly Bereaved Spouses." *American Journal of Psychiatry* 152 (1995): 22–30. [PubMed]
4. Holly G. Prigerson, Mardi J. Horowitz, Selby C. Jacobs, Colin M. Parkes, Mihaela Aslan, Karl Goodkin, Beverley Raphael, Samuel J. Marwit, Camille B. Wortman, Robert A. Neimeyer, and *et al.* "Prolonged Grief Disorder: Psychometric Validation of Criteria Proposed for DSM-V and ICD-11." *PLOS Medicine* 6 (2009): 1–12. [CrossRef] [PubMed]
5. American Psychiatric Association. *Diagnostic and Statistical Manual of Mental Disorders*, 5th ed. Washington: American Psychiatric Association, 2013.
6. Jason M. Holland, Robert A. Neimeyer, Paul A. Boelen, and Holly G. Prigerson. "The Underlying Structure of Grief: A Taxometric Investigation of Prolonged and Normal Reactions to Loss." *Journal of Psychopathology and Behavioral Assessment* 31 (2009): 190–201. [CrossRef]
7. Holly G. Prigerson, and Selby C. Jacobs. "Traumatic Grief as a Distinct Disorder: A Rationale, Consensus Criteria, and a Preliminary Empirical Test." In *Handbook of Bereavement Research.* Edited by Margaret Stroebe, Robert O. Hansson, Wolfgang Stroebe and Henk Schut. Washington: American Psychological Association, 2001, pp. 613–45.
8. Laurie A. Burke, Robert A. Neimeyer, Meghan E. McDevitt-Murphy, Maria R. Ippolito, and J. Matthew Roberts. "Faith in the Wake of Homicide: Religious Coping and Bereavement Distress in an African American Sample." *International Journal for the Psychology of Religion* 21 (2011): 289–307. [CrossRef]
9. Margaret Katherine Shear, Sharon Dennard, Montele Crawford, Mario Cruz, Bonnie Gorscak, and Linda Oliver. "Developing a Two-session Intervention for Church-based Bereavement Support: A Pilot Project." Paper presented at The 22nd International Society Traumatic Stress Studies, Hollywood, CA, USA, 4–7 November 2006, pp. 5–7.
10. Laurie A. Burke, and Robert A. Neimeyer. "Complicated Spiritual Grief I: Relation to Complicated Grief Symptomatology Following Violent Death Bereavement." *Death Studies* 38 (2014): 259–67. [CrossRef] [PubMed]
11. Laurie A. Burke, Robert A. Neimeyer, Amanda J. Young, Elizabeth Piazza Bonin, and Natalie L. Davis. "Complicated Spiritual Grief II: A Deductive Inquiry Following the Loss of a Loved One." *Death Studies* 38 (2014): 268–81. [CrossRef] [PubMed]
12. Wendy G. Lichtenthal, Laurie A. Burke, and Robert A. Neimeyer. "Religious Coping and Meaning-making Following the Loss of a Loved One." *Counseling and Spirituality* 30 (2011): 113–36.
13. Robert A. Neimeyer, and Laurie A. Burke. "Complicated Grief in the Aftermath of Homicide: Spiritual Crisis and Distress in an African American Sample." *Religions* 2 (2011): 145–64. [CrossRef]
14. Laurie A. Burke, Robert A. Neimeyer, Jason M. Holland, Sharon Dennard, Linda Oliver, and Margaret Katherine Shear. "Inventory of Complicated Spiritual Grief: Development and Validation of a New Measure." *Death Studies* 38 (2014): 239–50. [CrossRef] [PubMed]
15. Julie Juola Exline, Ann Marie Yali, and William C. Sanderson. "Guilt, Discord, and Alienation: The Role of Religious Strain in Depression and Suicidality." *Journal of Clinical Psychology* 56 (2000): 1481–96. [CrossRef]
16. Julie J. Exline, Crystal L. Park, Joshua M. Smyth, and Michael P. Carey. "Anger toward God: Social-Cognitive Predictors, Prevalence, and Links with Adjustment to Bereavement and Cancer." *Journal of Personality and Social Psychology* 100 (2011): 129–48. [CrossRef] [PubMed]
17. Terry Lynn Gall, Elizabeth Kristjansson, Claire Charbonneau, and Peggy Florack. "A Longitudinal Study on the Role of Spirituality in Response to the Diagnosis and Treatment of Breast Cancer." *Journal of Behavioral Medicine* 32 (2009): 174–86. [CrossRef] [PubMed]

18. Kenneth I. Pargament, Bruce W. Smith, Harold G. Koenig, and Lisa Perez. "Patterns of Positive and Negative Religious Coping with Major Life Stressors." *Journal for the Scientific Study of Religion* 37 (1998): 710–24. [CrossRef]
19. Todd W. Hall, and Keith J. Edwards. "The Spiritual Assessment Inventory: A Theistic Model and Measure for Assessing Spiritual Development." *Journal for the Scientific Study of Religion* 41 (2002): 341–57. [CrossRef]
20. Benjamin T. Wood, Everett L. Worthington, Jr., Julie Juola Exline, Ann Marie Yali, Jamie D. Aten, and Mark R. McMinn. "Development, Refinement, and Psychometric Properties of the Attitudes toward God Scale (ATGS-9)." *Psychology of Religion and Spirituality* 2 (2010): 148–67. [CrossRef]
21. Julie Juola Exline, and Alyce Martin. "Anger toward God: A New Frontier in Forgiveness Research." In *Handbook of Forgiveness*. Edited by Everett Worthington. New York: Routledge, 2005, pp. 73–88.
22. Robert A. Neimeyer, and Diana Sands. "Meaning Reconstruction in Bereavement: From Principles to Practice." In *Grief and Bereavement in Contemporary Society: Bridging Research and Practice*. Edited by Robert Neimeyer, Darcy Harris, Howard Winokuer and Gordon Thornton. New York: Routledge, 2011.
23. Kenneth I. Pargament, David S. Ensing, Kathryn Falgout, Hannah Olsen, Barbara Reilly, Kimberly Van Haitsma, and Richard Warren. "God Help Me (I): Religious Coping Efforts as Predictors of the Outcomes to Significant Negative Life Events." *American Journal of Community Psychology* 18 (1990): 793–824. [CrossRef]
24. Jason M. Holland, Joseph M. Currier, Rachel A. Coleman, and Robert A. Neimeyer. "The Integration of Stressful Life Experiences Scale (ISLES): Development and initial validation of a new measure." *International Journal of Stress Management* 17 (2010): 325–52. [CrossRef]
25. Ronnie Janoff-Bulman. *Shattered Assumptions*. New York: Simon and Schuster, 2010.
26. Philip Yancey. *Disappointment with God: Three Questions No One Asks Aloud*. Grand Rapids: Zondervan, 1988.
27. John R. Jordan. "Guided Imaginal Conversation with the Deceased." In *Techniques of Grief Therapy: Creative Practices for Counseling the Bereaved*. Edited by Robert A. Neimeyer. New York: Routledge, 2012.
28. Robert A. Neimeyer. "Chair Work." In *Techniques of Grief Therapy: Creative Practices for Counseling the Bereaved*. Edited by Robert A. Neimeyer. New York: Routledge, 2012.
29. Robert A. Neimeyer. "Correspondence with the Deceased." In *Techniques of Grief Therapy: Creative Practices for Counseling the Bereaved*. Edited by Robert A. Neimeyer. New York: Routledge, 2012.

Article

Belief into Action Scale: A Comprehensive and Sensitive Measure of Religious Involvement

Harold G. Koenig [1,2,3,*], **Zhizhong Wang** [4], **Faten Al Zaben** [2] and **Ahmad Adi** [1]

1   Department of Psychiatry, Duke University Medical Center, Durham, NC 27710, USA;
    ahmad.adi@dm.duke.edu
2   Department of Psychiatry, King Abdulaziz University, Jeddah 22254, Saudi Arabia; faten_zaben@yahoo.com
3   School of Public Health, Ningxia Medical University, Yinchuan 750004, China
4   Department of Epidemiology and Statistics, School of Public Health, Ningxia Medical University, Yinchuan
    750004, China; wangzhizhong@nxmu.edu.cn
*   Author to whom correspondence should be addressed; Harold.Koenig@duke.edu.; Tel.: +1-919-681-6633;
    Fax: +1-919-471-3624.

Academic Editor: Arndt Büssing
Received: 20 July 2015; Accepted: 19 August 2015; Published: 25 August 2015

Abstract: We describe here a new measure of religious commitment, the Belief into Action (BIAC) scale. This measure was designed to be a comprehensive and sensitive measure of religious involvement that could discriminate individuals across the religious spectrum, and avoid the problem of ceiling effects that have haunted the study of highly-religious populations. Many scales assess religious beliefs, where assent to belief is often widespread, subjective, and a superficial assessment of religious commitment. While people may say they believe, what does that mean in terms of action? This 10-item scale seeks to convert simple belief into *action*, where action is assessed in terms of what individuals say is most important in their lives, how they spend their time, and where they put their financial resources. We summarize here the psychometric characteristics of the BIAC in two very different populations: stressed female caregivers in Southern California and North Carolina, and college students attending three universities in Mainland China. We conclude that the BIAC is a sensitive, reliable, and valid measure of religious commitment in these two samples, and encourage research in other population groups using this scale to determine its psychometric properties more generally.

Keywords: religion; measurement; psychometric properties; DUREL; RCI-10; China

1. Introduction

The Belief into Action Scale (BIAC) [1] is a new scale developed in response to concerns that many religious measures only superficially assess the level of religiosity and often have ceiling effects in populations known to be highly religious (Blacks, other ethnic minorities, Middle Eastern groups, *etc.*) [2–4]. The BIAC was designed to increase the sensitivity in detecting differences in religious commitment by expanding response options so that both extremes of religiosity could be measured (from no involvement to a life centered on religious faith). The basis for the content of the BIAC is the importance of religion in a person's life. What individuals spend their time, talents, and financial resources on matters more than what they say matters to them.

The psychometric properties of the BIAC were originally tested in a sample of 251 middle-aged and older female caregivers (ages 40 to 75) of family members with severe disability due to stroke, dementia, or other neurological or medical problems [1]. Participants lived in either Los Angeles County, California, or in the Research Triangle of North Carolina (Durham-Raleigh-Chapel Hill), areas representing two opposite sides of the United States (U.S.). Subsequently, the BIAC has been administered in a number of populations in different areas of the United States (San Diego, California; Terre Haute, Indiana) and in other countries (China, Spain, Iran, Ghana, Brazil, Puerto Rico). The scale has now been translated into Spanish, Farsi, Arabic, Portuguese, and Chinese. In addition to the original validation study, the only other study that has so far reported the psychometric properties of the BIAC administered the scale to a sample of university students in Mainland China [5]. The present paper is a review of the findings in those studies and presents minimal new information not contained in those reports.

2. Scale Description and Content

The BIAC consists of 10 questions, each rated on a 1–10 scale (except the first question, which receives a value of 1 or 10 depending on the response). The total scale score, then, ranges from 10 to 100. The time of completion is less than two minutes. Each question was carefully chosen based on similar questions on other scales commonly used to assess religiosity [6].

The Question #1 directly asks the person to choose their highest priority in life, with common priorities among the response options. Relationship with, or connection to, God is one of the options. Other priorities include family, health, job, education, acquiring wealth, independence, and so forth. Depending on the dominant religion of the population being assessed, the word "God" may be replaced by Allah or HaShem or Buddha or Vishnu or whatever word is used to describe the Deity in that tradition. The Questions #2 and #3 assess degree of involvement in religious community activities (sometimes called organizational religiosity, as distinct from non-organizational or private religious activities). Question #4 is similar to Question #10 and examines the extent to which the respondent has consciously decided to place his/her life under the direction of God (or conform life to the teachings of their religious faith). The important word here is "decided". To what extent has the person made a *conscious* decision to surrender to God (a key theological teaching in Christian and Muslim faith traditions) or conform their will to God's will (based on religious teachings).

Questions #5 and #9 seek to determine whether use of personal financial resources (or time) is consistent with claims about the priority of God or religion in life. There is an old proverb that says, "if you want to know what is really important to someone, look at their checkbook." People usually spend their money on things they really value—such as family, friends, sports, cars or houses, other material possessions, vacations, business, other valued activities, or religion. Contributing money to or spending time volunteering for religious causes or supporting a religious community, then, indicates where the person directs their most precious resources (and may be a bit more objective in reflecting a person's priorities).

Questions #6, #7, and #8 assess level of involvement in private or non-organizational religious activities (as distinct from organizational ones). Time spent in private religious activities—such as watching religious TV or listening to religious radio or religious music, reading religious scriptures or other religious literature, and praying or meditating, are examples of non-organizational religious practices that are usually done alone. This is another good indication of how important religion is to a person and to what extent it is integrated into all of life (with regard to use of personal time). Involvement in organizational religious activities may be driven by a desire to socialize with others rather than devotion to religion or worship of God. Non-organizational religious activities, however, are not usually influenced by a desire for socialization.

In conclusion, then, the BIAC questions assess organizational and non-organizational religious activities, as well as degree of personal (intrinsic) devotion or commitment to one's religious faith (these are the three major dimensions of religiosity [7]). The expansion of possible response options (1 to 10) is intended to increase the sensitivity of each question and, as noted earlier, minimize ceiling effects (see Appendix A for the full questionnaire).

3. Scale Scores

In the original study conducted in 2013–2014, the BIAC was administered to a convenience sample of 246 stressed female caregivers (87% Christian) who were recruited by flyers and posters describing the study [1]. Of those, 238 (97%) complete the entire scale and of the eight remaining respondents, six completed eight or nine of 10 items. This suggests that the scale is acceptable to most participants who were drawn from both the West and East coasts of the U.S. While seven of the eight participants who did not complete all 10 items were from the West coast, the average score on the BIAC in North Carolina was 47.2 (SD = 21.5, 95% CI = 43.7–50.7), and was not significantly different from the average score of 45.1 (SD = 19.7, 95% CI = 41.2–49.0) obtained in Southern California (t value = 0.78, p = 0.44). Minority status, however, did make a difference. White Caucasians scored an average of 38.9 (SD = 20.2, 95% CI = 35.0–42.8), Hispanics 49.8 (SD = 17.3, 95% CI = 41.9–57.6), and Blacks 55.2 (SD = 18.7, 95% CI = 51.3–59.1) (F value = 17.7, p < 0.0001). Among participants with no religious affiliation, the average score was 13.3 (SD = 4.4, 95% CI = 9.2–17.3, range 10–22), compared to 47.4 for those with an affiliation (SD = 20.1, 95% CI = 44.9–50.1). There was no evidence for a ceiling effect, even among older (60+) Black women in the sample (median 55, range 15 to 81).

In a second study [5] conducted in 2014, the BIAC was administered to 1861 students identified using a cluster sampling method (those registered in the same class, usually 35–45 students, were defined as a cluster and were approached to participate in the study). Average age of respondents was 21.5 years and response rate was 97.8% (1861 out of 1902 students approached). Students attended Ningxia Medical University (NXMU) located in Ningxia province, an underdeveloped area in Western China (n = 1078); Southern Medical University located in Guangdong province, a well-developed area of Eastern China (n = 415); and Shaanxi University of Chinese Medicine located in Shaanxi province, a moderately developed area in Midwestern China (n = 408). Of those, 1812 (97%) completed 100% of questions on the BIAC and 18 (1%) completed at least 70% of questions, again indicating that the scale was well-tolerated. The average score for the total sample was 15.9 (SD = 8.8), with significantly higher scores in men compared to women (17.2, SD = 10.7, *vs.* 14.9, SD = 7.7, respectively, p < 0.001). Among students with no religious affiliation (66%), the average BIAC score was 12.4 (SD = 3.9); among those who were Muslim (18% of the sample), average score was 26.9 (SD = 11.1); and among those who were Christian (1.6%), average score was 29.6 (SD = 16.1). Among students who were affiliated with Buddhist, Tao, or Chinese religions (13% of the sample), average BIAC score was 16.8 (SD = 7.0). However, among those affiliated with these religions who indicated they had decided to conform their life to the teachings of their religious faith at least to a moderate degree, the average score was 34.7 (SD = 10.7), not greatly different from the average score in our sample of middle-age to older White Caucasian caregivers in the U.S. (average 38.9).

4. Psychometric Properties

The psychometric properties of the BIAC (reliability and validity) were determined in the two populations above, which we now describe.

4.1. Reliability

Reliability of a scale is the extent to which items on the scale are measuring the same thing (internal consistency or Cronbach's alpha) and whether responses to the items are similar when the scale is re-administered at different times in the same individuals (test-retest). In the original study of stressed female caregivers from North Carolina and California, internal reliability was high, as demonstrated by a Cronbach's alpha coefficient of 0.89 (95% CI = 0.86–0.91). Re-computing the alpha after removing individual items on the scale resulted in alphas ranging from 0.87 to 0.89. The test-retest reliability (assessed by the intra-class correlation coefficient or ICC) of individual items and total scale score after one week ranged from 0.66 to 0.97 for individual items and was 0.92 for the total score (n = 60). In the Chinese college student sample, the Cronbach's alpha was 0.83. When individual items were removed from the scale and alpha re-calculated, the values ranged from 0.80 to 0.84. The test-retest reliability (ICC) of individual items and the total score after two weeks ranged from 0.36 to 0.90 for individual items and was 0.86 for the total score (n = 133). Cronbach's alpha coefficients and ICCs that exceed 0.70 are considered satisfactory [8,9], suggesting that the BIAC is a reliable scale in diverse populations and religious groups.

4.2. Validity

Validity is the extent to which a scale really measures the theoretical concept or characteristic that it intends to measure. There are three basic types of validity: content validity, construct validity, and criterion validity. There is also a fourth type of validity when comparing a new measure to an existing measure called incremental validity.

4.2.1. Content Validity

The first type of validity, content or face validity, was discussed in the section above on the scale's description and content. The content of the items chosen for the BIAC make logical sense given the purpose of the scale.

4.2.2. Construct Validity

Construct validity is the extent to which a measure of a construct is related to things we expect the measure to be related to and is independent of constructs we expect the measure to be independent of. Construct validity is measured by convergent, discriminant, and factor analytic validity.

Convergent Validity

The correlation between a new scale and existing scales that have demonstrated validity is an indicator of convergent validity. In the caregiver study, religious affiliation was assessed, along with intrinsic religiosity (IR) that was measured by Hoge's 10-item Intrinsic Religiosity Scale [10], organizational (ORA) and non-organizational religiosity (NORA) by the five-item Duke University Religion Index (DUREL) [11,12] (that includes 3 items from the Hoge IR scale), religious support by Krause's 12-item Religious Support Scale (RSS) [13], and negative religious coping (NRC) by the seven-item subscale of the Brief RCOPE [14]. Correlations with the BIAC (and effect sizes, *i.e.*, Cohen's d, where d $\geq$ 0.80 is considered large and d $\leq$ 0.20 small) were r = 0.77 (d = 2.41) for IR, r = 0.76 (d = 2.34) for ORA, r = 0.60 (d = 1.50) for NORA, r = 0.67 (d = 1.81) for RSS, and, as predicted, r = –0.20 (d = 0.41) for NRC. These correlations indicate strong convergent validity for the BIAC in this largely Christian U.S. sample. Furthermore, as noted earlier, the average score among those acknowledging a religious affiliation (47.5, 95% CI = 44.9–50.1) was nearly four times higher than that of those indicating no religious affiliation (13.3, 95% CI = 9.2–17.3).

In the study of university students in Mainland China, other religious measures were the 10-item Religious Commitment Inventory [15] (RCI, with intrapersonal and interpersonal subscales) and religious affiliation. The correlations between the BIAC and the RCI subscales were high: r = 0.67 (d = 1.81) for intrapersonal religiosity and r = 0.60 (d = 1.50) for interpersonal religiosity. The total BIAC score also distinguished those with a religious affiliation from those without one (23.1, SD = 11.2, *vs.* 12.4, SD = 3.9, respectively, *p* < 0.0001).

Discriminant Validity

Discriminant validity is whether constructs or measures that are supposed to be unrelated are, in fact, unrelated. There has been a great deal of concern that measures of spirituality often include items that are actually measuring positive mental health or social connections, rather than anything distinctively spiritual, resulting in serious and concerning concept overlap [16]. In our U.S. caregiver study [1], the BIAC was only weakly related to depressive symptoms measured using the 20-item

CES-D ($r = -0.12$, $d = 0.24$), caregiver burden using the 22-item Zarit scale ($r = -0.19$, $d = 0.34$), social support network size ($r = 0.13$, $d = 0.26$), and physical health ($r = 0.01$, $d = 0.02$). Likewise, in the Mainland China study [5], the BIAC was only weakly correlated with purpose in life ($r = 0.01$, $d = 0.02$), quality of life ($r = -0.02$, $d = 0.04$), life satisfaction ($r = 0.02$, $d = 0.04$), and social interaction ($r = 0.10$, $d = 0.20$). These correlations suggest that the BIAC is measuring something quite different and distinct from mental, social, or physical health.

Factor Analytic Validity

Factor analysis determines if a measure of a construct behaves like theory says it should behave. In the caregiver study [1], principle components analysis (PCA, not rotated) revealed a single factor with an eigenvalue of 4.73 that explained 94.4% of the total variance (with factor loadings for individual items ranging from 0.545 to 0.797). This is consistent with the theory that the scale is measuring a single underlying construct that we call *religious commitment*. When PCA was repeated using an oblique rotation, two factors emerged but were highly correlated with each other ($r = 0.69$) and many items loaded equally on both factors. In the Chinese student study [5], PCA (oblique rotation) revealed three factors: a "God factor" representing a single item (Question #1), a "social factor" (Questions #2, #3, #4, #5), and a "personal factor" (Questions #6, #7, #8, #9, #10). The three-factor model explaining 66.3% of the total scale variance was identified in the first half of the sample (randomly split into two halves) and was verified in the second half of the sample. The three-factor model in the Chinese sample is consistent with the three major dimensions of religiosity that experts have identified (organizational, *i.e.*, social; non-organizational, *i.e.*, personal; and subjective, *i.e.*, God-centered commitment). The difference in the factor structure between the U.S. caregiver and Chinese samples may be due to the large difference in religiosity between the two populations, particularly the low religiosity in sample from China (a country where religious involvement has been discouraged for decades). The difference may also be due to the concept of God in eastern religions.

4.2.3. Criterion Validity

Criterion validity is the extent to which a measure is related to another measure of the construct that represents a "gold standard" or a more objective measure of the construct (clinical exam). Since there is no gold standard or as yet objective measure of religious commitment, criterion validity is difficult to establish for the BIAC. Criterion validity is established by concurrent validity and predictive validity.

Concurrent Validity

In the case where a new measure is being compared to an existing measure at one point in time (concurrent) and there is no gold standard or objective measure of the construct available, convergent validity may be used as a proxy for concurrent validity. Convergent validity (in Section 4.2.2) has already been discussed under construct validity above.

Predictive Validity

Predictive validity is the ability of a scale to predict over time important outcomes it should theoretically be able to predict. We would expect greater religious commitment (BIAC scores) to predict better mental and social health over time. Since we do not yet have longitudinal data on the BIAC, we do not yet have a measure of predictive validity for the scale.

4.2.4. Incremental Validity

As emphasized by Piedmont [17], a fourth type of validity called incremental validity measures the extent to which a new measure predicts important outcomes better than an existing measure. We now compare the BIAC with a well-established measure, the Duke University Religion Index [11]. The

DUREL is one of the most commonly-used measures of religiosity today with more than 1,130 citations on Google Scholar as of early August 2015; more than two-thirds of those studies were published since 2011. In the U.S. caregiver study [1], the BIAC and DUREL were correlated at r = 0.80 (d = 2.67). Table 1 examines the incremental validity of the BIAC in relationship to the DUREL in terms of correlations with several psychological and social outcomes (incremental validity meaning the amount of variance that the BIAC contributes to predicting the outcome above and beyond that accounted for by the DUREL). While only a small amount of variance (R-squared) is predicted by either measure in keeping with the discriminant validity of the DUREL and BIAC (1% to 3% and 1 to 10%, respectively), the findings suggest that the BIAC is considerably superior to the DUREL (75% to 300%) in terms of predicting psychosocial outcomes based on this cross-sectional work.

Table 1. Comparison of BIAC and DUREL with psychosocial outcomes in 245 female U.S. caregivers.

	DUREL		BIAC		
	R-Squared [1]	Partial F [2]	R-Squared [3]	Partial F [2]	R-Squared increase [4]
Psychosocial outcomes					
Mood (CES-D)	0.008	0.01	0.014	1.38	75%
Perceived stress (Cohen)	0.024 *	0.76	0.060 ***	9.06 **	150%
Caregiver burden (Zarit)	0.015 *	0.87	0.040 **	6.67 **	167%
Social support (SSQ-N)	0.006	0.37	0.018	2.86	200%
Social support (SSQ-S)	0.025 **	3.28	0.100 ****	19.22 ****	300%

Notes: BIAC = Belief into Action Scale; DUREL = Duke University Religion Index; CES-D = Center for Epidemiologic Studies—Depression; Zarit = Zarit Burden Interview; Cohen = Perceived Stress Scale; SSQ-N = Social Support Questionnaire-network size; SSQ-S = Social Support Questionnaire-satisfaction with support; [1] R-squared from model with only DUREL in model; [2] Type III SS from general linear model with both DUREL and BIAC included; [3] R-squared from model with both DUREL and BIAC included; [4] R-squared increase=percentage increase in R-squared with addition of BIAC to model with DUREL; * $p < 0.05$; ** $p \leq 0.01$; *** $p \leq 0.001$; **** $p \leq 0.0001$.

5. Discussion and Conclusions

Based on a study of stressed female caregivers from the U.S. and university students from Mainland China, the BIAC is a sensitive and comprehensive measure of religious commitment with solid psychometric characteristics that allow for assessment across a wide range of religious belief and activity. The relatively weak associations between the BIAC and mental and social health outcomes in stressed female caregivers appear to be stronger (by 75 to 300 percent) compared to a standard, widely-used measure of religiosity (DUREL), which may reflect the BIAC's greater sensitivity and, perhaps, greater accuracy. There is no evidence that the measure has a ceiling effect, even in Black older women who have long been known as the most religious age-gender-race group in America [18].

Although primarily designed for members of monotheistic religious traditions, the BIAC also performed fairly well in university students in Mainland China, a population at the other end of the religiosity spectrum affiliated with a variety of non-monotheistic religions or no religion. Given the limited populations that it has been studied in so far, more research is needed on the psychometric characteristics of the BIAC in other age, race, and gender groups located in secular and religious regions of the U.S. and other countries of the world, especially the Middle East. Several such studies are now ongoing (with a Muslim version of the BIAC in Arabic available). In particular, the factor structure of the BIAC needs evaluation in different religious and non-religious groups that include both men and women in order to determine if the one-factor, two-factor, or three-factor model best describes the structure of the scale. Most of the sample in the U.S. caregiver sample was Christian, which undoubtedly played a major role in the un-rotated single factor structure of the BIAC. The exact nature of the factor structure was called into question with the more diverse Chinese sample, underscoring the need for future research.

Appendix

Appendix A Belief into Action Scale

1. Please circle the highest priority in your life now? (most valued, prized) [circle only one]

    1. My health and independence
    2. My family
    3. My friendships
    4. Job, career or business
    5. My education
    6. Financial security
    7. Relationship with God
    8. Ability to travel & see the world
    9. Listening to music and partying
    10. Freedom to live as I choose

2. How often do you attend religious services? (circle a number below)

Never	Rarely	Couple times/yr	Every few mos	About once/mo	Several times/mo	About every wk	Every week	More than once/wk	Daily
1	2	3	4	5	6	7	8	9	10

3. Other than religious services, how often do you get together with others for religious reasons (prayer, religious discussions, volunteer work, *etc.*)?

Never	Rarely	Couple times/yr	Every few mos	About once/mo	Several times/mo	About every wk	Every week	More than once/wk	Daily
1	2	3	4	5	6	7	8	9	10

4. To what extent (on a 1 to 10 scale) have you decided to place your life under God's direction?

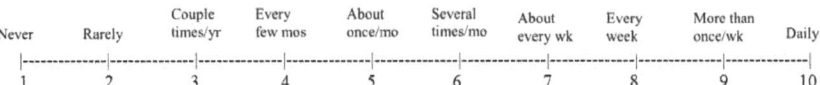

Not at all (really haven't thought about it)				To a moderate degree				Completely, totally	
1	2	3	4	5	6	7	8	9	10

5. What percentage of your gross annual income do you give to your religious institution or to other religious causes each year?

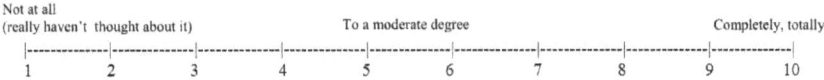

0%	Less than 1%	1%–2%	3%–4%	5%–6%	7%–8%	9%–10%	11%–12%	13%–14%	15% or more
1	2	3	4	5	6	7	8	9	10

6. On average, how much time each *day* (in 24 hours) do you spend listening to religious music or radio, or watching religious TV?

0 (never)	1–5 min	6–10 min	11–20 min	21–30 min	31–60 min	More than 1 hr, less than 2 hr	More than 2 hr, less than 3 hr	3–4 hrs	5 hrs or more
1	2	3	4	5	6	7	8	9	10

7. On average, how much time each *day* do you spend reading religious scriptures, books, or other religious literature?

0 (never)	1–5 min	6–10 min	11–20 min	21–30 min	31–60 min	More than 1 hr, less than 2 hr	More than 2 hr, less than 3 hr	3–4 hrs	5 hrs or more
1	2	3	4	5	6	7	8	9	10

8. On average, how much time each *day* do you spend in private prayer or meditation?

0 (never)	1–5 min	6–10 min	11–20 min	21–30 min	31–60 min	More than 1 hr, less than 2 hr	More than 2 hr, less than 3 hr	3–4 hrs	5 hrs or more
1	2	3	4	5	6	7	8	9	10

9. On average, how much time each *day* do you spend as a volunteer in your religious community or to help others for religious reasons?

0 (never)	1–5 min	6–10 min	11–20 min	21–30 min	31–60 min	More than 1 hr, less than 2 hr	More than 2 hr, less than 3 hr	3–4 hrs	5 hrs or more
1	2	3	4	5	6	7	8	9	10

10. To what extent (on a 1 to 10 scale) have you decided to conform your life to the teachings of your religious faith?

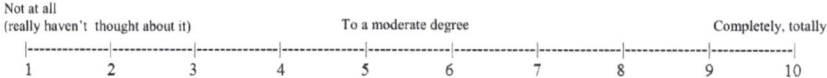

Not at all (really haven't thought about it)				To a moderate degree				Completely, totally	
1	2	3	4	5	6	7	8	9	10

Scoring instructions:

(1) Recode Q1 as follows: 7 = 10, all other answers = 1
(2) Sum recoded Q1 + Q2 thru Q10 to arrive at total score (range 10–100)

BIAC is also available in Arabic, Chinese, and Spanish

References

1. Harold G. Koenig, Bruce Nelson, Sally F. Shaw, Faten Al Zaben, Zhizhong Wang, and Salil Saxena. "Belief into Action Scale: A Brief but Comprehensive Measure of Religious Commitment." *Open Journal of Psychiatry* 5 (2015): 66–77. [CrossRef]
2. Will Slater, Todd W. Hall, and Keith J. Edwards. "Measuring religion and spirituality: Where are we and where are we going? " *Journal of Psychology & Theology* 29 (2001): 4–21.
3. Vicky Genia. "Evaluation of the Spiritual Well-Being Scale in a Sample of College Students." *The International Journal for the Psychology of Religion* 11 (2001): 25–33. [CrossRef]

4. James E. King, and Martha R. Crowther. "The measurement of religiosity and spirituality: Examples and issues from psychology." *Journal of Organizational Change Management* 17 (2004): 83–101. [CrossRef]
5. Zhizhong Wang, Hui Ma, Ye Rong, and Harold G. Koenig. "Psychometric properties of the Belief into Action Scale among university students in China." *Journal for the Scientific Study of Religion*, 2015. in submission.
6. Peter C. Hill, and Ralph W. Hood Jr. *Measures of Religiosity*. Birmingham: Religious Education Press, 1999.
7. Andrew Futterman, and Harold G. Koenig. "Measuring religiosity in later life: What can gerontology learn from the sociology and psychology of religion? Background paper." In Proceedings of Conference on Methodological Approaches to the Study of Religion, Aging, and Health, Co-Sponsored by National Institute on Aging and Fetzer Institute, Bethesda, MD, USA, 16–17 March 1995.
8. Lee J. Cronbach. "Coefficient alpha and the internal structure of tests." *Psychometrika* 16 (1951): 297–334. [CrossRef]
9. Patrick E. Shrout, and Joseph L. Fleiss. "Intraclass correlations: Uses in assessing rater reliability." *Psychological Bulletin* 86 (1979): 420–28. [CrossRef] [PubMed]
10. Dean R. Hoge. "A validated intrinsic religious motivation Scale." *Journal for the Scientific Study of Religion* 11 (1972): 369–76. [CrossRef]
11. Harold G. Koenig, George R. Parkerson Jr., and Keith G. Meador. "Religion index for psychiatric research." *The American Journal of Psychiatry* 154 (1997): 885–86. [PubMed]
12. Harold G. Koenig, and Arndt Büssing. "The Duke University Religion Index (DUREL): A five-item measure for use in epidemiological studies." *Religions* 1 (2010): 78–85. [CrossRef]
13. Neal Krause. "Religious support." In *Multidimensional Measurement of Religiousness/Spirituality for Use in Health Research: A Report of the Fetzer Institute/National Institute on Aging Working Group*. Kalamazoo: John E. Fetzer Institute, 1999, pp. 57–63.
14. Kenneth I. Pargament, Bruce W. Smith, Harold G. Koenig, and Lisa Perez. "Patterns of positive and negative religious coping with major life stressors." *Journal for the Scientific Study of Religion* 37 (1998): 710–24. [CrossRef]
15. Everett L. Worthington Jr., Nathaniel G. Wade, Terry L. Hight, Jennifer S. Ripley, Michael E. Mccullough, and Jack W. Berry. "The Religious Commitment Inventory-10: Development, refinement, and validation of a brief scale for research and counseling." *Journal of Counseling Psychology* 50 (2003): 84–96. [CrossRef]
16. Harold G. Koenig. "Concerns about measuring 'spirituality' in research." *Journal of Nervous & Mental Disease* 196 (2008): 349–55.
17. Ralph L. Piedmont. "Does spirituality represent the sixth factor of personality? Spiritual transcendence and the Five-Factor Model." *Journal of Personality* 67 (1999): 985–1014. [CrossRef]
18. Jeffrey S. Levin, Robert Joseph Taylor, and Linda M. Chatters. "Race and Gender Differences in Religiosity Among Older Adults: Findings From Four National Surveys." *Journal of Gerontology* 49 (1994): S137–45. [CrossRef] [PubMed]

 *religions*

Article

Reliance on God's Help Scale as a Measure of Religious Trust—A Summary of Findings

Arndt Büssing [1,*], Daniela Rodrigues Recchia [1] and Klaus Baumann [2]

[1]   Quality of Life, Spirituality and Coping, Institute for Integrative Medicine, Witten/Herdecke University,
      Gerhard-Kienle-Weg 4, 58313 Herdecke, Germany; Daniela.RodriguesRecchia@uni-wh.de
[2]   Caritas Science and Christian Social Work, Faculty of Theology, Albert-Ludwig University, Platz der
      Universität 3, 79098 Freiburg, Germany; Klaus.Baumann@theol.uni-freiburg.de
*   Author to whom correspondence should be addressed; arndt.buessing@uni-wh.de;
     Tel.: +49-2330-623-246; Fax: +49-2330-623-810.

Academic Editor: John P. Bartkowski
Received: 19 August 2015; Accepted: 25 November 2015; Published: 27 November 2015

Abstract: This paper gives a summary of findings from studies using the five-item *Reliance on God's Help* (RGH) scale, which was developed a decade ago as an integral part of a comprehensive measure to differentiate between external and internal adaptive coping strategies. It has been used for both healthy and diseased persons. We will summarize data on internal reliability scores and the distribution of mean values for the respective items in the different study samples. Also, we will present a structural equation model (SEM) to confirm the scale's validity. Our analysis shows that the RGH scale is a short, valid, and reliable measure of a person's strong basic trust in God (faith), regardless of what life brings. The items do not address aspects such as well-being, inner peace, or specific moods. Thus, it is important to note that the RGH scale was not *per se* associated with indicators of well-being or health-related quality of life, indicating distinct dimensions.

Keywords: Reliance on God's help; religious trust; faith; questionnaire; validation; chronic illness; healthy persons; life satisfaction; quality of life; well-being

---

1. Background

Since its beginnings, the psychology of religion [1] has had a strong current of research focused on investigating the functions of religious beliefs as they relate to cognitions, emotions, and behaviors, e.g., regarding physical and mental health, coping with critical life events, or managing stress in general [2]. According to the *Transactional Model of Stress* [3], when a person is confronted with significant health problems or life stressors, after at least two rounds of appraisal to assess the relevance of the stressor, its controllability, and the availability of coping resources, he or she may use distinct strategies to deal with these stressors. With respect to the *Locus of Control* concept [4,5], one may turn to external sources of help or may rely on personal (internal) resources to control the situation and stressor. In the case of illness, a common external resource of help might be a medical doctor. However, not all problems can be solved, and thus persons "have to adapt and find ways to maintain physical, emotional and spiritual health—despite their symptoms" [6]. Often, people may search for further ("more powerful") external sources and look to transcendent sources of help (*i.e.*, "God").

This strategy may be a reactive process in response to a stressor (resulting in prayers for help), a lifelong trained habit (in terms of a "trait"), or the conviction that faith is a stronghold and God is at one's side whatever life brings [6]. This can be regarded as a strong basic trust in God, who is expected to carry one through such phases of insecurity or illness. As a result, people who rely on theistic beliefs may pray for various reasons: to connect with the Sacred (communication), to become healthy again (invocation), or to articulate fears and worries without any further expectation of healing (which nevertheless may result in feelings of relief). Interestingly, research on this topic has shown that most patients with chronic diseases pray with the intention of finding relief from their suffering; they do not necessarily pray to receive healing, but to "positively transform the experience of their illness" [7].

In addition, such reliance on God's help does not necessarily mean that people passively wait for God to do the job; they also actively rely on their internal resources and consult medical doctors [8–10]. Such trust in God (referring to Proverbs 3:5) may imply the ability of a religious person to recognize God's presence in everything that happens, and therefore hold the conviction that God is at one's side, even in bad times. This may strengthen their hope, their confidence to utilize their own resources (with God's support), and their commitment to connect with God consciously through prayer.

2. The Reliance on God's Help Scale: Description of Items

To operationalize this trust in a transcendent (theistic) source, the *Reliance on God's Help* (RGH) scale (alternatively entitled *Trust in God's Help* scale) was developed about 10 years ago as part of a larger construct to address adaptive coping strategies related to the "locus of health control" concept [10,11]. The items were designed so as to be kept separate from aspects of psycho-emotional well-being, thankfulness, or feelings of spiritual peace or comfort. Conceptually, the five-item RGH scale is similar to SpREUK's [SpREUK is an acronym of the German translation of "Spiritual and Religious Attitudes in Dealing with Illness"] (religious) *Trust* scale and also uses one of its items [12,13]. From a theoretical point of view, the scale's topics differ from Pargament's concept of *Religious Coping* [14], which addresses the function of problem solving and differentiates between three styles: a deferring style (God will solve the problems), a self-directing style (use resources God has given to solve the problems on their own), and a collaborative style (problems are solved together with God) [15]. With the exception of one prayer item, the RGH scale does not refer to active coping strategies to restore health. Instead, it addresses the following topics:

Unconditional trust ("Whatever happens, I will trust in a higher power that carries me through")
Hopeful belief ("I have strong belief that God will help me")
Faith as a resource ("My faith is a stronghold, even in hard times")
Connection and effect/function ("I pray to become healthy again")
Behavioral correspondence ("I try to live in accordance with my religious convictions")

These items were scored on a five-point scale from disagreement to agreement, and the mean scores were transformed to a 100% level (transformed scale score).

3. Reliance on God's Help Scale: Internal Reliability Data and the Structural Equation Model

The internal reliability of the RGH scale was very good in most tested samples of healthy and diseased persons (Cronbach's alpha between 0.90 and 0.96) (Table 1). However, in a sample of Catholic pastoral workers, who all agreed with the statements, its internal reliability was acceptable yet lower (alpha = 0.78). Accuracy (corrected item—scale correlation) of the scale items was high in all samples (Table 1). Using the complete data sets, explorative factor analysis (Varimax rotation) of the scale (alpha = 0.96) determined one single factor which explained 84% of variance.

Table 1. Descriptive data with the RGH scale applied in different samples (data were calculated using the data sets of respective samples).

	Healthy persons [11] *	Chronic pain diseases [9]	Female cancer [8]	Depressive/addictive diseases [16]	Pastoral workers [17] *
Sample size (n)	3.593	448	390	110	5.460
Mean age (years)	63.9 ± 11.3	54.0 ± 14.9	59.7 ± 7.3	47.5 ± 10.1	-
Cronbach's alpha	0.90	0.94	0.96	0.94	0.78
Corrected Item—Scale Correlation	0.77 to 0.87	0.79 to 0.92	0.82 to 0.93	0.77 to 0.91	0.46 to 0.66
RGH Score (M ± SD)	54.7 ± 34.8	55.3 ± 33.1	56.5 ± 35.0	45.8 ± 34.0	83.8 ± 14.0
Agreement to Specific Statements	Scores (%): no—undecided—yes				
a35 "Whatever happens, I will trust in a higher power that carries me through"	34 16 50	30 23 47	27 16 57	36 26 39	2 4 94
a36 "I have strong belief that God will help me"	32 18 50	29 23 49	30 17 53	40 21 39	2 8 90
a37 "My faith is a stronghold, even in hard times"	31 18 51	29 22 49	30 15 55	40 20 40	2 8 90
a38 "I pray to become healthy again" **	40 16 45	35 16 49	34 13 54	54 12 34	2 6 93
a 39 "I try to live in accordance with my religious convictions"	37 17 46	35 19 46	36 20 44	49 20 32	8 9 83

* Subsample of the whole data set (n = 5830); ** For healthy pastoral workers, the phrasing was changed to "I pray that I am able to cope with arising problems".

In most tested samples, a majority indicated that they have trust in a higher power, that faith is a stronghold for them, and that they believe God will help them (Table 1), *i.e.*, about half of the enrolled persons would agree, and one-third would disagree. Nevertheless, this does not necessarily mean that all persons would pray to become healthy again (34%–54% would not); particularly, persons with depressive and/or addictive diseases are less likely to pray for this (Table 1).

To analyze how the RGH relates to these five items, we relied on a structural equation model (Figure 1) using the combined data sets (without pastoral workers to avoid systematic ceiling effects related to their profession). These five variables contributed significantly to explaining the RGH as they are components of a regression model with similar weights as the RGH. Moreover, they also have an unobserved common variance in between, which indicates communality between all five. The variables also correlated with each other. Interestingly, "strong belief that God will help" (a36) and "living in accordance with religious convictions" (a39) have a very weak negative relationship ($r = -0.16$).

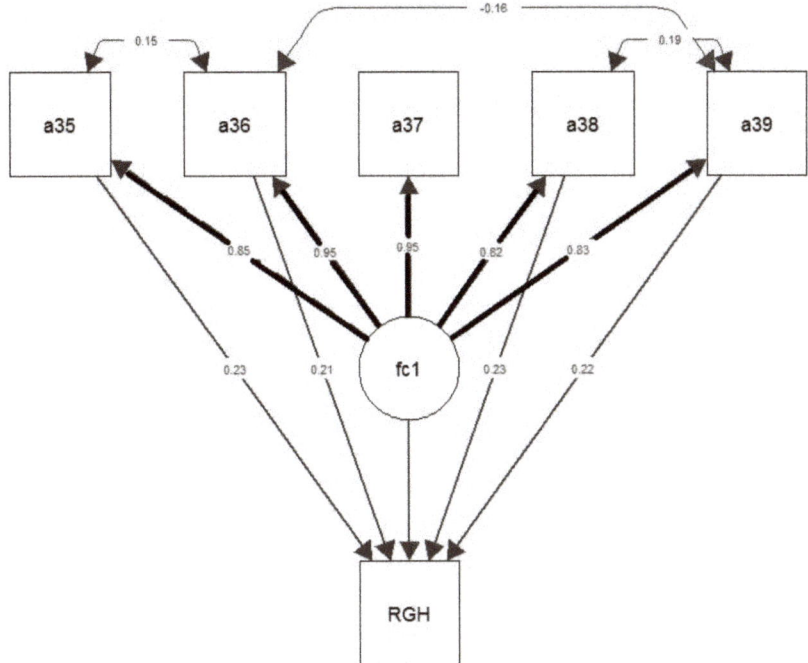

Small arrows between items and scale (RGH) describe regression coefficients (beta), thick arrows between items and factor (fc1) describe the standardized parameters from the factor analysis, while thin arrows between items describe correlations (r).

Figure 1. Structural equation model of RGH items (a35, a36, a37, a38, a39).

The structural equation model (SEM) presented below contains both the regression model for RGH and the factor analysis. The goodness of fit for this SEM model confirms its validity (CFI = 1.0, TLI = 0.99, RMSEA = 0.045, SRMR = 0.003).

In the following sections, we describe how the mean scores of the RGH scale were distributed in different samples, the influence of sociodemographic data, which variables may be related, and findings from previous studies and analyses [8–11,16,17].

4. Distribution of RGH Scores in Different Samples

In a large sample of German health insurance recipients [9], we analyzed the subgroup of healthy persons (mean age 64 ± 11 years of age; 70% male) derived from [11]. Here, the RGH scale had a mean score of 54.7 ± 34.8 (Table 1). Age had a relevant influence (F = 45.1; p < 0.0001), with the lowest scores in younger persons (<40 years: 43.2 ± 32.8) and the highest in older persons (>80 years: 71.5 ± 32.0). Women had higher RGH scores than men (60.1 ± 35.6 *versus* 52.5 ± 34.2; F = 35.8; p < 0.001); however, level of education had no relevant influence (F = 1.2; ns.). Within the larger sample [11], the subgroup of patients with cancer had higher RGH scores (61.4 ± 34.0) than those with other chronic diseases (54.0 ± 34.4) or healthy individuals (54.8 ± 34.8). These differences were statistically significant (F = 6.1; p < 0.0001).

In patients with chronic pain diseases (mean age 53.9 ± 15.9 years; 84% female; 77% Christian affiliation, 5% other, 18% none) [9], the RGH scale had a mean score of 55.3 ± 33.1 (Table 1). Here, women had significantly higher scores than men (F = 5.3; p = 0.022).

In a sample of cancer patients (mean age 59.7 ± 7.3; all but one were female; 69% Christians, 31% no religious denomination) [8], the RGH score was 56.5 ± 35.0 (Table 1). As one would expect from the aforementioned findings, patients with a Christian affiliation scored significantly higher on the RGH scale than in those without a religious denomination (72.2 ± 25.2 *versus* 22.6 ± 28.0; $F = 299.5$; $p < 0.0001$), indicating criterion validity.

In patients with depressive and/or addictive disorders (mean age 47.5 ± 10.1; 51% women; 68% Christians, 1% other, 31% no religious denomination) [16], the scale's mean score was lowest (45.8 ± 34.0) (Table 1). In this sample, there were no significant effects related to gender ($F = 1.1$; n.s.). Still, religious denomination had an influence ($F = 36.2$; $p < 0.0001$). Interestingly, patients with addictive diseases had higher scores (59.3 ± 37.1) than those with depressive (41.2 ± 31.9) or unspecified psychiatric diseases (36.9 ± 29.8) ($F = 3.6$; $p = 0.030$).

The mean RGH score in healthy and diseased samples (6550 persons) is 55.1 ± 34 (ranging from 0 to 100; 25% percentile at 25, 75% percentile at 85).

To test the RGH scale with a positively selected sample, we used it in a study of Catholic pastoral workers, assuming that this group would have very high RGH scores [17]. From the larger sample, we analyzed a subgroup of 5460 persons (54% were aged between 45–65 years; 76% were male, all Christians). As expected, the scale's mean score was very high (83.8 ± 14.0). Gender had no significant influence within this sample ($F = 0.4$; n.s.). However, underlying profession ($F = 25.2$; $p < 0.0001$) and age ($F = 4.2$; $p < 0.0001$), with the highest RGH scores in very old persons (>85 years: 88.5 ± 11.7) and the lowest in younger ones (<35 years: 82.7 ± 13.1), had an influence.

5. Correlation between RGH Scores and Measures of Religiosity

In patients with chronic diseases [9], RGH scores were strongly associated with SpREUK's religious *Trust* scale ($r = 0.77$). Both scales are not identical (although they share one item), but have similar motifs (Table 2).

Table 2. Synoptic comparison of RGH and SpREUK's *Trust* scale items (with same scoring options).

RHG scale	SpREUK's *Trust* scale [13]
Whatever happens, I will trust in a higher power which carries me through.	Whatever happens, I will trust in a higher power which carries me through
I have strong belief that God will help me.	In my mind, I am connected with a "higher source".
My faith is a stronghold, even in hard times.	I have faith in spiritual guidance in my life.
I pray to become healthy again.	I am convinced that death is not an end.
I try to live in accordance with my religious convictions.	In my mind, I am a religious individual.

Moreover, the RGH also correlated moderately with SpREUK's *Search* for Spiritual Support Scale ($r = 0.47$), and to a lesser extent also with the positive interpretation of illness (*Reappraisal*; $r = 0.30$). With respect to the frequency of engagement in various spiritual practices, RGH correlated strongly and best with religious practices ($r = 0.64$) and gratitude/awe ($r = 0.59$) [9]. These findings indicate construct validity.

Support that the RGH is in fact a measure of religious trust and is relevant particularly for spiritual/religious persons comes from further data which shows that patients with chronic pain diseases who regard themselves as both religious and spiritual (R+S+) had the highest RGH scores (72.9 ± 27.9). Those who regard themselves as religious but not as spiritual (R+S−; 68.1 ± 26.2) followed, and then those who see themselves as spiritual but not religious (R−S+) (41.4 ± 32.1). Patients who regarded themselves as neither religious nor spiritual (R−S−) had the lowest scores (27.0 ± 24.6), indicating that they do not rely on this source [9]. These results differ significantly ($F = 59.5$; $p < 0.0001$) and again suggest good construct validity.

6. Methodological Issues: RGH is not Associated with Health-Related Measures

We believe that this compact and circumscribed scale may be beneficial in health studies. Several multidimensional instruments on spirituality, particularly when used as a one-scale measure rather than differential subscales, tend to correlate considerably with mental components of quality of life measures. Thus, to avoid "false positive" associations between RGH and measures of psychological quality of life and life satisfaction, the items of the RGH were created as to not conceptually overlap with measures of psycho-emotional well-being or feelings of spiritual peace or comfort. In our samples of persons with chronic diseases, cancer, and also healthy individuals [6], there were only marginal associations between the RGH and health-related quality of life, as measured by the Medical Outcomes Study Short-Form Health Survey SF-12 questionnaire. Also, in female cancer patients [8], the RGH was either not at all or only marginally related to cancer-related fatigue ($r = 0.08$), life satisfaction ($r = 0.09$), anxiety (0.08), depressive symptoms ($r = -0.15$), and SF-12's mental health component ($r = -0.13$). Similarly, in patients with depressive and/or addictive diseases [16], the RGH was weakly—but significantly—associated with life satisfaction ($r = 0.24$). However, the weak association for depression scores ($r = -0.13$) failed to reach a level of significance.

These findings stand in contrast to results obtained with other measures of religiosity such as the *Daily Spiritual Experience Scale* (DSES). The DSES addresses specific experiences such as feeling God's presence, feeling God's love, a desire to be closer to God, finding strength/comfort in God, but also being touched by the beauty of creation, *etc.* [18,19]. One may thus assume that in religious persons the DSES is a measure of spiritual (or better, religious) well-being. In fact, in Catholic pastoral workers [17], the DSES was significantly associated with life satisfaction ($r = 0.38$), stress perception ($r = -0.29$), and depressive symptoms ($r = -0.29$).

Also "spiritual well-being" as measured with the *Functional Assessment of Chronic Illness Therapy—Spiritual Well-being Scale* (FACIT-Sp) [20,21] with its sub-constructs:

- *faith* (*i.e.*, find comfort in faith; find strength in faith; difficult times have strengthened faith; know that whatever happens with illness, things will be okay),
- *meaning* (*i.e.*, have a reason for living; life has been productive; feel a sense of purpose in life; life lacks meaning and purpose), and
- *peace* (feel peaceful; have trouble feeling peace of mind; able to reach down deep inside myself in order to feel comfort; feel a sense of harmony)

should correlate with measures of health. These items clearly address a person's well-being, and thus one may assume inverse associations, particularly with mental health. Indeed, in female cancer survivors it is particularly the (non-religious) *peace* component which is moderately associated with anxiety ($r = -0.48$) and depression ($r = -0.45$). To a lesser extent, the (existential) component *meaning* correlated with anxiety ($r = -0.22$) and depression ($r = -0.32$), whereas the *faith* sub-construct was only marginally associated with depression or anxiety ($r < 0.20$) [22].

Thus, specific scales intended to measure 1) spirituality in its wider context or 2) religiosity in its more specific, faith-associated context may be associated because the constructs overlap (*i.e.*, well-being, inner peace). On the other hand, they may not be associated because both measure different and independent dimensions. The latter seems to be true for the RGH scale and for the (religious) *faith* component of the FACIT-Sp.

7. Conclusions

Developed a decade ago as an integral part of a comprehensive measure to differentiate between external and internal adaptive coping strategies, our analysis has shown that the RGH scale is a unique measure of a person's strong basic trust in God (faith), regardless of what happens. It was used in several published studies among both healthy and diseased individuals. Our summary of findings about this short instrument indicates that the five-item RGH is a valid and reliable instrument to measure religious trust among persons with a theistic religious background. So far, there have been no longitudinal studies that have analyzed changes in the RGH during phases of existential crisis or its adjustment across illness trajectories. It is important to note, however, that this instrument is not *per se* associated with indicators of well-being or health-related quality of life, indicating clearly distinct dimensions. In other words, subjective religiousness consists of various dimensions, elements, and functions with different effects and meanings to the different individuals. Even empirically, religiosity cannot be reduced completely to coping or health-related functions [1].

Acknowledgments: We are grateful to all colleagues and collaborators, and to Karin Jors for her help as a native speaker.

Conflicts of Interest: The authors declare no conflict of interest.

References

1. Klaus Baumann. "The birth of human sciences, especially psychology." In *L'uomo moderno e la chiesa-atti del congresso (analecta gregoriana, 317)*. Edited by Paul Gilbert. Rome: Gregorian & Biblical Press, 2012, pp. 391–408.

2. Harold G. Koenig, Dana King, and Verna Benner Carson. *Handbook of Religion and Health*, 2nd ed. Oxford: Oxford University Press, 2010.

3. Richard S Lazarus, and Susan Folkman. *Stress, Appraisal, and Coping*. New York: Springer, 1984.

4. Julian B. Rotter. "Generalized expectancies for internal *versus* external control of reinforcement." *Psychological Monographs: General & Applied* 80 (1966): 1–28. [CrossRef]

5. Hannah Levenson. "Multidimensional locus of control in psychiatric patients." *Journal of Consulting and Clinical Psychology* 41 (1973): 397–404. [CrossRef] [PubMed]

6. Arndt Büssing. "Health-related quality of life and reliance on god's help." In *Encyclopedia of Quality of Life and Well-Being Research*. Edited by Alex C. Michalos. Dordrecht: Springer, 2014, pp. 2801–7.

7. Karin Jors, Arndt Büssing, Nield Christian Hvidt, and Klaus Baumann. "Personal prayer in patients dealing with chronic illness: A review of the research literature." *Evidence-based Complementary and Alternative Medicine* 2015 Article 927973. (2015). [CrossRef] [PubMed]

8. Arndt Büssing, Julia Fischer, Thomas Ostermann, and Peter F. Matthiessen. "Reliance on god's help, depression and fatigue in female cancer patients." *The International Journal of Psychiatry in Medicine* 38 (2008): 357–72. [CrossRef] [PubMed]

9. Arndt Büssing, Nadja Keller, Andreas Michalsen, Susanne Moebus, Gustav Dobos, Thomas Osterman, and Peter F. Matthiessen. "Spirituality and adaptive coping styles in german patients with chronic diseases in a cam health care setting." *Journal of Complementary and Integrative Medicine* 3 (2006): 1553–3840. [CrossRef]

10. Arndt Büssing, Thomas Ostermann, and Peter F. Matthiessen. "Wer kontrolliert die Gesundheit?—Adaptive Krankheitsverarbeitungsstile bei Patienten mit chronischen Erkrankungen." *Deutsche Zeitschrift für Onkologie* 40 (2008): 140–56.

11. Arndt Büssing, Thomas Ostermann, and Peter F. Matthiessen. "Adaptive coping and spirituality as a resource in cancer patients." *Breast Care* 2 (2007): 195–202.

12. Arndt Büssing, Thomas Ostermann, and Peter F. Matthiessen. "Role of religion and spirituality in medical patients: Confirmatory results with the SpREUK questionnaire." *Health and Quality of Life Outcomes* 3 (2005): 10. [CrossRef] [PubMed]

13. Arndt Büssing. "Spirituality as a resource to rely on in chronic illness: The SpREUK questionnaire." *Religions* 1 (2010): 9–17. [CrossRef]

14. Kenneth I. Pargament. *The Psychology of Religion and Coping: Theory, Research, Practice*. New York: Guilford Press, 1997.

15. Russel E. Phillips III, Quinten K. Lynn, Craig D. Crossley, and Kenneth I. Pargament. "Self-directing religious coping: A deistic god, abandoning god, or no god at all? " *Journal For The Scientific Study Of Religion* 43 (2004): 409–18.

16. Arndt Büssing, and Götz Mundle. "Reliance on god's help in patients with depressive and addictive disorders is not associated with their depressive symptoms." *Religions* 3 (2012): 455–66. [CrossRef]

17. Eckhard Frick, Arndt Büssing, Klaus Baumann, Wolfgang Weig, and Christoph Jacobs. "Do self-efficacy expectation and spirituality provide a buffer against stress-associated impairment of health? A comprehensive analysis of the german pastoral ministry study." *Journal of Religion and Health*. Published electronically 27 March 2015. Available online: http://link.springer.com/article/10.1007/s10943-015-0040-7. [CrossRef]

18. Lynn G. Underwood, and Jeanne A. Teresi. "The daily spiritual experience scale: Development, theoretical description, reliability, exploratory factor analysis, and preliminary construct validity using health-related data." *Annals of Behavioral Medicine: A Publication of the Society of Behavioral Medicine* 24 (2002): 22–33. [CrossRef]

19. Lynn Underwood. "The daily spiritual experience scale: Overview and results." *Religions* 2 (2011): 29–50. [CrossRef]

20. Amy H. Peterman, George Fitchett, Marianne J. Brady, Lesbia Hernandez, and David Cella. "Measuring spiritual well-being in people with cancer: The functional assessment of chronic illness therapy—Spiritual well-being scale (FACIT-Sp)." *Annals of Behavioral Medicine* 24 (2002): 49–58. [CrossRef] [PubMed]

21. Jason M. Bredle, John M. Salsman, Scott M. Debb, Benjamin J. Arnold, and David Cella. "Spiritual well-being as a component of health-related quality of life: The functional assessment of chronic illness therapy—Spiritual well-being scale (FACIT-Sp)." *Religions* 2 (2011): 77–94. [CrossRef]

22. Andrea L. Canada, Patricia E. Murphy, George Fitchett, Amy H. Peterman, and Leslie R. Schover. "A 3-factor model for the FACITt-Sp." *Psycho-oncology* 17 (2008): 908–16. [CrossRef] [PubMed]

Article

The Internal Consistency Reliability of the Katz-Francis Scale of Attitude toward Judaism among Australian Jews

Patrick Lumbroso [1], Kirill Fayn [1], Niko Tiliopoulos [2] and Leslie J. Francis [3,*]

1   School of Psychology, University of Sydney, New South Wales 2006, Australia;
     plum1148@uni.sydney.edu.au (P.L.); kfayn@uni.sydney.edu.au (K.F.)
2   Faculty of Science, University of Sydney, New South Wales 2006, Australia; niko.tiliopoulos@sydney.edu.au
3   Warwick Religions and Education Research Unit, Centre for Education Studies, The University of Warwick,
     Coventry CV4 7AL, UK
*   Correspondence: leslie.francis@warwick.ac.uk; Tel.: +44-247-652-2539

Academic Editor: Arndt Büssing
Received: 16 March 2016; Accepted: 14 September 2016; Published: 30 September 2016

Abstract: The Katz-Francis Scale of Attitude toward Judaism was developed initially to extend among the Hebrew-speaking Jewish community in Israel a growing body of international research concerned to map the correlates, antecedents and consequences of individual differences in attitude toward religion as assessed by the Francis Scale of Attitude toward Christianity. The present paper explored the internal consistency reliability and construct validity of the English translation of the Katz-Francis Scale of Attitude toward Judaism among 101 Australian Jews. On the basis of these data, this instrument is commended for application in further research.

Keywords: psychology; religion; Australia; Judaism; attitude; Katz-Francis Scale of Attitude toward Judaism

1. Introduction

The measurement-based approach to the empirical psychology of religion, as reviewed for example by Spilka, Hood, Hunsberger, and Gorsuch [1] and Hood, Hill and Spilka [2], remains dominated by studies shaped within Christian or post-Christian contexts. Reviews of instruments developed for research within the empirical psychology of religion confirm the paucity of scales designed specifically for application within other religious traditions [3,4].

One highly productive strand of research within the measurement-based approach to the empirical psychology of religion within Christian or post-Christian contexts has focused on the affective dimension of religion as operationalized through the Francis Scale of Attitude toward Christianity. Developed first in English in the late 1970s, as reported by Francis [5,6], the Francis Scale of Attitude toward Christianity is currently available in Arabic [7], Czech [8], Chinese [9,10], Dutch [11], French [12,13], German [14,15], Greek [16], Italian [17], Norwegian [18], Portugese [19], Romanian [20], Slovenian [21], Spanish [22], Swedish [23], and Welsh [24,25].

In order to extend this strand of research beyond the confines of the Christian and post-Christian context, three related instruments have been developed for application in Islamic, Hindu and Jewish contexts: The Sahin-Francis Scale of Attitude toward Islam [26], the Santosh-Francis Scale of Attitude toward Hinduism [27], and the Katz-Francis Scale of Attitude toward Judaism [28]. In order to develop the Katz-Francis Scale of Attitude toward Judaism, the 24-items of the original Francis Scale of Attitude toward Christianity were discussed by a group of theologians and religious educators representing both the Jewish tradition from Bar-Ilan University and the Christian tradition from the University of Wales, Bangor. The items were first developed in English, then translated into Hebrew and then back-translated into English to check the reliability of the translation.

In their foundation study, Francis and Katz [28] confirmed the internal consistency reliability and construct validity of this instrument among 618 Hebrew-speaking undergraduates attending Bar-Ilan University. Alpha coefficients of 0.98 were reported among female students and of 0.97 among male students [29]. Significant positive correlations with synagogue attendance were reported among both female students ($r = 0.35$) and male students ($r = 0.72$) and with prayer were reported among both female students ($r = 0.51$) and male students ($r = 0.79$).

The internal consistency reliability and construct validity of the Hebrew form of the Katz-Francis Scale of Attitude toward Judaism was confirmed by Yablon, Francis, and Robbins [30] in an independent study conducted among 284 Hebrew-speaking female students at Bar-Ilan University. In this study an alpha coefficient of 0.94 was reported, together with significant positive correlations with synagogue attendance ($r = 0.37$) and with prayer ($r = 0.60$).

2. Research Question

The Katz-Francis Scale of Attitude toward Judaism, reported by Francis and Katz [28] and further tested by Yablon, Francis, and Robbins [30] was developed in Hebrew and has so far only been employed and tested in Israel. Against this background the aim of the present study was to establish and test an English language version of the instrument for use among Jewish communities in the English-speaking world. The opportunity to do this was provided by a study among Australian Jews.

3. Method

3.1. Participants

Participants were 101 members of the Australian Jewish community with females comprising 68% of the sample. The sample was acquired through synagogues in Sydney and Melbourne and through the Maccabi sporting clubs.

Of the female respondents, 12% were under the age of twenty, 28% were in their twenties, 8% were in their thirties, 8% in their forties, 12% in their fifties, 18% in their sixties, and 14% were in their seventies or older; 21% attended synagogue never or almost never, 8% attended only on Yom Kippur, 25% attended mainly on high holidays, 21% attended during all or most of the festivals, 23% attended weekly but not daily, and 2% attended synagogue daily; 27% prayed never or almost never, 6% prayed only on Yom Kippur, 12% prayed mainly on high holidays, 14% prayed during all or most of the festivals, 20% prayed weekly but not daily, and 20% prayed daily; 53% did not follow Kashrut, 17% followed Kashrut during Passover, 15% followed Kashrut at home, and 15% followed Kashrut all the time.

Of the male respondents, 12% were under the age of twenty, 33% were in their twenties, 12% were in their thirties, 10% in their forties, 10% in their fifties, 12% in their sixties, and 12% were in their seventies or older; 29% attended synagogue never or almost never, 12% attended only on Yom Kippur, 35% attended mainly on high holidays, 4% attended during all or most of the festivals, 16% attended weekly but not daily, and 4% attended synagogue daily; 34% prayed never or almost never, 8% prayed only on Yom Kippur, 22% prayed mainly on high holidays, 6% prayed during all or most of the festivals, 10% prayed weekly but not daily, and 20% prayed daily; 60% did not follow Kashrut, 13% followed Kashrut during Passover, 19% followed Kashrut at home, and 9% followed Kashrut all the time.

3.2. Measures

The Katz-Francis Scale of Attitude toward Judaism [28], based on the Francis Scale of Attitude toward Christianity [31,32], is a 24-item Likert type instrument, employing a 5-point response scale: Agree strongly, agree, not certain, disagree and disagree strongly. The individual items are concerned with an affective response toward God, bible, prayer, synagogue, and the Jewish religion. In this study questions containing the word "bible" were adjusted by substituting "torah" instead, a word which is more appropriate to the Jewish faith.

Behavioral elements of religion were also assessed. Synagogue attendance was assessed on a 6-point scale: Never or almost never, only on Yom Kippur, mainly on high holidays, during all or most of the festivals, weekly but not daily and daily. Personal prayer was assessed on a 6-point scale: never or almost never, only on Yom Kippur, mainly on high holidays, during all or most of the festivals, weekly but not daily and daily. Observance of Kashrut Jewish dietary laws was assessed on a 4-point scale: I don't follow them, only during Passover, mainly in my home, and all the time.

3.3. Procedure

Participants were tested at the synagogue, in the Maccabi club rooms and at their home. The questionnaire was completed by individuals and in groups in quiet settings where participants were not allowed to discuss their answers.

3.4. Data Analysis

The data was analysed using the SPSS statistical package particularly the scale reliability and correlations analyses.

4. Results and Discussion

Table 1 presents the item rest of test correlation coefficients in respect of all 24 scale items, together with the alpha coefficient for females and for males separately. Table 1 also presents the loadings on the first factor of the unrotated solution proposed by principal-component analysis, together with the percentage of variance explained by the first factor for females and for males separately. Furthermore, the dataset possessed near perfect sampling adequacy, as assessed through the Kaiser-Meyer-Olkin (KMO) statistic (KMO = 0.94). These sets of statistics support the conclusion that the scale is characterized by homogeneity, unidimensionality, and internal consistency reliability among females and males. The alpha coefficients (0.97 and 0.97) are of similar order to those reported by Francis and Katz [28], which ranged between 0.97 and 0.98. The proportions of variance accounted for by the first factor are also similar to those reported by Francis and Katz [28], which ranged between 61.8% and 66.9%. A two-factorial solution was also assessed; however, it was rejected since (a) the variance explained by the second factor was rather low (7.56%) and (b) the makeup of that factor was meaningless.

Table 1. The Katz-Francis scale of attitude toward Judaism.

	Female		Male	
	r	*f*	*r*	*f*
I find it boring to learn the Torah *	0.71	0.66	0.57	0.71
I know that my religion helps me	0.63	0.61	0.70	0.83
Saying my prayers helps me a lot	0.73	0.82	0.78	0.89
The synagogue is very important to me	0.63	0.74	0.61	0.82
I think going to synagogue is a waste of my time *	0.61	0.90	0.66	0.82
I want to love G_d	0.86	0.78	0.82	0.87
I think synagogue services are boring *	0.59	0.82	0.51	0.78
I think people who pray are stupid *	0.55	0.57	0.70	0.75
G_d helps me to lead a better life	0.90	0.86	0.90	0.87
I like to learn about G_d very much	0.74	0.58	0.54	0.75
G_d means a lot to me	0.86	0.80	0.87	0.93
I believe that G_d helps people	0.80	0.73	0.84	0.84
Prayer helps me a lot	0.83	0.89	0.80	0.92

Table 1. *Cont.*

	Female		Male	
	r	*f*	*r*	*f*
I know that I am very close to G_d	0.79	0.82	0.86	0.88
I think praying is a good thing	0.83	0.74	0.86	0.84
I think the Torah is out of date *	0.66	0.49	0.64	0.64
I believe that G_d listens to prayers	0.79	0.85	0.82	0.85
G_d doesn't mean anything to me *	0.80	0.68	0.88	0.85
G_d is very real to me	0.89	0.88	0.84	0.82
I think saying prayers does no good *	0.75	0.72	0.86	0.89
The idea of G_d means much to me	0.90	0.85	0.77	0.76
I believe that my religion still helps people	0.65	0.76	0.60	0.72
I know that G_d helps me	0.86	0.83	0.88	0.86
I find it hard to believe in G_d *	0.84	0.75	0.72	0.83
Alpha/percent of variance	0.97	61.9%	0.97	61.3%

Notes: * Reverse-coded items; r correlation between item and sum of other items; f factor loading.

Steps towards assessing the construct validity of this scale can be made by assessing the extent to which certain predictions about the theoretical variations in attitude scores are reflected empirically [33,34]. While attitudes alone may not be simple or direct predictors of behavior [35,36], substantial evidence suggests a fairly close relationship between attitude toward religion and religious behavior, as demonstrated, for example, by Francis, Lewis, Philipchalk, Brown, and Lester [32]. For this reason, the construct validity of the Francis Scale of Attitude toward Christianity has generally been established by means of correlation with indices of religious behavior. In the case of Judaism, the path between attitudinal predisposition and religious behavior can be considered as not dissimilar from the case of Christianity. For this reason, three behavioral measures of religious practice were included in the current survey, namely measures of personal prayer, synagogue attendance, and observation of the dietary laws of Kashrut. Significant positive correlations were found between scores recorded on the Katz-Francis Scale of Attitude toward Judaism and all three behavioral measures among both men and women. For men the following correlations were reported: prayer, $r = 0.72$; synagogue, $r = 0.67$; Kashrut, $r = 0.44$. For women the following correlations were reported: prayer, $r = 0.71$; synagogue, $r = 0.71$; Kashrut, $r = 0.59$. These statistics support the construct validity of the attitude scale.

5. Conclusions

The present study set out to build on the work of Francis and Katz [28] and Yablon, Francis, and Robbins [30] who constructed and tested the Hebrew language Katz-Francis Scale of Attitude toward Judaism, rooted in the theory and empirical research pioneered by the Francis Scale of Attitude toward Christianity [32]. The objective of the present study was to examine the internal consistency reliability and construct validity of an English language version of this instrument among a sample of Australian Jews. Data provided by 101 members of the Australian Jewish community accessed through synagogues in Sydney and Melbourne and through the Maccabi sporting clubs reported highly satisfactory statistics of internal consistency reliability and construct validity among both men and women. On this basis the scale can be commended for further empirical studies concerned to map the personal and social correlates of individual differences in attitude toward Judaism among Jews living in Australia.

This instrument can also be commended for application and examination among the Jewish community in other English-speaking countries and for translation and testing in other languages.

Author Contributions: Patrick Lumbroso, Kirill Fayn and Niko Tiliopoulos jointly conceived and designed the project, conducted the data analyses, and organized the argument. Leslie J Francis served as project leader and assisted with the contextualization and writing.

Conflicts of Interest: The authors declare no conflict of interest.

References

1. Bernard Spilka, Ralph W. Hood, Bruce Hunsberger, and Richard L. Gorsuch. *The Psychology of Religion: An Empirical Approach*, 3rd ed. New York: Guilford Press, 2003.

2. Ralph W. Hood, Peter C. Hill, and Bernard Spilka. *The Psychology of Religion: An Empirical Approach*, 4th ed. New York: The Guilford Press, 2009.

3. Peter C. Hill, and Ralph W. Hood., eds. *Measures of Religiosity*. Birmingham: Religious Education Press, 1999.

4. Marsha Cutting, and Michelle Walsh. "Religiosity scales: What are we measuring in whom? " *Archive for the Psychology of Religion* 30 (2008): 137–53. [CrossRef]

5. Leslie J. Francis. "Attitude and longitude: A study in measurement." *Character Potential* 8 (1978): 119–30.

6. Leslie J. Francis. "Measurement reapplied: Research into the child's attitude towards religion." *British Journal of Religious Education* 1 (1978): 45–51. [CrossRef]

7. Salim J. Munayer. "The Ethnic Identity of Palestinian Arab Christian Adolescents in Israel." Unpublished Doctoral Dissertation, University of Wales, Oxford Centre for Mission Studies, Wales, UK, 2000.

8. Leslie J. Francis, Michael Quesnell, and Christopher Alan Lewis. "Assessing attitude toward Christianity among adolescents in the Czech Republic: The Francis Scale." *Irish Journal of Psychology* 31 (2010): 125–34. [CrossRef]

9. Leslie J. Francis, Christopher Alan Lewis, and Peter Ng. "Assessing attitude toward Christianity among Chinese speaking adolescents in Hong Kong: The Francis Scale." *North American Journal of Psychology* 4 (2002): 431–40.

10. Niko Tiliopoulos, Leslie J. Francis, and Yixin Jiang. "The Chinese translation of the Francis Scale of Attitude toward Christianity: Factor structure, internal consistency reliability and construct validity among Protestant Christians in Shanghai." *Pastoral Psychology* 62 (2013): 75–79. [CrossRef]

11. Leslie J. Francis, and Chris A. M. Hermans. "Internal consistency reliability and construct validity of the Dutch translation of the Francis Scale of Attitude toward Christianity among adolescents." *Psychological Reports* 86 (2000): 301–7. [CrossRef] [PubMed]

12. Christoper Alan Lewis, and Leslie J. Francis. "Evaluer l'attitude d'étudiantes universitaires françaises à l'égard du Christianisme: L'Echelle de Francis." *Sciences Pastorals* 22 (2003): 179–90.

13. Christopher Alan Lewis, and Leslie J. Francis. "Reliability and validity of a French translation of a short scale of attitude toward Christianity." *Pastoral Psychology* 52 (2004): 459–64. [CrossRef]

14. Leslie J. Francis, and Manfred Kwiran. "Werthaltungen (einstellungen) gegenüber dem christentum bei deutschen heranwachsenden: Die Francis-Skala." *Braunschweiger Beiträge* 89 (1999): 50–54.

15. Leslie J. Francis, Hans Georg Ziebertz, and Christopher Alan Lewis. "The psychometric properties of the Francis Scale of Attitude toward Christianity among German students." *Panorama* 14 (2002): 153–62.

16. Athena Youtika, Stephen Joseph, and Deborah Diduca. "Personality and religiosity in a Greek Christian Orthodox sample." *Mental Health, Religion and Culture* 2 (1999): 71–74. [CrossRef]

17. Giuseppe Crea, Roberto Baioco, Salvatore Ioverno, Gabriele Buzzi, and Leslie J. Francis. "The psychometric properties of the Italian translation of the Francis Scale of Attitude toward Christianity: A study among Catholic adolescents." *Journal of Beliefs and Values* 35 (2014): 118–22. [CrossRef]

18. Leslie J. Francis, and Trond Enger. "The Norwegian translation of the Francis Scale of Attitude toward Christianity." *Scandinavian Journal of Psychology* 43 (2002): 363–67. [CrossRef] [PubMed]

19. Ana Verissimo Ferreira, and Félix Neto. "Psychometric properties of the Francis Scale of Attitude toward Christianity among Portugese university students." *Psychological Reports* 91 (2002): 995–98. [CrossRef] [PubMed]

20. Leslie J. Francis, Dan Ispas, Mandy Robbins, Alexandra Ilie, and Dragos Iliescu. "The Romanian translation of the Francis Scale of Attitude toward Christianity: Internal consistency reliability, re-test reliability and construct validity among undergraduate students within a Greek Orthodox culture." *Pastoral Psychology* 58 (2009): 49–54. [CrossRef]

21. Sergej Flere, Rudi Klanjsek, Leslie J. Francis, and Mandy Robbins. "The psychometric properties of the Slovenian translation of the Francis Scale of Attitude toward Christianity: A study among Roman Catholic undergraduate students." *Journal of Beliefs and Values* 29 (2008): 313–19. [CrossRef]

22. Adalberto Campo-Arias, Heidi Celina Oviedo, Carmen Elena Diaz, and Zuleima Cogollo. "Internal consistency of a Spanish translation of the Francis Scale of Attitude toward Christianity short form." *Psychological Reports* 99 (2009): 1008–10. [CrossRef] [PubMed]

23. Jonas Eek. *Religious Facilitation through Intense Liturgical Participation: A Quasi-Experimental Study of Swedish Pilgrims to Taizé*. Lund: University of Lund Studies in Psychology of Religion, 2001.

24. Thomas E. Evans, and Leslie J. Francis. "Measuring attitude toward Christianity through the medium of Welsh." In *Research in Religious Education*. Edited by Leslie J. Francis, William K. Kay and William S. Campbell. Leominster: Fowler Wright Books, 1996, pp. 279–94.

25. Leslie J. Francis, and Enlli M. Thomas. "The reliability and validity of the Francis Scale of Attitude toward Christianity among Welsh speaking 9–11 year olds." *The Psychologist in Wales* 16 (2003): 9–14.

26. Abdullah Sahin, and Leslie J. Francis. "Assessing attitude toward Islam among Muslim adolescents: The psychometric properties of the Sahin-Francis Scale." *Muslim Educational Quarterly* 19 (2002): 35–47.

27. Leslie J. Francis, Yashoda Romil Santosh, Mandy Robbins, and Savita Vij. "Assessing attitude toward Hinduism: The Santosh-Francis Scale." *Mental Health, Religion and Culture* 11 (2008): 609–21. [CrossRef]

28. Leslie J. Francis, and Yaacov J. Katz. "Measuring attitude toward Judaism: The internal consistency reliability of the Katz-Francis Scale of Attitude toward Judaism." *Mental Health, Religion and Culture* 10 (2007): 309–24. [CrossRef]

29. Lee J. Cronbach. "Coefficient alpha and the internal structure of tests." *Psychometrika* 16 (1951): 297–334. [CrossRef]

30. Yaacov Yablon, Leslie J. Francis, and Mandy Robbins. "The Katz-Francis Scale of Attitude toward Judaism: Internal consistency reliability and construct validity among female undergraduate students in Israel." *Pastoral Psychology* 63 (2014): 73–78. [CrossRef]

31. Leslie J. Francis, and Michael T. Stubbs. "Measuring attitudes towards Christianity: From childhood to adulthood." *Personality and Individual Differences* 8 (1987): 741–43. [CrossRef]

32. Leslie J. Francis, John M. Lewis, Ronald Philipchalk, Laurence B. Brown, and David Lester. "The internal consistency reliability and construct validity of the Francis scale of attitude towards Christianity (adult) among undergraduate students in the UK, USA, Australia and Canada." *Personality and Individual Differences* 19 (1995): 949–53. [CrossRef]

33. Lee J. Cronbach, and Paul E. Meehl. "Construct validity in psychological tests." *Psychological Bulletin* 52 (1955): 281–302. [CrossRef] [PubMed]

34. Robert E. Orton. "The foundations of construct validity: Towards an update." *Journal of Research and Development in Education* 21 (1987): 22–35.

35. Icek Ajzen. *Attitudes, Personality and Behaviour*. Milton Keynes: Open University Press, 1988.

36. J. Richard Eiser, and Joop van der Pligt. *Attitudes and Decisions*. London: Routledge, 1988.

 *religions*

Article

Validity and Reliability of a Revised Scale of Attitude towards Buddhism (TSAB-R)

Phra Nicholas Thanissaro

WRERU, Centre for Education Studies, University of Warwick, Coventry CV4 7AL, UK;
p.n.thanissaro@warwick.ac.uk; Tel.: +44-24-7652-3800

Academic Editor: Arndt Büssing
Received: 26 February 2016; Accepted: 20 April 2016; Published: 28 April 2016

Abstract: The empirical properties of a revised 24-item instrument called the Thanissaro Scale of Attitude towards Buddhism (TSAB-R) designed to measure Buddhist affective religiosity are described. The instrument was tested on adolescents and teenagers in the UK. Discriminant validity of the instrument was found satisfactory in relation to Buddhist affiliation and content validity in relation to religious involvement with temple attendance, scripture reading, meditation, having had a religious or spiritual experience and religious style. Unlike Christians, for Buddhists, affective religiosity was found to vary independently from age and sex. The differential between heritage and convert religious style of Buddhism was linked to the perceived affective religiosity of the Buddhist features of the home shrine and bowing to parents. Factor analysis revealed two subscales within the instrument for intellectual and affective components. With confirmation of the validity and reliability of the revised scale, the instrument is commended for measurement of Buddhist affective religiosity with adults and children down to the age of 13 years.

Keywords: Buddhism; religiosity; quantitative measure; affective religiosity

1. Introduction

Modelling the religious sphere of life has led to the development of over 125 measurement scales [1]. Broadly speaking, the four core aspects of religiosity amenable to measurement include: religious belief, attitude to religion, religious participation and affiliation ([2], pp. 129–30). Since the majority of these measures have been grounded in monotheistic religions, it cannot be assumed they can be extrapolated to a non-theistic religion like Buddhism. Since some Buddhists question the salience of (dogmatic) belief to Buddhism [3], it is likely that the relationship between attitude towards religion, participation and affiliation would hold the key to measurement of Buddhist religiosity.

Preliminary work with attitude towards Buddhism has borrowed from the principles of the Francis Scale of Attitude toward Christianity (FSAC) [4]. Research with adolescents in the UK resulted in the design and reliability testing of a 24-item, 5-point Likert attitude scale for Buddhism known as the Thanissaro Scale of Attitude towards Buddhism (TSAB)—an instrument designed to measure the affective aspect of Buddhist religiosity as well as the intellectual response to Buddhist tenets [5]. Given that many aspects of Buddhist teachings such as karma and meditation elicit positive attitudes even outside the community of those self-identifying as Buddhist, the scale was designed on the basis of an exercise in discriminant validity: containing Buddhism-based attitude questions with the biggest differential between Buddhists and non-Buddhist views. The designer of TSAB had no chance to test the validity of the scale directly with Buddhists and commended this task to future research along with comparison of the affective aspect of Buddhism with other individual differences and dimensions of religiosity.

It is a challenge to find shared identity in the diverse Buddhist community. Often there seem to be more differences from one Buddhist to another, than between Buddhists and non-Buddhists. One of the biggest sources of internal diversity is seen in the heritage-convert dichotomy for Buddhists in western society—while some of these Buddhists have ethnic roots in the countries of Asia (so-called "heritage Buddhists") (e.g., [6], p. 199), others have converted to Buddhism independent of their family's influence (so-called "convert" Buddhists) (e.g., [7], pp. 42–49). These different routes into Buddhist faith result in major differences in religious style.

For most religions, participation is measured by frequency of place of worship attendance frequency, personal prayer and scripture reading. For Buddhists, equivalents can be found for all three of these modes of religious participation. Scripture reading would mean study of the Buddhist sutras or the Tipiṭaka in translation and chanting of tracts of Buddhist verses in the relevant scriptural language—with 55% of Buddhists involved with this form of practice to some extent. For Buddhists, attendance at a place of worship for those of heritage style would mean visits to Buddhist temples, but for those of convert style it might mean joining activities at meditation centres or Buddhist centres, with 98% of Buddhists involved in this practice to some extent, making it the most ubiquitous expression of religious participation—being practised intensively by heritage and convert Buddhists alike. For Buddhists, meditation would mean sitting cross-legged to cultivate mindfulness, with 82% of Buddhists involved in this practice to some extent ([8], p. 311).

It is only fair however, in the Buddhist case, additionally to include religious aspects of everyday life beyond the formalized expressions of religion—since when Buddhists were questioned about their faith, many considered non-formal aspects important to their Buddhist identity, not just their "cultural" identity. Having had a religious or spiritual experience found in 48% of Buddhists, means self-report of phenomena such as meditation inner experience, insight, wonder or other-worldly contact. Having a Buddhist shrine (reported by 70% of Buddhists), means displaying a raised shelf or set of tables in the home with Buddhist iconography and has also been used as a proxy for Buddhists affiliation in a Chinese study [9]. Bowing to parents means physically expressing respect to parents by lowering the head as more than just a gesture, and was found in 57% of Buddhists.

The expectations for validity based on previous experience with FSAC are that attitude towards religion would be more positive in those who are younger, in females, in those who self-identify as belonging to that religion and in those who participate most frequently in religious activities such as prayer, scripture reading or attendance at a place of worship ([10], p. 191). To test these expectations in the Buddhist context, the discriminant validity of TSAB-R was measured in a comparison between the scores of those adhering and those not adhering to Buddhism. In a test of content validity, statistical links between Buddhist affective religiosity and other dimensions of religiosity were explored for bowing to parents, scripture reading, having a home shrine, meditating, having had a religious or spiritual experience and temple attendance. The empirical properties of the instrument were tested in relation to other individual differences such as age, sex and religious style. Finally, the reliability of the revised scale was revisited and a confirmatory factor analysis performed.

2. Methodology

2.1. Sample

Buddhist teenagers participating in this study were derived from a tiny religious minority of 0.2%–0.4% in the British population. The sample size for the inter-religious comparison (*viz.* the "discriminant validity" heading in the findings section below) was 518. In this sample the experimental group consisted of 166 self-identifying Buddhist adolescents aged between 13- and 15-years-old derived from the dataset described by Thanissaro [8]. This sample contained 95 male (57%) and 71 female (43%) participants. The comparison group numbering 352, derived from the dataset described by Thanissaro [11], consisted of adolescents attending London schools who did *not* self-identify as Buddhists, also with ages between 13- and 15-years-old. This comparison group consisted of 225 male (64%) and 127 female (36%) participants. The self-identifying religion of the comparison group included

42% Christian, 34% no religion, 13% Muslim, 5% Hindu, 4% unspecified (not Buddhist), 1% Jewish and 1% Sikh.

For the intra-Buddhist comparisons (*viz.* all *but* the "discriminant validity" heading in the findings section below), the sample size was 417. These were teenagers attending temples in Britain or displaying an interest in Buddhist keywords[1] on their Facebook page, all of whom self-identified as Buddhists. The sample consisted of 225 male (54%) and 192 females (46%) aged between 13 and 20 and included Buddhists of Asian (52%), White (34%), Mixed (11%) Chinese (2%) and Black (1%) ethnicity. In terms of the temple institutions attended, to give some idea of Buddhist denominations included, the sample comprised Sinhalese (23%), Thai (16%), Tibetan (12%), Burmese (11%), Vietnamese (9%), Japanese (5%), Bangladeshi (3%), Western (2%), Chinese (2%), Nepalese (2%) and Cambodian (1%). Since the definition of heritage-style Buddhism is having a connection with Asian Buddhism through one's parents, Buddhists of Asian-Indian, Asian-Pakistani, Asian-Bangladeshi, Any Other Asian and Chinese ethnicity were allocated to the "heritage" Buddhist teenager category (hereafter abbreviated to "HBT"). Buddhists of White, Black-African and Black-Caribbean ethnicity were allocated to the "convert" Buddhist teenager category (hereafter abbreviated to "CBT"). In this sample, of those for whom religious style could be ascertained,[2] 61% were heritage and 39% were convert. Although it is likely that attitude towards Buddhism could be tested more easily in an adult age-group who would have a more fluent command of the English vocabulary, this research project was hosted in an education faculty and of necessity worked with adolescents and teenagers.

2.2. Instrument

A composite questionnaire deployed general questions on ethnicity, age, sex and religious affiliation. Multiple choice items allowed participants to indicate whether and how often they meditated, bowed to parents, attended a place of worship or read the scriptures. It was asked whether the respondents had a Buddhist shrine at their home and whether they had had a religious or spiritual experience. This general section was followed by the TSAB-R, which like TSAB, is a set of 24 statements relating to Buddhism. Respondents rated their level of agreement with the statements using a five-point Likert scale (Agree strongly—Agree—Not Certain—Disagree—Disagree Strongly) (*see* Figure A1 *for print example*). Differences between the TSAB and TSAB-R relate to reduction of verbosity in the original questions. Following the numerical order in which TSAB-R questions appear in Table 1, simplifications of language were made to questions 1, 8, 9, 10, 15, 17, 20, 21 and 22. Question 23 was converted into a second reverse-coded item. Special attention was given to the original "Sangha Day" question which after the testing of three variations to avoid the compound wording used in the TSAB ([8], p. 339) was adjusted to the wording "I like how Buddhists encourage people to become friends" for question 6.

---

[1] The keywords included the words: arhat (Buddhism), Buddhism, Buddhism Theravada, Buddhist, Buddhist meditation, Burmese Buddhist temple, Dhammakaya meditation, Dhammakaya movement, Foundation for the Preservation of the Mahayana Tradition, FWBO, Gautama Buddha, interbeing, Karma Kagyu, Mahayana, merit (Buddhism), New Kadampa Tradition, Order of Interbeing, Samatha, Soka Gakkai International SGI, Theravada, Theravada Buddhism, Theravada Buddhist, Tibetan Buddhism, Triratna Buddhist Community, Vietnamese Family of Buddhism, Vipassana, Vipassana meditation, Zen, Thich Nhat Hanh, Buddhism in Bangladesh, Buddhahood, Diamond Way Buddhism, Buddha's Dharma, Pure Land Buddhism, Buddha's Light International Association.
[2] Not possible where ethnicity was "mixed".

Table 1. Comparison of attitude towards Buddhism between adolescents of no religion, non-Buddhist religion and Buddhist religion.

		None *	Non-B. *	Budd.	χ^2	$p <$
1.	I like how Buddhists train their minds through prayer and meditation	16	15	77	192.4	0.001
2.	I like the way Buddhists offer flowers and incense to statues of Buddha	18	11	80	221.1	0.001
3.	Eightfold Path seems a good way to achieve happiness	17	15	67	137.4	0.001
4.	I admire Buddhists for respecting all living things	24	16	87	220.9	0.001
5.	I find it inspiring to hear Buddhist stories	19	23	75	134.3	0.001
6.	I like how Buddhists encourage people to become friends	13	15	72	196.0	0.001
7.	Spending time as a Buddhist monk is beneficial to the world at large	11	6	54	139.6	0.001
8.	I like how some Buddhists spend time in meditation as monks or nuns	14	12	66	153.2	0.001
9.	Buddhists should have respect for those worthy of respect	20	17	74	151.5	0.001
10.	I like the Buddhist idea of having a calm mind	37	31	86	126.7	0.001
11.	I respect Buddhists for giving food and money to their monks	30	18	85	187.9	0.001
12.	I respect the Buddhist idea that understanding is more important than belief	28	16	77	159.9	0.001
13.	It is important for Buddhists to spend time meditating	18	13	76	189.2	0.001
14.	It is necessary for us to share what we have with others	26	25	72	103.6	0.001
15.	Enjoying life or hating it depends on how we see the world	36	31	71	66.8	0.001
16.	Spending time meditating is a constructive use of one's time	12	11	54	109.2	0.001
17.	Buddhists should not to kill any sort of animal	18	17	71	143.5	0.001
18.	It is necessary for us to give support to the poor and the needy	32	28	88	157.4	0.001
19.	Nirvana is the ultimate peace	10	4	60	185.8	0.001
20.	Buddhists should avoid drinking alcohol	25	24	54	45.6	0.001
21.	Buddhists should look after their parents in their old age	26	23	83	160.1	0.001
22.	People who have helped us a lot deserve our special respect	40	27	82	121.0	0.001
23.	If a person does good deeds, good things will come back to them	58	67	66	118.4	0.001
24.	I would enjoy killing any sort of animal [®]	64	66	1	187.1	0.001

* from ([11], p. 242), Yates correction applied throughout; [®] indicates "reverse-coding" of the question.

2.3. Procedure

Surveys were distributed in the UK in the period 2013–2014 in paper and online formats and completed in the participants' own time. For those unable to complete the paper survey immediately, a stamped addressed envelope was provided to facilitate return. For the online version of the survey a Qualtrics web-based survey was hosted on the St Mary's Centre website (www.st-marys-centre.org.uk). Teenagers were directed to this survey by clicking sidebar advertising banners that appeared on their Facebook page if they belonged to a Buddhism-related interest group. The online sample was limited to those both resident in the UK and falling within the target age-group. For all items excepting those that were reverse coded[3] "Agree Strongly" was coded by a score of "5", "Agree" by "4", "Not Certain" by "3", "Disagree" by "2" and "Disagree Strongly" by "1"—the aggregate of the 24 items produces scores ranging from 120 indicating the most positive attitude towards Buddhism down to 24 indicating the least positive. Results were compared by Chi-square for single-item categorical measures and independent samples *t*-test for continuous scale scores in comparison between groups by the relevant routines of the SPSS statistical package [12].

3. Findings

In this section, findings have been subdivided into four subheadings: firstly, a test of validity, in terms of Buddhist affiliation and religious participation (bowing to parents, home shrine, meditation, having had a religious or spiritual experience, temple attendance and scripture reading), secondly a test of statistical links between TSAB-R and the individual differences of sex, age and religious style, thirdly the revised scale is revisited for an assessment of internal consistency reliability and finally a Principal Component Analysis of the instrument is performed.

3.1. Validity

3.1.1. Discriminant Validity: Buddhist Affiliation

As shown in Table 1, Buddhists had significantly more positive attitude, item-by-item on every one of the 24 questions on the Scale of Attitude towards Buddhism in comparison with adolescents of no religion and adolescents of a non-Buddhist religion. Only on item 23 which was fielded as a reverse coded item in the Buddhist sample, were non-Buddhist responses more similar to the Buddhist responses than to the response of those of no religions. These results strongly support the validity of those questions as Buddhist attitude identifiers. Taken together as a scale, the mean Scale of Attitude towards Buddhism score was greater for Buddhist adolescents ($M_{buddhist}$ = 97.04, S.D. = 12.04) than for adolescents of non-Buddhist religions ($M_{non-buddhist}$ = 75.98, S.D. = 8.54) a difference that was highly significant (t[396] = 20.41, $p < 0.001$). Similarly, the mean Scale of Attitude towards Buddhism score was greater for Buddhist adolescents ($M_{buddhist}$ = 97.04, S.D. = 12.04) than for adolescents of no religion ($M_{no\_religion}$ = 75.32, S.D. = 12.55) a difference that was also highly significant (t[284] = 14.78, $p < 0.001$).

3.1.2. Content Validity: Religious Participation

To examine whether the instrument covered all facets of the social construct of Buddhist religiosity, the presence or absence of diverse available formal and implicit expressions of Buddhist participation were compared in terms of TSAB-R.

Temple attendance: A significantly lower TSAB-R score was found for those who attended a temple weekly (M_{weekly} = 94.69, S.D. = 15.17) than for those who did not attend the temple this often ($M_{non-weekly}$ = 97.76, S.D. = 10.73, t[380] = 2.38, $p < 0.05$).

---

[3]   For reverse-coded items, the inverse scoring applies with AS = 1 … to … DS = 5.

Scripture reading: Being a reader of the Buddhist scriptures corresponded with a significantly more positive attitude towards Buddhism (M_{reader} = 97.75, S.D. = 12.92) compared to those who did not read the scriptures ($M_{non-reader}$ = 94.33, S.D. = 13.45, $t[393]$ = −2.63, $p < 0.01$).

Meditation: A significantly higher TSAB-R score was found for those who meditated daily (M_{daily} = 100.43, S.D. = 12.21) than for those who did not meditate this often ($M_{non-daily}$ = 95.36, S.D. = 13.25, $t[414]$ = −3.03, $p < 0.01$), however comparison of TSAB-R scores between those who meditated monthly ($M_{monthly}$ = 97.31, S.D. = 12.62) and those who meditated less than monthly ($M_{non-daily}$ = 95.02, S.D. = 13.78), were not significantly different ($t[414]$ = −1.47, NS).

Having had a religious or spiritual experience: According to the work of Thanissaro [13], those who had had a religious or spiritual experience were significantly more positive in their attitude towards Buddhism (M_{rse+} = 97.39, S.D. = 13.81) than those who had *not* had a religious or spiritual experience (M_{rse-} = 94.71, S.D. = 12.35, $t[415]$ = −2.06, $p < 0.05$).

Bowing to parents: According to the work of Thanissaro [14], for heritage Buddhist teenagers, the TSAB-R score for those bowing to parents (M_{bowing} = 98.29, S.D. = 11.70) was not significantly more positive than for heritage Buddhist teenagers who did not bow to their parents ($M_{no\ bowing}$ = 94.66, S.D. = 12.28, $t[224]$ = 1.87, N.S.). For convert Buddhist teenagers however, the TSAB-R score for those bowing to parents (M_{bowing} = 99.92, S.D. = 15.06) *was* significantly more positive than for other convert Buddhist teenagers who did not bow to their parents ($M_{no\ bowing}$ = 92.56, S.D. = 14.96, $t[144]$ = 2.31, $p < 0.05$).

Having a home shrine: For heritage teen Buddhists, having a shrine corresponded with a significantly higher mean score on the TSAB-R ($M_{with\ shrine}$ = 98.55, S.D. = 11.50) than that of those without a shrine ($M_{no\ shrine}$ = 91.13, S.D. = 12.46, $t[224]$ = −3.30, $p < 0.01$). For convert teen Buddhists however, having a shrine did not correspond with a significant difference in score on the TSAB-R ($M_{with\ shrine}$ = 96.64, S.D. = 14.60) as compared with those who had no shrine ($M_{no\ shrine}$ = 92.40, S.D. = 15.27, $t[142]$ = −1.68, NS).

3.2. Individual Differences

To test extrapolation of trends in conjunction with individual differences observed with FSAC and also to ascertain the performance of the instrument across differences of religious style, TSAB-R scores were tested against sex, age and religious style.

Sex: No sex-differences were apparent for TSAB-R scores, with no significant difference between the male mean TSAB-R score (M_{male} = 95.97, S.D. = 12.82) and the female (M_{female} = 96.47, S.D. = 13.47, $t[415]$ = −0.381, NS).

Age: The mean TSAB-R score for those in their early teens (13- to 16-year-olds) (M_{early_teen} = 97.07, S.D. = 12.22) was not significantly different from that of those in their late teens (17- to 20-year-olds)(M_{late_teen} = 95.18, S.D. = 14.30, $t[378]$ = 1.436, NS).

Religious Style: The mean TSAB-R score for HBT was higher (M_{hbt} = 97.53, S.D. = 11.89) than for CBT (M_{cbt} = 93.92, S.D. = 15.20) which was a significant difference ($t[256]$ = 2.430, $p < 0.05$).

3.3. Reliability of the Revised Scale

The study was able to verify the internal consistency reliability of TSAB-R using the usual measures of reliability [15,16]. Cronbachs's alpha coefficient for all 24 items of Buddhist attitude together was 0.901, with item-total reliabilities ranging from 0.324 to 0.785—well within the bounds of acceptability since Kline [17] indicates that an alpha-coefficient of over 0.8 is acceptable in psychological testing. Table 2 shows the contributing reliabilities for each item, arranged in decreasing order of reliability.

Table 2. Reliability of the revised Scale of Attitude towards Buddhism (TSAB-R).

	Item Rest of Test Correlation
I like how Buddhists train their minds through prayer and meditation	0.785
I like the Buddhist idea of having a calm mind	0.772
I like how Buddhists encourage people to become friends	0.739
It is necessary for us to give support to the poor and the needy	0.726
I admire Buddhists for respecting all living things	0.725
I like how some Buddhists spend time in meditation as monks or nuns	0.699
I find it inspiring to hear Buddhist stories	0.670
I would enjoy killing any sort of animal [R]	0.668
It is important for Buddhists to spend time meditating	0.664
Buddhists should look after their parents in their old age	0.654
Spending time meditating is a constructive use of one's time	0.638
Eightfold Path seems a good way to achieve happiness	0.632
I respect the Buddhist idea that understanding is more important than belief	0.619
Nirvana is the ultimate peace	0.598
I respect Buddhists for giving food and money to their monks	0.586
People who have helped us a lot deserve our special respect	0.571
I like the way Buddhists offer flowers and incense to statues of Buddha	0.555
It is necessary for us to share what we have with others	0.542
Buddhists should have respect for those worthy of respect	0.537
Enjoying life or hating it depends on how we see the world	0.525
Buddhists should not kill any sort of animal	0.523
Spending time as a Buddhist monk is beneficial to the world at large	0.513
If a person does good deeds, bad things will come back to them [R]	0.406
Buddhists should avoid drinking alcohol	0.324
Alpha coefficient for all 24 items together =	0.901

[R] Indicates that this item was reverse scored for correlation purposes.

3.4. Factor Analysis

A principal component analysis (PCA) was conducted on the 24 items with orthogonal rotation (Promax). The Kaiser-Meyer-Olkin measure verified the sampling adequacy for the analysis, KMO = 0.96 which is well above the acceptable limit [18]. Bartlett's test of sphericity χ^2 (276) = 5279.79, $p < 0.001$ indicated that correlations between items were sufficiently large for PCA. An initial analysis was run to obtain eigenvalues for each component in the data. Four components had eigenvalues over Kaiser's criterion of 1, however factor analysis identified only two components that corresponded with reliable sub-scales and in combination accounted for 49.58% of the total variance. Table 3 shows the factor loadings after rotation. The items that cluster on the same components suggest that component 1 represents "Intellect" and component 2 "Affect".

Table 3. Summary of exploratory factor analysis results for TSAB-R (*n* = 417).

Item	Rotated Factor Loadings	
	Intellect	Affect
Spending time meditating is a constructive use of one's time	0.84	−0.12
It is important for Buddhists to spend time meditating	0.75	−0.01
I like how Buddhists train their minds through prayer and meditation	0.72	0.15
I like how some Buddhists spend time in meditation as monks or nuns	0.71	0.05
Nirvana is the ultimate peace	0.66	0.00
Eightfold Path seems a good way to achieve happiness	0.58	0.11
I find it inspiring to hear Buddhist stories	0.55	0.18
I like how Buddhists encourage people to become friends	0.51	0.30
Spending time as a Buddhist monk is beneficial to the world at large	0.50	0.02
I respect the Buddhist idea that understanding is more important than belief	0.36	0.33
Enjoying life or hating it depends on how we see the world	0.33	0.25
If a person does good deeds, bad things will come back to them	−0.32	−0.12
I like the Buddhist idea of having a calm mind	0.40	0.47
It is necessary for us to give support to the poor and the needy	−0.00	0.82
I would enjoy killing any sort of animal	0.04	−0.79
I admire Buddhists for respecting all living things	0.09	0.74
People who have helped us a lot deserve our special respect	−0.07	0.71
Buddhists should look after their parents in their old age	0.10	0.64
I respect Buddhists for giving food and money to their monks	0.01	0.63
Buddhists should have respect for those worthy of respect	0.09	0.50
It is necessary for us to share what we have with others	0.20	0.40
Buddhists should not kill any sort of animal	0.20	0.37
I like the way Buddhists offer flowers and incense to statues of Buddha	0.24	0.38
Buddhists should avoid drinking alcohol	0.18	0.18
Eigenvalues	10.68	1.22
% of variance	44.48	5.10
α	0.910	0.757

Factor loadings over 0.40 appear in **bold**; Extraction method: Principal Axis Factoring; Rotation method: Promax with Kaiser Normalization.

4. Discussion

4.1. Discriminant Validity

TSAB-R was able to discriminate accurately between adolescents self-identifying as being of Buddhist, non-Buddhist or no religion on the basis of their affective religiosity, both on individual questions and with the scale as a whole, commending the choice of questions on the TSAB-R both as effective Buddhist identifiers and meaningful across the range of Buddhist styles.

4.2. Content Validity

That TSAB-R covers all aspects of the construct of affective Buddhist religiosity has been borne out in the statistical linking of higher scores with more frequent participation in many forms of Buddhist practice, whether it was temple attendance, scripture reading, meditation or having a religious or spiritual experience. The strongest link between participation and affective religiosity was for the practice of meditation, specifically daily meditation, which is interesting considering the popularity of meditation and mindfulness practices even outside the community of those self-identifying as Buddhist. Another expectation from Christian affective religiosity is that scores would be higher amongst females and those of a younger age group. For Buddhist affective religiosity however, there was no sex-difference or age-difference between scores.

4.3. Complexity Introduced by the Heritage-Convert Dichotomy

The differences in scores between heritage and convert Buddhists may indicate that as an instrument, TSAB-R is slightly weighted towards the heritage style of Buddhism or that CBT are actually less affective in their religiosity than HBT. In any case, such differences would be masked if affiliation were the only indicator of Buddhist religiosity. Nonetheless, instead of having to consider HBT and CBT samples separately, direct comparison can be made to see the relative importance of different forms of practice to each style with TSAB-R as a common variable. As has been seen from the findings, bowing to parents linked to the affective religiosity for CBT but not for HBT, but the opposite was true in the case of having a Buddhist shrine in the home. It may be that the perpetuating or plausibility structures communicating the culture of Buddhism between generations differ depending on the style of Buddhism practised.

4.4. Emancipatory Apologetic for the Instrument

As Buddhists are relatively unfamiliar with quantitative analysis of their religiosity, and mindful of Wilfred Cantwell-Smith's advice that no statement about Buddhist doctrine is valid unless Buddhists can respond, "Yes! That is what we hold" ([19], p. 97), a few words of reassurance about this scale are probably required. Reflecting on whether this instrument measures something that would be recognizable to Buddhists, rather than having value only as an academic hermeneutic, I would consider TSAB-R scores represent steadfastness of the ten-forms of Right View [as they appear in the Sāleyyaka Sutta ([20], pp. 347–48) rather than strength of belief. This affective aspect of being Buddhist might correspond with faith or "piety" although not necessarily corresponding with translation of such piety into religious participation—which would be measured by a different sort of instrument.

4.5. Commendation for Further Use

Given the limitations of drawing conclusions about Buddhist religiosity based solely on 'saying one is a Buddhist' TSAB-R offers a new dimension for the consideration of Buddhists' religiosity, and also those in the category of Buddhist sympathizers and those with multiple religious affiliations. The validity testing contained in this paper indicates potential for the instrument to distinguish between Buddhist and non-Buddhist affective religiosity while also predicting a higher degree of "readiness" to participate in Buddhist activities. It would be instructive to plot TSAB-R scores over the full course of the lifespan and Buddhist mentors would find it useful to measure the influence of nurture, formation and other educational interventions on elevating affective Buddhist religiosity in their students, in a way that has not been previously possible. TSAB-R is thus commended here for further use amongst adults and children down to the age of 13—in the English wording tested here or in translation.

4.6. Suggestions for Further Research

Since PCA indicates that two subscales of "intellect" and "affect" may vary to some extent independently within this scale of Buddhist religiosity, in future research it would be helpful to consider these two aspects of religiosity separately, for example in their relative emphasis in heritage and convert styles of Buddhism. Also, as the wording of the TSAB-R questions is reasonably accessible to respondents who are not themselves Buddhist, the instrument would lend itself to inter-religious comparison of attitude towards Buddhism. It would also be instructive to field the instrument in countries where Buddhism has a more dominant presence outside the Western context where TSAB-R has been designed.

Conflicts of Interest: The author declares no conflict of interest.

Appendix A

INSTRUCTIONS

Please read each sentence carefully and see if you agree or disagree with it. You have to draw one ring on each line.

If you Agree Strongly, put a ring around	**AS**	A	NC	D	DS
If you Agree, put a ring around	AS	**A**	NC	D	DS
If you are Not Certain, put a ring around	AS	A	**NC**	D	DS
If you Disagree, put a ring around	AS	A	NC	**D**	DS
If you Disagree Strongly, put a ring around	AS	A	NC	D	**DS**

I like how Buddhists train their minds through prayer and meditation	AS	A	NC	D	DS
I like the way Buddhists offer flowers and incense to statues of Buddha	AS	A	NC	D	DS
Eightfold Path seems a good way to achieve happiness.............................	AS	A	NC	D	DS
I admire Buddhists for respecting all living things	AS	A	NC	D	DS
I find it inspiring to hear Buddhist stories..	AS	A	NC	D	DS
I like how Buddhists encourage people to become friends..........................	AS	A	NC	D	DS
Spending time as a Buddhist monk is beneficial to the world at large	AS	A	NC	D	DS
I like how some Buddhists spend time in meditation as monks or nuns	AS	A	NC	D	DS
Buddhists should have respect for those worthy of respect	AS	A	NC	D	DS
I like the Buddhist idea of having a calm mind..	AS	A	NC	D	DS
I respect Buddhists for giving food and money to their monks	AS	A	NC	D	DS
I respect the Buddhist idea that understanding is more important than belief	AS	A	NC	D	DS
It is important for Buddhists to spend time meditating	AS	A	NC	D	DS
It is necessary for us to share what we have with others	AS	A	NC	D	DS
Enjoying life or hating it depends on how we see the world	AS	A	NC	D	DS
Spending time meditating is a constructive use of one's time	AS	A	NC	D	DS
Buddhists should not kill any sort of animal	AS	A	NC	D	DS
It is necessary for us to give support to the poor and the needy	AS	A	NC	D	DS
Nirvana is the ultimate peace...	AS	A	NC	D	DS
Buddhists should avoid drinking alcohol..	AS	A	NC	D	DS
Buddhists should look after their parents in their old age...........................	AS	A	NC	D	DS
People who have helped us a lot deserve our special respect.....................	AS	A	NC	D	DS
If a person does good deeds, bad things will come back to them	AS	A	NC	D	DS
I would enjoy killing any sort of animal..	AS	A	NC	D	DS

Figure A1. Revised Scale of Attitude towards Buddhism (TSAB-R).

References

1. Peter C. Hill, and Ralph W. Hood. *Measures of Religiosity*. Birmingham: Religious Education Press, 1999.
2. Leslie J. Francis. "Comparative empirical research in religion: Conceptual and operational challenges within empirical theology." In *Empirical Theology in Texts and Tables: Qualitative, Quantitative and Comparative Perspectives*. Edited by Leslie J. Francis, Mandy Robbins and Jeff Astley. Brill: Leiden, 2009, pp. 127–52.
3. Stephen Batchelor. *Buddhism without Beliefs: A Contemporary Guide to Awakening*. New York: Riverhead, 1997.
4. Leslie J. Francis. "Attitude and longitude: A study in measurement." *Character Potential: A Record of Research* 8 (1978): 119–30.
5. Phra Nicholas Thanissaro. "Measuring attitude towards Buddhism and Sikhism: Internal consistency reliability for two new instruments." *Mental Health, Religion & Culture* 14 (2011): 797–803. [CrossRef]
6. Joyce Miller. "The Forest Hermitage: An Ethnographic Study of a Buddhist Community in Warwickshire." Master's Thesis, University of Warwick, Coventry, UK, 1992.
7. Jan Nattier. "Visible & Invisible: The Politics of Representation in Buddhist America." *Tricycle, the Buddhist Review* 5 (1995): 42–49.

8. Phra Nicholas Thanissaro. "Temple-going Teenagers: Religiosity and Identity of Buddhists growing up in Britain." Ph.D. Thesis, University of Warwick, Coventry, UK, 2016.
9. Xinzhong Yao, and Paul Badham. *Religious Experience in Contemporary China*. Cardiff: University of Wales Press, 2007.
10. William K. Kay, and Leslie J. Francis. *Drift from the Churches: Attitude toward Christianity during Childhood and Adolescence*. Cardiff: University of Wales Press, 1996.
11. Phra Nicholas Thanissaro. "Religious Education and Attitudes to Buddhism & Sikhism." Master's Thesis, University of Warwick, Coventry, UK, 2010.
12. SPSS Inc. *SPSS User's Guide*, 2nd ed. New York: McGraw-Hill, 1988.
13. Phra Nicholas Thanissaro. "The spirituality of Buddhist teenagers: Religious/spiritual experiences and their associated triggers, attributes and attitudes." *International Journal of Children's Spirituality* 20 (2015): 219–33. [CrossRef]
14. Phra Nicholas Thanissaro. "Buddhist teen bowing to parents: Straddling the border between private and public religion." *Usuteaduslik Ajakiri* 69 (2016): 110–26.
15. Lee J. Cronbach. "Coefficient alpha and the internal structure of tests." *Psychometrika* 16 (1951): 297–334. [CrossRef]
16. Robert F. DeVellis. *Scale Development: Theory and Applications*. London: Sage Publications, 1991, vol. 26.
17. Paul Kline. *The Handbook of Psychological Testing*. London: Routledge, 1999.
18. Graeme D. Hutchinson, and Nick Sofroniou. *The Multivariate Social Scientist: Introductory Statistics Using Generalized Linear Models*. London: Sage, 1999.
19. William Cantwell Smith. *Towards a World Theology: Faith and the Comparative History of Religion*. Maryknoll: Orbis, 1981.
20. Pali Text Society. *The Middle Length Sayings*. Translated by Isaline B. Horner. Lancaster: Pali Text Society, 2007, vol. 1.

Article

Exploratory Psychometric Properties of the Farsi and English Versions of the Spiritual Needs Questionnaire (SpNQ)

Nazi Nejat [1], Lisa Whitehead [2,*] and Marie Crowe [3]

[1] School of Nursing and Midwifery, Arak University of Medical Sciences, Arak 6941-7-38481, Iran; n.nejat@arakmu.ac.ir

[2] School of Nursing and Midwifery, Edith Cowan University, Joondalup, WA 6027, Australia

[3] Centre for Postgraduate Nursing Studies, University of Otago, Christchurch 8140, New Zealand; marie.crowe@otago.ac.nz

* Correspondence: l.whitehead@ecu.edu.au; Tel.: +61-863-042-641

Academic Editor: Arndt Büssing
Received: 28 February 2016; Accepted: 14 June 2016; Published: 28 June 2016

Abstract: The aim of this study was to translate and test the psychometric properties of a Farsi and an English version of the spiritual needs questionnaire (SpNQ) a measure originally developed in German. The World Health Organization guideline for translating and validating questionnaires was used. Participants were recruited from hospitals in Iran and New Zealand during an outpatient follow-up appointment after cancer treatment. People diagnosed with cancer in Iran (68) and New Zealand (54) completed and returned the SpNQ (at time 1) and within the two week time period (time 2). Cronbach's alpha ranged from 0.79 to 0.92, except for the existentialistic domain of the SpNQ (0.53–0.54). The coefficient of variation (CV) indicated minimal random variation between the assessments; the measures were generally stable, except for the item "existentialistic". The translated versions of the SpNQ have the potential to support a comprehensive assessment of cancer patients' spiritual needs.

Keywords: cancer; spiritual care; needs

---

1. Background

The provision of holistic care is recognised and promoted as best practice in caring for people with cancer [1], and involves assessing and treating physical, emotional and spiritual needs [2]. Spirituality has been defined as "an inherent quality of all humans that drives the search for meaning and purpose in life" and "involves relationships with oneself, others and a transcendent dimension" ([3], p. 324). Taylor [4] states spirituality reveals itself as spiritual needs in three levels: intrapersonal, interpersonal and transpersonal. The need to have purpose, hope and transcend challenges is an example of intrapersonal spiritual needs. The desire to forgive and be forgiven and to love and be loved by others illustrates an interpersonal level of need. Examples of transpersonal spiritual needs include the desire to relate to and worship an ultimate other (often God).

In recent years, an increasing number of studies have shown that spirituality and/or religiosity can be a source of comfort for cancer patients [5,6] and is linked to self-esteem, sense of hope, a sense of meaning and purpose, and the provision of emotional comfort [6]. Spirituality is a much broader concept than religion, although it may be expressed through religion [7]. Koenig [2] believes that spirituality and religion can be used interchangeably, because most research linking spirituality to health has measured religious beliefs or practices.

There is a growth in the evidence of a positive association between spirituality and other health outcomes [8], which suggests the importance of considering spiritual needs in health care [9]. There is also interest in the relationship between spiritual needs and mental and physical health [10], and the role and importance of religion and spirituality in health care practice [6]. Spiritual needs have been defined by the Institute of Medicine as "the needs and expectations that humans have to find meaning, purpose and value in their life" ([11], p. 40). Health care professionals, through better understanding of patients' spiritual needs, will develop effective spiritual interventions [10] and provide spiritual care to promote spiritual health through addressing patients' spiritual needs [4]. Therefore it is important that ongoing assessment of spiritual needs continues throughout the course of treatment and beyond for patients [1].

It is well documented that living with cancer often increases an individual's awareness of the spiritual dimension of the self and intensifies their spiritual needs [12]. They frequently and increasingly use spiritual and/or religious resources, and spiritual healing to improve their health and cope with cancer [13,14]. Moreover, the literature supports the benefits of spiritual care, including improvement in quality of life [15], and increased overall patient satisfaction [16].

However, there are few measures for assessing spiritual needs in patients with chronic illnesses [17] such as cancer, especially in non-English language and among different religions [18]. Therefore, there is a need to explore the psychometric properties of measures for different languages, cultures and religions. The Spiritual Needs Questionnaire (SpNQ) was originally developed in German [19], and this paper reports on the psychometric properties of the English version and Farsi version of the SpNQ respectively.

Islam is the main religion in Iran, followed by 99% of the population [20]. The other religions include Christianity, Zoroastrianism and Judaism [21] Religion and spirituality play an important role in the Iranian life. As Fasihi Harandy et al. ([22], p. 94) state "Islamic teaching and ideology in Iran heavily emphasizes the 'will of God' by indicating that the birth, life and death of all creatures are in" God's hand, and with many quotations in the Holy Qur'an indicating this belief. Muslims believe that dying is a passage from this world to resurrection, and the spirit continues to live after death [23]. From a Muslims' point of view, there are no differences between spirituality and religion (thought and activities) [23], while in Western society, spirituality is seen as a more comprehensive concept than religion and incorporates finding purpose and meaning of life [24,25].

New Zealand is a highly secular country [26,27], but there is evidence that spirituality is important for patients with cancer [1]. The 2013 census showed that four out of ten New Zealanders (35.3%) declare themselves to be non-religious. The most common religion was Christianity (48.9%) [28]. Māori (indigenous people of New Zealand) have had an important role in promoting spirituality in the health agenda in New Zealand [26], because spirituality has special meaning for Māori. They believe that everything has a type of soul and "when considering health and wellbeing, mind, body and spirit are inseparable" ([29], p. 5).

The study was conducted in two countries, Iran (researcher's home country) and New Zealand (location of PhD study) because of the contrasts in terms of religion, culture and delivery of health care services. This allowed for the exploration of differences and similarities in psychometric properties of the SpNQ across two very different cultures and countries where little research in this area has been conducted.

2. Materials and Methods

2.1. Translation and Validation of the Questionnaires

The translation and validation of the questionnaires were performed using the World Health Organization process for the translation and adaptation of instruments [30]. After receiving written permission from the original authors of the instruments, the original scales in German were translated into Farsi and English by a person fluent in German and Farsi or German and English. Then three bilingual experts (German and English or German and Farsi) identified and resolved inadequate expressions and concepts resulting from the translation of the scales. In the next step, the two experts fluent in both languages translated the questionnaires back into the language. The discrepancies in both translations (forward and backward) were discussed with an emphasis on conceptual and cultural equivalence, and some minor revisions were made in the Farsi and English versions of the questionnaires. Pre-testing of the instruments was then performed.

2.2. Participants

The study was conducted within New Zealand and Iran. Participants were recruited from a large tertiary hospital in New Zealand and a large cancer hospital in Iran. Participants were recruited (convenience sampling) from hospitals during their hospital visit and were identified by nurses. The researcher described the study to patients as part of a wider study where the first step was validation of the questionnaires (SpNQ). Participants were further fluent in either Farsi or English and clinical staff ensured that study information was not given to those exhibiting high levels of distress during their outpatient visit.

The researcher asked all participants, (who accepted to participate in the research) people diagnosed with cancer in Iran (89 patients) and New Zealand (85 patients) to complete a demographic and clinical characteristics questionnaire and the SpNQ, either at the clinic or at home and to return these to the researcher or the nurse manager in the hospital as soon as they were able. Participants were asked to complete the same questionnaires two weeks later. In Iran, 68 patients completed and returned both questionnaires within the two week time period. In New Zealand, 61 patients completed the questionnaire (SpNQ) at time 1 and 54 patients completed it at time 2.

Eligibility to participate was restricted to people diagnosed with cancer; aged between 18 and 80 years; aware of their diagnosis; and physically and mentally capable of participating in the study. The study was approved by the Upper South A Regional Ethics Committee in New Zealand, and the Ethics Committee of Arak Medical Sciences University in Iran.

2.3. Measures

The Spiritual Needs Questionnaire (SpNQ) was designed to explore people's spiritual needs and can be used in both secular and religious societies by avoiding exclusive religious terminology. Respondents indicate whether a need exists or not in relation to four domains and the strength of the need on a four point Likert scale.

The (SpNQ was originally developed with 210 adults living with chronic pain (67%), cancer (28%), and other chronic conditions (5%). Factor analysis supported four factors which explained 67% of the variance: Religious needs, i.e., praying for and with others, and by themselves, participating in religious ceremonies (six items), Need for inner peace i.e., spending time in a place of peace and tranquility, (five items), Existentialistic needs i.e., reflecting on life and finding meaning in illness or suffering, (five items); and Actively giving i.e., passing on your life experiences to others; (three items).

The questionnaire has been translated into a number of languages with publications on the Polish [31], and Chinese versions [32]. The internal consistency estimates for the SpNQ range from 0.82 to 0.90 [5] for the German version, 0.74 to 0.92 for the Polish version and 0.51 to 0.81 for the Chinese version. The first paper [19] indicated that for people with chronic pain conditions and cancer, the need for Inner Peace was of strongest relevance, followed by Actively Giving. In Poland, 275 people with chronic diseases who identified as Catholic completed the questionnaire and needs in all four areas were found to be relatively high and people living with chronic pain expressing higher levels of need related to Existential Needs and Inner Peace Needs compared with those living with other chronic conditions. In China, 168 people living with chronic conditions completed the Chinese version of the SpNQ. The 17 item SpNQ-Ch had a similar factorial structure as the original version, with two main and three minor factors which accounted for 64% of the variance. In this study people with cancer (63%), chronic pain (10%) and other chronic conditions, needs relating to Giving/Generosity and Inner Peace were rated highly and Religious Needs and Reflection/Release needs lower.

The Duke University Religion index (DUREL) is a five-item measure of religious involvement, was developed in English by Koenig (1997–1998) [33], and "was designed to measure religiosity in Western religions (e.g., Christianity, Judaism and Islam)" ([34], p. 84).

The questionnaire assesses three major dimensions of religious involvement that consists of three parts including organizational religiosity (one-item) that assesses frequency of attendance at religious meetings. The second part assesses non-organizational or private religiosity (one-item). The third part includes assessing intrinsic religiosity that assesses religious beliefs and experiences (three-items) [34].The DUREL has an overall score range from 5 to 27. However, since it consists of three subscales and measures three dimensions of religiosity, computing a total score is not recommended by authors [34].

This scale is widely used as a religiosity scale with strong psychometric properties across medical and community setting [35]. Validated Farsi [36] and English [34] version of Duke University Religion Index (DUREL) were used in this study.

2.4. Statistical Analysis

The internal consistency was assessed using Cronbach's alpha for each subscale within the questionnaire with the coefficient criteria set at 0.7. The best method to evaluate the internal consistency is Cronbach's alpha and reliability coefficients higher than 0.7 are deemed adequate, but coefficients >0.8 are preferable [37]. The reliability of the scales was measured by Pearson or Spearman correlation coefficients by a test re test approach with a two-week interval as recommended [37].

The correlation coefficients of the scales (stability of the tests over time) were evaluated by paired sample *t*-test and Wilcoxon signed ranks test (for some measures that were not-normally distributed, including DUREL in Iran, and SpNQ at time 2 and DUREL at both time points in New Zealand) as appropriate.

The convergent validity of the Farsi and English version of the SpNQ 2.1 were assessed with validated Farsi [36] and English [34] version of Duke University Religion Index (DUREL) respectively.

The relationship between spiritual needs of participants in Iran (as measured by the SpNQ) and religiosity (as measured by the DUREL scale) were evaluated using Pearson correlation and Spearman's rho (for some measures that did not have normal distribution, including DUREL) as appropriate. The relationship between spiritual needs of participants in New Zealand (as measured by the SpNQ) and religiosity (as measured by the DUREL scale) was assessed using Pearson correlation and Spearman rho (for some measures that were 'non-normal' including SpNQ at time 2 and DUREL at both time points) as appropriate.

3. Results

3.1. Participants in Iran

In Iran, a convenience sample of 89 patients agreed to participate in the study, and 68 patients completed and returned the questionnaires within the two week time period. The mean age of participants was 53.60 (*SD* = 13.28) years; 51.5% were men and 48.5% women. Most participants were married (91.2%), the majority had a primary school level education (72.1%), 38.2% were employed and 42.6% managed the home. All participants in Iran (*n* = 68, 100%) were Muslim. The most prevalent cancer type was leukaemia (30.9%), and the time since diagnosis was less than six months (30.9%) (Table 1).

Table 1. Characteristics of Iranian and New Zealand participants with cancer.

Participant Characteristics	Iran (*n*)	Iran (%)	NZ (*n*)	NZ (%)
Age				
Age range	18–77		35–82	
Mean age	53.60 (SD = 13.28)		65.01 (SD = 12.90)	
Gender				
Male	35	51.47	29	53.70
Female	33	48.52	25	46.29
Marital Status				
Married	62	91.17	42	77.77
Never been married	5	7.35	6	11.11
Widowed	1	1.47	4	7.40
Never been married	-	-	2	3.70
Education Level				
No school completed	21	30.88	4	7.40
Primary school completed	28	41.17	18	33.33
High school graduate	18	26.47	29	53.70
University degree	1	1.47	3	5.55
Employment				
Employed	7	10.29	20	37.03
Self employed	19	27.94	5	9.25
Retired	8	11.76	20	37.03
Home duties	29	42.46	3	5.55
Unable to work	2	2.94	6	11.11
Unemployed	3	4.41	-	-
Religion				
Moslem	68	100	-	-
Christian	-	-	51	94.45
No religion	-	-	2	3.70
Prefer not to say	-	-	1	1.85
Type of Cancer				
Lung	6	8.82	6	11.11
Stomach	4	5.88	2	3.70
Colorectal	8	11.76	13	24.07
Breast	8	11.76	13	24.07
Leukaemia	21	30.88	-	-
Ovarian	4	5.88	-	-
Prostate	-	-	6	11.11
Other	17	25.00	14	25.92
Time since Diagnosis				
⩽6 months	21	30.88	1	1.85
7–12 months	17	25.00	23	42.59
13–24 months	18	26.47	24	44.44
>24 months	-	-	6	11.11

3.2. Participants in New Zealand

In New Zealand, a convenience sample of 85 patients agreed to participate in the study, and 61 patients completed the SpNQ at time 1 and 54 patients completed it at time 2. The mean age was 65.01 (SD = 12.90) years; 53.7% were male and 46.3% female, 46.3% were employed, and 37% retired. The majority were married (77.8%) and had a high school education (53.7%). Fifty one New Zealand participants (94.45%) had a Christian affiliation, two (3.70%) had none, and one (1.85%) preferred not to say. Colorectal (24.1%) and breast (24.1%) cancers were the most prevalent cancer type. The time since cancer diagnosis was less than six months for 42.6% and between 1 and 2 years for 44.4% of the patients (Table 1).

3.3. Results of Translation and Validation of the Questionnaires

Amongst Iranian participants, religious needs were rated highly, followed by Inner Peace. In New Zealand, the highest rating was associated with Inner Peace followed by Religious Needs.

Internal consistency was assessed using Cronbach's alpha for each subscale within the questionnaire, with the coefficient criteria set at 0.7. Cronbach's alpha and reliability coefficients higher than 0.7 are deemed adequate, but coefficients >0.8 are preferable [37]. The reliability of all scales was measured by Pearson or Spearman correlation coefficients using a test re-test approach with a two-week interval as recommended [37].

The reliability of SpNQ scales in Iran and New Zealand, showed acceptable to high internal consistency using Coefficient of Cronbach's alpha ranging from 0.794 to 0.920 (Table 2). The questionnaires subscales achieved acceptable to high internal consistency (0.72–0.94) at both time points in both countries except for the existentialistic domain of SpNQ (0.53–0.54) in Iran (Table 2).

Table 2. Cronbach's alpha for all dimensions of the scales in Iran and New Zealand.

Cronbach's Alpha	Time 1	Time 2
SpNQ (Iran)	0.797	0.794
Religious Needs	0.877	0.874
Need for inner peace	0.824	0.822
Existentialistic needs	0.543	0.534
Actively giving	0.851	0.875
SPNQ (New Zealand)	0.920	0.916
Religious needs	0.945	0.948
Need for inner peace	0.788	0.809
Existentialistic needs	0.764	0.726
Actively giving	0.772	0.780

The coefficient of variation (CV) measures the level of random variation, with a higher level (expressed as a percentage) indicating increased random variation. Where the measurement has been taken between two time points in close proximity, the systematic change between the two time-points should be minimal, i.e., the CV% small. The accepted level is <15%. This was observed in general across the measures in both countries, indicating minimal random variation between the assessments; the measures are generally stable. The subscales with higher than expected CV were the subscale "existentialistic" in Iran and in New Zealand (Tables 3 and 4).

Table 3. Cronbach's alpha and Coefficient of variation for spiritual needs questionnaire (SpNQ) in Iran.

Subscale	Mean Time 1	α	Mean Time 2	α	Mean Diff.	SD Diff.	Coefficient of Variation %
Religious	15.67	0.877	15.70	0.874	−0.03	0.07	2.50
Inner peace	9.89	0.824	9.94	0.822	−0.05	0.06	7.97
Existentialistic	5.89	0.543	5.67	0.534	0.22	0.10	17.35
Actively giving	6.17	0.851	6.22	0.857	−0.05	−0.006	7.58

Table 4. Cronbach's alpha and Coefficient of variation for SpNQ in New Zealand.

Subscale	Mean Time 1	α	Mean Time 2	α	Mean Diff.	SD Diff.	Coefficient of Variation %
Religious	7.00	0.945	6.25	0.948	0.75	0.03	9.80
Inner peace	8.98	0.788	8.07	0.809	0.91	−0.31	9.92
Existentialistic	5.13	0.764	4.14	0.726	0.99	0.14	19.06
Actively giving	6.03	0.772	5.40	0.780	0.63	−0.15	14.17

The correlation coefficients of the scales (stability of the tests over time) were evaluated by paired sample *t*-test and Wilcoxon signed rank test (for some measures that were not-normally distributed including DUREL in Iran, and SpNQ at time 2 and DUREL at both time points in New Zealand) as appropriate. No statistically significant difference in spiritual needs of participants in New Zealand from time 1 ($M = 27.92$, $SD = 14.09$) to time 2 ($M = 23.88$, $SD = 13.96$), $t(53) = 1.72$, $p > 0.05$ (two-tailed) were noted. The mean decrease was 4.04 with a 95% confidence interval ranging from −0.65 to 8.72. Additionally, the Wilcoxon signed rank test did not reveal a statistically significant difference between the two time points $z = −1.58$, $p > 0.05$ with a small effect size ($r = 0.2$).

The relationship between spiritual needs of participants in Iran (as measured by the SpNQ) and religiosity (as measured by the DUREL scale) was evaluated using Pearson correlation and Spearman's rho (for some measures that did not have normal distribution, including DUREL) as appropriate. A weak positive correlation between two scales, $r = 0.10$, $n = 68$, $p > 0.05$ was noted. The Spearman's rho correlation also revealed a small positive correlation, $r = 0.17$, $n = 68$, $p > 0.05$.

The relationship between spiritual needs of participants in New Zealand (as measured by the SpNQ) and religiosity (as measured by the DUREL scale) was assessed using Pearson correlation and Spearman's rho (for some measures that were 'non-normal' including SpNQ time 2 and DUREL at both time points) as appropriate. A strong positive correlation (Pearson) between two scales in time 1, $r = 0.673$, $n = 61$, $p < 0.005$ and time 2, $r = 0.559$, $n = 54$, $p < 0.005$ was noted. The Spearman's rho correlation also revealed a strong positive correlation in time 1, $r = 0.658$, $n = 61$, $p < 0.005$ and time 2, $r = 0.524$, $n = 54$, $p < 0.005$.

4. Discussion

There is no universally agreed definition of spirituality, however, there is some agreement that religion and spirituality are different but connected concepts [38]. Spirituality contains two different dimensions: individuals' relationship with the transcendent (God) and the relationship with oneself, others and nature [39]. In the Islamic context, there is no distinction between spirituality and religion, and religion provides the spiritual way of life [40]. The present study assessed the psychometric properties of the Farsi and English version of the SpNQ among cancer patients in Iran and New Zealand. The study suggests initial validity and reliability of the SpNQ in both languages and countries.

The coefficient of Cronbach's alpha was above 0.79 for the total score and above 0.72 for subscales at both time points in both countries except for the existentialistic domain of SpNQ (0.53–0.54) in Iran (Table 2). The low internal consistency of the existentialistic domain resulted from participant responses clustering. For example, for most Iranian participants the future was more important than the past, and people knew the meaning of their illness and did not report any need to talk about the meaning of life. Additionally, all Iranian participants believed in life after death and did not report any need to talk about it.

The coefficient of variation (CV) was higher than expected only for subscale "existentialistic" in Iran (17.35) and in New Zealand (19.06). It is well documented that living with cancer often increases an individual's awareness of the spiritual dimension of the self and intensifies their spiritual needs [12]. Cancer creates an existential crisis, and often initiates spiritual questioning about life and death. This existential domain reflects previous life experiences and involves the need for finding answers to questions about the meaning of life, illness, and life after death [5]. Cancer patients often report their spiritual needs as finding meaning and hope [41], and drawing meaning from the suffering [42] that are related to existential domain. These needs may develop overtime as a result of increasing space of possibilities and uncertain future regarding to pending death, finality of life [43], and life after death. The differences between two time points are likely to be related to both the subjective nature of this domain and real changes in response over even a short time period during certain stages of cancer. An existential feeling is a space of possibilities and is likely to be a dynamic area, where people's thoughts, feelings and attitudes will change frequently especially around diagnosis, treatment and follow-up appointments and life events. Additionally the cancer experience is a dynamic entity. Thus, it is not surprising that the domain was found to be unstable when people are confronted with life-threatening illnesses and are undergoing major change.

The results of test retest reliability of the questionnaires (SpNQ 2.1) in both countries indicated that the questionnaires were not sensitive to change in two weeks, (except the existential subscale) and test re-test stability was partially confirmed. A weak positive correlation between SpNQ and DUREL in Iran and a strong positive correlation between SpNQ and DUREL in New Zealand were noted.

The results showed that the main subscales of SpNQ were not significantly influenced by cultural or religious differences, except for the existentialistic domain This may be particularly true for those with specific religious beliefs and attitudes [32]. The Farsi and English version of SpNQ are congruent with its original version.

The findings of this study reflect those of earlier studies with comparable internal consistency. In relation to needs, the New Zealand data reflected the findings of the German study, the Polish study and the Chinese version where needs related to Inner Peace needs were rated highly. Whilst participants in Iran rated Inner Peace as important the importance placed on Religious Needs far exceeded those of all earlier studies.

This study had some limitations. There were no analyses on how many patients did not fill out the SpNQ in both countries, so the sample should be regarded as a convenience sample. Additionally, this study is limited by the small sample size and the level of analysis that could be undertaken.

Additionally the scale was completed only by Muslims in Iran, and mostly by Christians or those with no religion in New Zealand and has not been validated with other religions.

5. Conclusions

The psychometric properties of the Farsi version of the SpNQ questionnaires in Iran, and the English version of SpNQ questionnaire in New Zealand were assessed in this study. The study showed that the SpNQ questionnaire is a promising tool to measure spiritual needs of patients with cancer and could be used in Iran, New Zealand and other Muslim countries in addition to Christian countries [5], and nonreligious societies [32].

Since the psychometric properties of the Farsi version of the SpNQ questionnaires in Iran, and the English version of SpNQ in New Zealand were assessed with small sample sizes, future studies in both countries with larger sampling, minority religion and ethnic groups are necessary to enable more thorough statistical evaluation of the translations of the SpNQ.

In the existential domain, low internal consistency appears to be related to a clustering of responses in Iran. Hence, caution should be taken in using the SpNQ to assess spiritual needs in Iran or other cultural or religious contexts, and needs further exploration.

Author Contributions: Nazi Nejat, Lisa Whitehead and Marie Crowe conceived designed the study. Nazi Nejat conducted data collection. Nazi Nejat, Lisa Whitehead and Marie Crowe analyzed the data. Nazi Nejat and Lisa Whitehead wrote the paper.

Conflicts of Interest: The authors declare no conflict of interest. The founding sponsors had no role in the design of the study; in the collection, analyses, or interpretation of data; in the writing of the manuscript, and in the decision to publish the results.

Abbreviations

The following abbreviations are used in this manuscript:

SpNQ   Spirituality Needs Questionnaire
DUREL   Duke University Religion Index

References

1. Egan, Richard, Roz McKechnie, Jan Jobson, Peter Herbison, and Rose Richards. "Exw2Perspectives on psychosocial and spiritual cancer support services in New Zealand." *Journal of Psychosocial Oncology* 31 (2013): 659–74. [CrossRef] [PubMed]
2. Koenig, Harold G. "Religion, spirituality, and medicine: Application to clinical practice." *JAMA* 284 (2000): 1708. [CrossRef] [PubMed]
3. Hermann, Carla. "A guide to the spiritual needs of elderly cancer patients." *Geriatric Nursing* 21 (2000): 324–25. [CrossRef] [PubMed]
4. Taylor, Elizabeth Johnston. "Prevalence and associated factors of spiritual needs among patients with cancer and family caregivers." *Oncology Nursing Forum* 33 (2006): 729–35. [CrossRef] [PubMed]
5. Büssing, Arndt, H. J. Balzat, and P. Heusser. "Spiritual needs of patients with chronic pain diseases and cancer-validation of the spiritual needs questionnaire." *European Journal of Medical Research* 15 (2010): 266. [CrossRef] [PubMed]
6. Thune-Boyle, Ingela C., Jan A. Stygall, Mohammed R. Keshtgar, and Stanton P. Newman. "Do religious/spiritual coping strategies affect illness adjustment in patients with cancer? A systematic review of the literature." *Social Science & Medicine* 63 (2006): 151–64. [CrossRef] [PubMed]
7. Hampton, Diane M., Dana E. Hollis, Dudley A. Lloyd, James Taylor, and Susan C. McMillan. "Spiritual needs of persons with advanced cancer." *American Journal of Hospice and Palliative Medicine* 24 (2007): 42–48. [CrossRef] [PubMed]
8. McSherry, Wilfr. *The Meaning of Spirituality and Spiritual Care within Nursing and Health Care Practice*. London: Quay Books, 2007.
9. Speck, Peter, Irene Higginson, and Julia Addington Hall. "Spiritual needs in health care." *British Medical Journal* 329 (2004): 123–24. [CrossRef] [PubMed]
10. Galek, Kathleen, Kevin J. Flannelly, Adam Vane, and Rose M. Galek. "Assessing a patient's spiritual needs: A comprehensive instrument." *Holistic Nursing Practice* 19 (2005): 62–69. [CrossRef] [PubMed]
11. Murray, Scott A., Marilyn Kendall, Kirsty Boyd, Allison Worth, and T. Fred Benton. "Exploring the spiritual needs of people dying of lung cancer or heart failure: A prospective qualitative interview study of patients and their carers." *Palliative Medicine* 18 (2004): 39–45. [CrossRef] [PubMed]
12. Taylor, Elizabeth Johnston. "Spiritual needs of patients with cancer and family caregivers." *Cancer Nursing* 26 (2003): 260–66. [CrossRef] [PubMed]
13. Pargament, Kenneth I. *The Psychology of Religion and Coping: Theory, Practice and Research*. New York: Guilford Press, 1997.
14. Wyatt, Gwen K., Laurie L. Friedman, Charles W. Given, Barbara A. Given, and Kathryn Christensen Beckrow. "Complementary therapy use among older cancer patients." *Cancer Practice* 7 (1999): 136–44. [CrossRef] [PubMed]
15. Balboni, Tracy A., Lauren C. Vanderwerker, Susan D. Block, M. Elizabeth Paulk, Christopher S. Lathan, John R. Peteet, and Holly G. Prigerson. "Religiousness and spiritual support among advanced cancer patients and associations with end-of-life treatment preferences and quality of life." *Journal of Clinical Oncology* 25 (2007): 555–60. [CrossRef] [PubMed]
16. Clark, Paul Alexander, Maxwell Drain, and Mary P. Malone. "Addressing patients' emotional and spiritual needs." *Joint Commission Journal on Quality and Patient Safety* 29 (2003): 659–70.
17. Büssing, Arndt, and Harold G. Koenig. "Spiritual needs of patients with chronic diseases." *Religions* 1 (2010): 18–27. [CrossRef]
18. Koenig, Harold G. *Spirituality and Health Research: Methods, Measurements, Statistics, and Resources*. Philadelphia: Templeton Foundation Press, 2011.

19. Büssing, Arndt, Annina Janko, Klaus Baumann, Niels Christian Hvidt, and Andreas Kopf. "Spiritual needs among patients with chronic pain diseases and cancer living in a secular society." *Pain Medicine* 14 (2013): 1362–73. [CrossRef] [PubMed]
20. Rezaei, Mahboubeh, Mohsen Adib-Hajbaghery, Naima Seyedfatemi, and Fatemeh Hoseini. "Prayer in Iranian cancer patients undergoing chemotherapy." *Complementary Therapies in Clinical Practice* 14 (2008): 90–97. [CrossRef] [PubMed]
21. Taylor, Andrew, and Margaret Box. *Multicultural Palliative Care Guidelines.* Canberra: Palliative Care Australia, 1999.
22. Fasihi-Harandy, Tayebeh, Fazlollah Ghofranipour, Ali Montazeri, Monireh Anoosheh, Mohsen Bazargan, Eesa Mohammadi, Fazlollah Ahmadi, and Shamsaddin Niknami. "Muslim breast cancer survivor spirituality: Coping strategy or health seeking behavior hindrance? " *Health Care for Women International* 31 (2009): 88–98. [CrossRef] [PubMed]
23. Cheraghi, Mohammad Ali, Sheila Payne, and Mahvash Salsali. "Spiritual aspects of end-of-life care for Muslim patients: Experiences from Iran." *International Journal of Palliative Nursing* 11 (2005): 468–74. [CrossRef] [PubMed]
24. Laubmeier, Kimberly K., Sandra G. Zakowski, and John P. Bair. "The role of spirituality in the psychological adjustment to cancer: A test of the transactional model of stress and coping." *International Journal of Behavioral Medicine* 11 (2004): 48–55. [CrossRef] [PubMed]
25. Vachon, Mary L. S. "Meaning, spirituality, and wellness in cancer survivors." *Seminars in Oncology Nursing* 24 (2008): 218–25. [CrossRef] [PubMed]
26. Egan, Richard, Rod MacLeod, Chrystal Jaye, Rob McGee, Joanne Baxter, and Peter Herbison. "What is spirituality? Evidence from a New Zealand hospice study." *Mortality: Promoting the Interdisciplinary Study of Death and Dying* 16 (2011): 307–24. [CrossRef]
27. Lambie, Deborah, Richard Egan, Shayne Walker, and Rod Macleod. "How spirituality is understood and taught in New Zealand medical schools." *Palliative and Supportive Care* 13 (2013): 53–58. [CrossRef] [PubMed]
28. Statistics New Zealand. *2013 Census QuickStats about Culture and Identity.* Wellington: Statistics New Zealand, 2014.
29. Nikora, Linda Waimarie Ngahuia Te Awekotuku, and Virginia Tamanui. "Home and the Spirit in the Māori World." Paper presented at the He Manawa Whenua:Indigenous Research Conference, University of Waikato, Hamilton, New Zealand, 30 June–3 July 2013.
30. World Health Organisation. "Process of Translation and Adaptation of Instruments." 2014. Available online: http://www.who.int/substance_abuse/research_tools/translation/en/ (accessed on 20 February 2014).
31. Büssing, Arndt, Iwona Pilchowska, and Janusz Surzykiewicz. "Spiritual needs of Polish patients with chronic diseases." *Journal of Religion and Health* 54 (2015): 1524–42. [CrossRef] [PubMed]
32. Büssing, Arndt, Xiao-feng Zhai, Wen-bo Peng, and Chang-quan Ling. "Psychosocial and spiritual needs of patients with chronic diseases: Validation of the Chinese version of the Spiritual Needs Questionnaire." *Journal of Integrative Medicine* 11 (2013): 106–15. [CrossRef] [PubMed]
33. Koenig, Harold G. *Developing the Duke Religion Index. Center for the Study of Religion, Spirituality and Health.* Durham: Duke University Medical Center, 1997–1998.
34. Koenig, Harold G., and Arndet Büssing. "The Duke University Religion Index (DUREL): A five-item measure for use in epidemological studies." *Religions* 1 (2010): 78–85. [CrossRef]
35. Saffari, Mohsen, Harold G. Koenig, Ghader Ghanizadeh, Amir H. Pakpour, and Donia R. Baldacchino. "Psychometric properties of the Persian spiritual coping strategies scale in hemodialysis patients." *Journal of Religion and Health* 53 (2014): 1025–35. [CrossRef] [PubMed]
36. Saffari, Mohsen, Isa Mohammadi Zeidi, Amir H. Pakpour, and Harold G. Koenig. "Psychometric properties of the Persian version of the Duke University Religion Index (DUREL): A study on Muslims." *Journal of Religion and Health* 52 (2013): 631–41. [CrossRef] [PubMed]
37. Polit, Denise F., and Cheryl Tatano Beck. *Essentials of Nursing Research: Appraising Evidence for Nursing Practice*, 8th ed. Philadelphia: Wolters Kluwer/Lippincott/Williams & Wilkins Health, 2014.
38. Weaver, Andrew J., Kenneth I. Pargament, Kevin J. Flannelly, and Julia E. Oppenheimer. "Trends in the scientific study of religion, spirituality, and health: 1965–2000." *Journal of Religion and Health* 45 (2006): 208–14. [CrossRef]

39. Markani Khorami, Abdolah, Mohammad Khodayari Fard, and Farideh Yaghmaei. "Spirituality as experienced by Muslim oncology nurses in Iran." *British Journal of Nursing* 21 (2012): S20–25. [CrossRef]
40. Karimollahi, Mansooreh, Heidar Ali Abedi, and Alireza Yousefi. "Spiritual needs as experienced by Muslim patients in Iran: A qualitative study." *Research Journal of Medical Sciences* 1 (2007): 183–90. [CrossRef]
41. Moadel, Alyson, Carole Morgan, Anne Fatone, Jennifer Grennan, Jeanne Carter, Gia Laruffa, Anne Skummy, and Janice Dutcher. "Seeking meaning and hope: Self-reported spiritual and existential needs among an ethnically-diverse cancer patient population." *Psycho-Oncology* 8 (1999): 378–85. [CrossRef]
42. Käppeli, Silvia. "Between suffering and redemption." *Scandinavian Journal of Caring Sciences* 14 (2000): 82–88. [CrossRef] [PubMed]
43. Karlsson, Magdalena, Febe Friberg, Catarina Wallengren, and Joakim Öhlén. "Meanings of existential uncertainty and certainty for people diagnosed with cancer and receiving palliative treatment: A life-world phenomenological study." *BMC Palliative Care* 13 (2014): 28. [CrossRef] [PubMed]

Article

Bifactor Models of Religious and Spiritual Struggles: Distinct from Religiousness and Distress

Nick Stauner [1,*], Julie J. Exline [1], Joshua B. Grubbs [1], Kenneth I. Pargament [2], David F. Bradley [1] and Alex Uzdavines [1]

[1] Department of Psychological Sciences, Case Western Reserve University, Cleveland, OH 44106, USA; julie.exline@case.edu (J.J.E.); jbg49@case.edu (J.B.G.); dfb43@case.edu (D.F.B.); alex.uzdavines@case.edu (A.U.)

[2] Department of Psycholog, Bowling Green State University, Bowling Green, OH 43403, USA; kpargam@bgsu.edu

* Correspondence: ngs21@case.edu; Tel.: +1-216-368-2686

Academic Editor: Arndt Büssing
Received: 5 March 2016; Accepted: 30 May 2016; Published: 7 June 2016

Abstract: The Religious and Spiritual Struggles Scale (RSS) measures important psychological constructs in an underemphasized section of the overlap between religion and well-being. Are religious/spiritual struggles distinct from religiousness, distress, and each other? To test the RSS' internal discriminant validity, we replicated the original six-factor measurement model across five large samples (N = 5705) and tested the fit of a restricted bifactor model, which supported the mutual viability of multidimensional and unidimensional scoring systems for the RSS. Additionally, we explored a bifactor model with correlated group factors that exhibited optimal fit statistics. This model maintained the correlations among the original factors while extracting a general factor from the RSS. This general factor's strong correlations with religious participation and belief salience suggested that this factor resembles religiousness itself. Estimating this general factor seemed to improve Demonic and Moral struggles' independence from religiousness, but did not change any factor's correlations with neuroticism, depression, anxiety, and stress. These distress factors correlated with most of the independent group factors corresponding to the original dimensions of the RSS, especially Ultimate Meaning and Divine struggles. These analyses demonstrate the discriminant validity of religious/spiritual struggles and the complexity of their relationships with religiousness and distress.

Keywords: religion; spirituality; struggle; bifactor; measurement; latent; confirmatory factor analysis; distress; depression; anxiety

1. Introduction

Religious and spiritual (R/S) aspects of life present a variety of challenges. Over the course of the lifespan many people experience *R/S struggle*, defined as tension and conflict about sacred matters within oneself, with others, and with the supernatural [1,2]. R/S struggles occur commonly, though not often severely [3,4]. A growing subdomain of psychological research on R/S examines the causes, consequences, and subjective experience of R/S struggle (for reviews, see [1,2,5–8]). Over 80 new publications related to R/S struggle have appeared since the turn of the millennium [8]. Exline [1] reviewed the broad relationships between R/S struggle and health outcomes of both psychological and physical natures.

Although many people experience religion and spirituality as a source of comfort (e.g., [9]), meaning [10], or help in coping [11], this dominant trend may overshadow the difficulties people experience in their R/S relationships, behaviors, and identity development. R/S struggle foreshadows losses in both mental and physical health [12,13], and relates positively to depression [14], suicidality [15], and even higher mortality rates [13]. These findings have appeared robustly across religious traditions and socio-demographic groups thus far [4,16]. R/S struggle might ultimately hold the potential for personal growth and transformation, although only a few empirical studies have shown support for this position as of yet [17]. Better insight on R/S struggle might clarify the roles it plays in suffering and growth and inspire new means of therapeutic intervention or new public health initiatives. Further evidence of R/S struggle's relevance to well-being may help emphasize the need to address R/S struggles directly in counseling contexts rather than only treating its symptoms or circumstances [18].

To advance understanding of R/S struggle through quantitative empirical research, Exline, Pargament, Grubbs, and Yali [19] developed the Religious and Spiritual Struggles (RSS) Scale. The RSS measures a range of normative R/S struggles. This multidimensional measure demonstrated good psychometric qualities, including predictive validity and an efficient measurement model. This original model comprises six correlated dimensions:

(1)   Divine: conflict or insecurity in one's relationship with God
(2)   Demonic: persecution or temptation by the devil or evil spirits
(3)   Interpersonal: conflicts with people or groups related to religion/spirituality
(4)   Moral: concerns with the morality of one's actions and desires
(5)   Ultimate Meaning: doubting the importance, purpose, or meaning of one's life as a whole
(6)   Doubt: discomfort with religious or spiritual doubts and questions

Exline and colleagues also estimated a total RSS score from the mean of all subscales' 26 items.

All RSS factors correlate positively with depressive symptoms, anxiety, state anger, and loneliness [19]. Most RSS factors relate positively and moderately to other measures of R/S struggle constructs, such as anger at God and religious fear, guilt, and doubt. The Divine, Demonic, and Moral subscales appear to converge with attributions of R/S struggles to God, the devil or evil spirits, or oneself, respectively. RSS factors also relate negatively with life satisfaction and meaning in life, admitting some exceptions due in part to domain specificity. For example, meaning in life relates most strongly to meaning struggle, but does not relate to moral struggle. Conversely, moral struggle relates to attributions of personal responsibility for specific R/S struggles, but meaning struggle does not. In original analyses, religiousness also related more to Demonic and Moral struggles than to Ultimate Meaning struggle or to total RSS scores; religiousness did not relate to other RSS factors.

These nuances motivate further study of distinctions among the six subdomains of the RSS, especially with respect to distress and religiousness. Does the RSS merely measure religious expressions of ordinary distress, or expressions of religiousness from particularly distressed people? Neither seems likely given the modest strength of correlations among these constructs as measured independently [19–21], as well as evidence of moderators of these relationships [22]. Nonetheless, these theoretical simplifications warrant further disproof if one must reject them and conceptualize R/S struggles as independent constructs.

1.1. Measurement Methodology

Exline and colleagues [19] found good fit statistics for the first-order measurement model of the RSS' six correlated latent factors in confirmatory factor analysis (CFA). Nonetheless, these analyses left some room for doubts. Primarily, the latent factor model did not test the viability of a second-order factor corresponding to the total RSS score. Strong correlations among the first-order factors ($rs = 0.31$–0.66, median $= 0.51$) build evidence for a second-order factor that could represent R/S struggle in general, but a CFA of this model can more precisely quantify support for any single factor that affects all six dimensions of the RSS, which could also include religiousness or distress. Secondarily, model estimation and evaluation methods did not accommodate the ordinal measurement of skewed latent distributions inherent in the design of the RSS and the nature of R/S struggles, which are rarely severe, especially in non-clinical populations [20,21].

Finally, original replications did not test the invariance of the measurement model to ensure that the RSS assessed the same set of constructs in each population without interference from group-specific response biases. The original analyses pooled data from three university samples into one combined sample. These samples shared many demographic features: majorities of each sample were women and ethnically white, and ages varied very little. However, religious affiliations and regions varied somewhat more. One sample came from a university located on the Pacific coast with an institution-level affiliation to Christianity, whereas the others came from religiously unaffiliated universities in the Midwest. Any heterogeneity in latent structures for the RSS and other factors across these samples may have undermined the original analyses' accuracy. We intend to address each of these limitations throughout this study.

1.1.1. Model Configuration

Second-order factor models can test the validity of a general latent factor that explains why a set of first-order factors correlate. This is a popular method for validating total scores for questionnaires with several subscales, such as the RSS. However, Reise, Moore, and Haviland [23] recommend confirmatory bifactor analysis to compare unidimensional and multidimensional scale scoring alternatives. In a restricted bifactor model, the general factor represents a hypothetical cause of any covariance common to all indicators (in our case, 26 RSS items), which also load on separate, orthogonal group factors. A second-order factor model nests within this less constrained bifactor model and often produces poorer model fit statistics, because it requires that indicators relate to the second-order factor in fractional proportion to their first-order factors' loadings on the second-order factor (the *proportionality constraint*).

For example, "Felt troubled about doubts or questions about religion or spirituality" could only relate to a second-order factor of general R/S struggle as strongly as it relates to other Doubt struggle items in general (*i.e.*, its *factor loading*), and only as strongly as Doubt struggle relates to second-order R/S struggle (the second-order factor loading). Realistically, neither of these correlations would equal 1.0, so the product of these loadings (the correlation between the item and the second-order factor) would necessarily be the smallest of these three numbers, potentially by an inaccurately large margin. For instance, if this item loaded strongly on its first-order factor (e.g., $\lambda_{Doubt} = 0.80$), and latent Doubt struggle loaded moderately on the second-order factor (e.g., $\lambda_{general} = 0.50$), this model would limit the item's correlation with the second-order factor to moderate strength at most (implied $\lambda_{general} = 0.40$). Though the proportionality constraint prohibits indicators from relating more strongly to the second-order factor than to their first-order factors, a bifactor model allows either correlation (loading) to exceed the other.

If a single latent general factor truly affects responses to all RSS items, it may disproportionately affect some items belonging to a single group factor (e.g., the aforementioned Doubt struggle item). The proportionality constraint arises from an implication of second-order models: first-order factors completely mediate all effects of the second-order factor on the items. A second-order model could allow limited exceptions to the proportionality constraint and incorporate some direct effects by estimating direct loadings on the general factor for some items, but each additional loading would increase the model's likelihood of empirical underidentification and the estimator's chances of failing to converge or produce valid parameter estimates. Only bifactor models facilitate estimation of direct, unmediated effects from a general factor on all items at once.

Bifactor models achieve this advantage through an alternate assumption: instead of assuming that first-order group factors fully mediate the effects of a general factor, a bifactor model assumes that the general factor does not relate to the group factors at all. This too may limit the model's accuracy, but probably to a lesser degree in the case of the RSS. We do not posit some distal, latent influence on all R/S struggles that only affects item responses indirectly through its effects on latent R/S struggles.

Instead, we would expect some mixture of domain-specific influences on struggles of particular kinds (e.g., skepticism could produce doubt) and broader, general, unrelated influences on all struggles, such as distress or religiousness, or perhaps something more unique to R/S struggle.

The proportionality constraint may also distort loadings at either level if indicators that share a first-order factor vary in relatedness to other indicators that share the second-order factor. For example, if one indicator (e.g., cloud cover) represents a unique part of a first-order factor (climate) that varies independently of the second-order factor (latitude), that indicator should load strongly on the first-order factor, but not relate to the second-order factor, unlike other indicators (sunlight intensity). Nonetheless, a second-order factor model implies that the indicator's correlation with the second-order factor equals the product of the indicator's loading and the first-order factor's loading on the second-order factor. Such conflicts between empirical reality and second-order models of covariance structure contribute to overall misfit for second-order models, but need not invalidate bifactor models. We do not suspect the RSS of containing any items that relate only to a first-order group factor and not to any general factor, but we cannot rule this out without estimating general factor loadings, nor do we see benefits to imposing the proportionality constraint on a bifactor model of the RSS. For these reasons, we favored bifactor models in our analyses.

A bifactor model's two sets of loadings also provide a quantitative basis for judging whether a single general factor or multiple group factors explain greater overall amounts of indicators' covariance. If a general factor explains most of the covariance in a set of measures (as distress or religiousness could in the RSS), this result favors a unidimensional model over a multidimensional model, and *vice versa*. If indicators load with similar and adequate strength on both general and group factors, this supports the viability of both measurement models.

Our application benefits from this additional advantage of bifactor models over second-order models. After establishing the validity of a general factor of R/S struggle, the six original dimensions of the RSS will need to demonstrate their uniqueness from this primary common factor to retain discriminant validity. In other words, if R/S struggles cohere well enough across the original six dimensions to be described by one scale score representing general R/S struggle, do we still need to think of more specific dimensions (e.g., Doubt struggle) as meaningfully unique from this broader dimension of R/S struggle in general? If the group factors retain some uniqueness, could religiousness or distress then render any of these dimensions redundant, if not the entire RSS?

1.1.2. Model Estimation

The original CFA of the RSS [19] used maximum likelihood estimation on Likert-type rankings treated as interval data for the purpose of these and other correlation analyses. Instead, Reise and colleagues [23] recommend *polychoric correlations* for CFA of Likert scale data (see also [24]). The two-stage polychoric correlation procedure first estimates values of latent, continuous, normally distributed dimensions to stand in for observed responses on ordinal (including Likert-type) scales, then calculates bivariate correlations between these estimated values. Because polychoric correlations use standard normal latent distributions, they equal the latent covariances.

Most people report low levels of R/S struggles (as measured with other questionnaires) [20,21], indicating *positively skewed* distributions (with more frequent responses toward the low ends of their scales). Thus we expected to violate the assumption of normal latent distributions when using polychoric correlations. Latent variables with nonnormal distributions bias polychoric correlations upward very slightly (bias < 2%) [25,26]. However, measuring continuous latent variables with a small number of ordered options (as many Likert-type scales do, including the RSS) introduces much greater downward bias in product-moment correlations estimated between the latent variables, even if they follow normal distributions [27–29]. Thus as an alternative to CFA estimation using covariance matrices, polychoric correlation matrices usually introduce less bias than they correct, which helps survey data meet assumptions of the popular maximum likelihood (ML) estimator.

Nonetheless, several authors [24,26,30–35] argue against ML estimation of common factor models based on polychoric correlations. ML estimation using polychoric correlations generates conservatively biased fit statistics and standard errors [36], and may result in more convergence errors and improper solutions [37]. Unweighted least squares estimation [38] with mean and variance adjustments (ULSMV) [39] seems marginally preferable to ML for polychoric covariances of ordinal data [40,41].[1] If ULSMV estimation fails to converge, diagonally weighted least squares estimation (WLSMV) may produce a comparably robust alternative solution with only marginally more susceptibility to bias [42].

The original CFA of the RSS reported no convergence issues with ML estimation, but did not use all available data simultaneously [19], which may have circumvented any such problems that might have arisen in a more complex model. The measurement model's fit statistics also suggested room for marginal improvements. Could this have resulted from the downward bias of ML estimation, a lack of polychoric correlations, or an ignored general factor? This study examined these possibilities.

1.1.3. Measurement Invariance

When comparing correlations across samples, using multi-group structural equation modeling (SEM) with invariant measurement models can help ensure that differences in correlations across samples do not result from biased measurement. Establishing that items load on the same factors (*configural invariance*) with the same strengths (*metric invariance*) across samples enables direct comparison of latent correlations by eliminating the possibility that certain items only relate to latent factors of interest in some samples, not all. For instance, if the Interpersonal struggle item, "Felt angry at organized religion", related much more strongly to latent Interpersonal struggle in populations with specific R/S affiliations than in unaffiliated populations, this would cause latent correlations to reflect the influence of this particular item more strongly in the affiliated populations. Constraining loading estimates to equality across samples prevents the meanings of correlations from varying across samples, but worsens SEM fit statistics if the loadings vary greatly across samples [43].

Since sampling error causes loading estimates to vary across samples from even a single population, measurement invariance tests retain the null hypothesis of identical measurement across groups unless separate estimation of parameters in each group improves SEM fit statistics significantly. Cheung and Rensvold [44] recommend using a minimal improvement threshold with the comparative fit index, ΔCFI > 0.01, as an indication of significant variance in parameters being tested. This method can also test the invariance of items' thresholds used in polychoric correlations (*strong invariance*), which enables unbiased comparisons of latent means to determine which populations tend to score lower or higher than others. Testing the invariance of items' residual variances or uniquenesses (*strict invariance*) matters as well when using *classical test theory* assumptions to score a questionnaire by averaging or summing numerical responses, because this scoring method includes all common and unique item variance in its scale scores. Since Exline and colleagues [19] used this classical test theory scoring method, the exactness of their comparisons across samples depends on classical test theory's assumptions of strict measurement invariance. Measurement invariance tests would help to address any concern that strict invariance does not hold; if it does, this will facilitate general comparisons of RSS data across diverse populations.

1.2. The Present Study

These improvements on conventional methods raise interesting questions within the basic CFA replication paradigm. The original CFA of the RSS measurement model [19] used ML estimation; will the model still fit well using ULSMV estimation from polychoric correlations in a larger sample? Will a bifactor structure improve the model's fit? Will the items' dual loadings favor a unidimensional or

---

[1]   If available, the polychoric instrumental variable estimator would offer further improvements on ULSMV estimation.

multidimensional model? Will bifactor models replicate across samples as accurately as the simpler, original measurement model?

The RSS provides an especially intriguing opportunity to investigate the psychological implications of a bifactor measurement model. As a newly explored set of psychological constructs, the RSS has yet to resolve its placement in the overlapping domains of distress and religiousness/spirituality. Thus far, the Demonic, Moral, and Ultimate Meaning subscales have exhibited stronger relationships with religiousness than the Divine, Interpersonal, and Doubt subscales, whereas relationships with depressive symptoms, anxiety, anger, and loneliness appear relatively consistent across all subscales [19]. The unidimensional or second-order models of the RSS produce a total score that correlates more strongly to these measures of mental health than to religiousness, unlike the Demonic and Moral subscales. All these correlations are positive, yet Ultimate Meaning struggle correlates negatively with religiousness.

How will forcing orthogonality among the group factors of the RSS in a bifactor model affect their correlations with measures of distress and religiousness? Will these measures relate more strongly to the general factor of the RSS than to its group factors? If so, this would imply that religiousness or distress relate to R/S struggle in general, not just some of its specific domains. If estimating a general factor reduces the group factors' correlations with religiousness or distress by partialing out their common covariance, this would improve the group factors' independence from these potential confounds.

Happily, these questions have arisen after we completed collection of data on all measures of interest in five large studies of subtly different populations, providing a wealth of information and no shortage of statistical power for these analyses. Hence, we adopt a coordinated or integrative data analytic strategy based on exploration and replication [45–47]. We only employ null hypothesis significance tests to arbitrate analytic decisions, rather than using them as the basis of psychological inferences, and we emphasize effect sizes throughout, following the lead of modern methodologists (e.g., [48]).

2. Method

2.1. Participants and Procedure

Survey protocols varied across samples and collection times (all during 2012–2015; Exline *et al.* [19] used data from Fall 2012 and Spring 2013 as their Study 2). We recruited participants in three of our five samples from undergraduate introductory psychology courses held at three universities in the USA. Undergraduates received partial course credit for participating online in a larger survey. Two of these universities are in the Great Lakes region of the Midwest; one is large and public ($N = 1946$ with some RSS data), the other midsized and private ($N = 1019$). The third is a private Christian university near the Pacific coast ($N = 1102$). The west coastal Christian undergraduates tended to participate earlier in their educations than the others, and the Midwestern private undergraduates tended to participate later (Table 1).

Table 1. Educational statuses across samples.

Sample	Freshmen	Sophomores	Juniors	Seniors	Others
WCC	76%	16%	4%	2%	2%
MWU	61%	23%	9%	4%	2%
MWR	53%	27%	11%	8%	1%
	High School or Less	**Partial College**	**Two-Year, Trade, or Technical**	**Bachelor's**	**Master's**
GMT	11%	31%	8%	36%	12%
NMT	14%	34%	11%	31%	10%

Note: WCC = west coastal Christian university; MWU = Midwestern public university; MWR = Midwestern private university; GMT = general MTurk; NMT = nontheistic MTurk.

2.1.1. Amazon Mechanical Turk Samples

We recruited adult internet workers from the USA through Amazon Mechanical Turk (MTurk) for our two other studies' samples. MTurk is a web platform and online marketplace that allows individuals to offer monetary compensation, processed via Amazon, to adult workers in exchange for completing tasks of various length, including surveys. Its worker population provides survey data of comparable or superior validity to undergraduate samples, and tends to represent a more diverse range of ages, locations, and of course, occupations and educational backgrounds [49–57]. MTurk workers over-represent nonreligious subpopulations [58], which, consistent with the goals of this project, allows for increased power to detect differences related to nonreligious participants in samples. MTurk has proven useful in a number of prior studies of religion-based constructs [19].

Participants for one MTurk survey responded to an advertisement on the MTurk database for a survey entitled "Two-Part Study of Personality, Beliefs, and Behavior" that offered $3.00 USD in MTurk credit for completing the survey. To ensure that participants provided adequate attention to the survey task, rather than answering at random or without regard to instructions and item content, we included several attention check items (e.g., in a longer measure, including an item that instructs participants to "Please select 'disagree'" for that item). Participants who fail attention checks might not be providing meaningful, reliable data in response to other items. Thus, among 1397 consenting participants, we excluded 12% (*n* = 172) who failed an attention check, and an additional 25 who failed another attention check (3% of those who received it). Of the 1200 participants who satisfied our screening criteria, 1158 (97%) continued this survey past the RSS.

Participants in the other MTurk survey responded to an offer to earn $2.00 upon completion. As in the general MTurk sample, we used attention check items to ensure that participants provided adequate attention, and we excluded participants who failed attention checks. Among 2062 consenting adult participants, we excluded 6% (*n* = 124) who failed an attention check.

We then assessed belief in the existence of a god or gods using a forced-choice item modified from the General Social Survey. This second MTurk survey only invited complete responses from participants who expressed doubt or disbelief that any gods exist. Henceforth we refer to this as the nontheistic MTurk sample, and to the other as the general MTurk sample. To avoid self-selection bias, we titled this survey "Emotions, Beliefs, and Attitudes", emphasizing its content rather than its intent as a study of nonbelief. The consent form specified that the survey would include questions related to religious/nonreligious matters, among other topics.

We excluded 60% (1139 of 1904 continuing participants) who expressed at least some belief in a god or gods (*i.e.*, selected "I find myself believing in a god or gods at some of the time, but not at others," "While I have doubts, I feel that I do believe in a god or gods," or "I know that a god or gods really exist, and I have no doubts about it"). Among the remaining 765 participants, 19% endorsed, "I know that no god or gods exist, and I have no doubts about it," 33% endorsed, "While it is possible that a god or gods exist, I do not believe in the existence of a god or gods," 32% endorsed, "I don't know whether there is a god or gods, and I don't believe there is any way to find out," and 17% endorsed, "I don't know whether there is a god or gods, but it may be possible to find out." Last, we excluded 25 more participants who failed another attention check (5% of those who received it). Of the 740 nontheistic participants who passed these attention checks, 638 (86%) continued the survey past the RSS. In both MTurk samples, as in the university samples, we only report other statistics regarding participants who provided at least some RSS data.

2.1.2. Demographics

Respondents in the MTurk samples tended to participate later in life and across a more even distribution of ages than the university samples' undergraduates (Table 2). Majorities of all samples' participants identified as women by birth, ethnically white, heterosexual, born in the USA, and raised to speak English (Tables 2–4). Majorities of the university samples reported no romantic relationship at the time of participation. The MTurk samples reported more evenly distributed relational statuses.

Table 2. Ages, genders, ethnicities, birthplaces, and first languages across samples.

Sample	Age		Gender		Ethnicity					Born in the USA	English as First Language
	Median	MAD	Women	Men	White	Asian	Black	Latin	Other or Multiple		
WCC	18	1	63%	37%	67%	10%	8%	4%	10%	89%	86%
MWU	19	1	66%	34%	63%	15%	6%	6%	10%	97%	98%
MWR	19	1	54%	46%	65%	15%	8%	2%	9%	80%	81%
GMT	31	6	60%	39%	74%	5%	8%	5%	8%	96%	97%
NMT	29	6	51%	46%	77%	3%	3%	5%	12%	93%	96%

Note: WCC = west coastal Christian university; MWU = Midwestern public university; MWR = Midwestern private university; GMT = general MTurk; NMT = nontheistic MTurk; MAD = median absolute deviation. In the MTurk samples, 1% (GMT) and 3% (NMT) designated genders other than man or woman from birth (e.g., transgender and withheld options).

Table 3. Sexual orientations and relationship statuses across samples.

Sample	Sexual Orientation				Relationship Status					
	Hetero-Sexual	Bisexual	Homosexual	Other or Withheld	Single	In a Relationship	Cohabiting	Married	Divorced	Other or Withheld
WCC	97%	1%	—	2%	74%	24%	—	1%	—	1%
MWU	92%	3%	3%	2%	54%	43%	2%	—	—	1%
MWR	93%	3%	2%	2%	64%	33%	1%	—	—	1%
GMT	87%	7%	3%	3%	29%	19%	15%	36%	6%	2%
NMT	79%	10%	7%	6%	36%	20%	15%	23%	3%	2%

Table 4. Religious affiliations across samples.

Sample	Christian: Unspecified/Other	Protestant	Catholic	Jewish	Buddhist	Hindu	Muslim	Other	Mixed	Agnostic	None	Atheist
WCC	66%	30%	2%	0%	0%	0%	—	0%	—	—	1%	0%
MWU	24%	19%	30%	1%	0%	0%	0%	0%	1%	7%	9%	4%
MWR	13%	12%	18%	4%	2%	4%	2%	2%	1%	13%	14%	8%
GMT	15%	19%	11%	2%	2%	1%	1%	6%	3%	17%	10%	13%
NMT	2%	3%	5%	1%	3%	1%	—	1%	1%	24%	19%	22%

Note: WCC = west coastal Christian university; MWU = Midwestern public university; MWR = Midwestern private university; GMT = general MTurk; NMT = nontheistic MTurk; MAD = median absolute deviation. In the MTurk samples, 1% (GMT) and 3% (NMT) designated genders other than man or woman from birth (e.g., transgender and withheld options).

Religion distributions varied across samples. Large majorities affiliated with Christianity in the west coastal Christian and Midwestern public university samples (Table 4). The Midwestern private university and general MTurk samples represented Christian and unaffiliated students more evenly. In the nontheistic MTurk sample, 21% listed a religious affiliation, nonbelief in divine entities notwithstanding. Each non-Christian affiliation comprised less than 5% of each sample.

2.2. Measures

2.2.1. Religious and Spiritual Struggles (RSS) Scale [13]

The RSS measured the extent to which participants had experienced six dimensions of R/S struggle over their previous few months with 26 statements (four per dimension except Divine and Doubt, which have five items each) rated on a five-point Likert-type scale with the following options: *not at all/does not apply, a little bit, somewhat, quite a bit,* and *a great deal.*[2] *Divine struggle* subsumes relational problems with God (e.g., "felt angry at God"), including perceptions and fears of abandonment and punishment. *Demonic struggle* subsumes supernatural evil interference (e.g., "felt attacked by the devil or evil spirits") including temptation. *Interpersonal struggle* subsumes conflict with religious people and groups (e.g., "felt angry at organized religion"), including victimization and ostracism. *Moral struggle* subsumes personal ethical difficulties (e.g., "felt torn between what I wanted and what I knew was morally right") and guilt. *Ultimate meaning struggle* subsumes doubts about personal and existential significance (e.g., "felt as though my life had no deeper meaning"). *Doubt struggle* subsumes distressing uncertainty about R/S beliefs (e.g., "felt confused about my religious/spiritual beliefs").

2.2.2. Religiousness

Previous studies (e.g., [3,59,60]) have used the following measures of religiousness in research on attitudes toward God. They have demonstrated good internal reliability and convergent validity with other religious constructs.

Religious Belief Salience (RBS) [61]

Four statements (e.g., "My religious/spiritual beliefs lie behind my whole approach to life") rated for agreement on a 12-point Likert-type scale measured the personal significance of participants' religious beliefs. Verbal anchors only appeared above the options we ranked lowest (*does not apply; I have no religious/spiritual beliefs*), second lowest (*strongly disagree*), and highest (*strongly agree*) for ordinal quantitative analyses.

Religious Participation (RP) [9]

Participants rated their frequencies of eight behaviors (e.g., "prayed or meditated", "thought about religious/spiritual issues") in the previous week on a six-point Likert-type scale with the following options: *not at all, once, a few times, on most days, daily,* and *more than once per day.* We excluded the last two items pertaining to hearing from God from all analyses because only relatively recent participants received them.

---

[2] Throughout we list the lowest-ranked response options first and the highest-ranked options last. Most of our analyses did not treat these data as numeric. When using maximum likelihood estimation, we assigned the lowest-ranked option a value of one and increased this by one unit for each rank (e.g., a five represented the highest-ranked option on a five-point scale).

2.2.3. Distress

Center for Epidemiologic Studies—Depression scale (CES-D) [62]

Participants rated their frequencies of eight depressive symptoms during the past week (e.g., "felt depressed", "felt lonely") on a four-point Likert-type scale with the following options: *rarely or none of the time (less than 1 day); some or a little of the time (1–2 days); occasionally or a moderate amount of time (3–4 days);* and *most or all of the time (5–7 days).* Two additional items rated on the same scale represented an absence of or reprieve from depression ("felt hopeful about the future" and "were happy"). This measure has been validated for many populations (e.g., [63,64]).

Generalized Anxiety Disorder Seven-Item Scale (GAD-7) [65]

Participants rated their frequencies of seven anxiety-related problems during the past two weeks (e.g., "trouble relaxing", "becoming easily annoyed or irritable") on a four-point Likert-type scale with the following options: *not at all, several days, more than half the days,* and *nearly every day.* A large German study validated this measure for the general population [66].

Perceived Stress Scale [67]

Participants rated their frequencies of seven stressful experiences during the past month (e.g., "felt nervous and 'stressed'", "been upset because of something that happened unexpectedly") on a five-point Likert-type scale with the following options: *never, almost never, sometimes, fairly often,* and *very often.* Three additional items rated on the same scale represented a sense of control and ease ("felt that things were going your way", "felt that you were on top of things", and "been able to control the irritations in your life"), the theoretically opposite pole of the latent stress dimension. Recent research has validated this measure for undergraduates [68].

Big Five Inventory—Neuroticism Subscale [69]

Participants rated 44 statements about themselves for agreement on a five-point Likert scale ranging from *strongly disagree* to *strongly agree.* These statements measure the five most essential traits in personality theory [70]. We focused on *neuroticism,* the characteristic tendency to experience frequent or intense negative emotions, impulses, and thoughts. This construct shares heritable influences with anxiety [71]. Only eight items pertained to neuroticism (e.g., "I am depressed, blue"), three of which indicate low neuroticism or high emotional stability (e.g., "I am relaxed and handle stress well"), the theoretically opposite pole of the latent neuroticism dimension. This measure converges well with other neuroticism measures [72]. We only used data from the other 36 items to identify participants with excessively invariant response patterns.

3. Results

We conducted all analyses in R [73]. We report only standardized loadings and correlations instead of raw covariances.

3.1. Exclusion Criteria

Before conducting primary analyses, we excluded participants with insufficiently effortful responding (IER) patterns based on the number of identical responses each participant gave across all items of the RSS. We ignored the lowest response option, *not at all/does not apply,* since many people might legitimately experience no R/S struggles whatsoever. We found an absolute minimum of participants across all samples ($n = 8$ of $N = 5863$) chose the same option (excluding the lowest) 23 out of 26 possible times. We assumed this represented the most extreme degree of invariant responding that might occur legitimately. This threshold also resembles the highest empirically derived cutoff that identified IER with 99% specificity for a 300-item questionnaire (25) [74]. Thus we excluded

106 participants (1.8%) who gave the same response between 2 and 5 to at least 24 RSS for clear IER, but retained 842 participants (14.4%) who chose the lowest response option, *not at all/does not apply*, for at least 24 questions. Preferring to retain invalid responses rather than exclude valid responses, we implemented this screening technique (*long string*) [75] more permissively than Johnson [76], who used it to exclude 3.5% of another Web-based survey's participants. Four of our samples would have set a lower threshold by our criterion: absolute minima within samples occurred first at 17 (*n* = 0), 17 (1), 19 (0), 21 (3), and 24 (0) identical responses.

We also excluded participants who failed an attention check embedded in the RSS. The participants of both MTurk studies and the 900 most recent participants from the university samples received an item with the RSS that instructed them to choose a specific response option. Of the 2697 participants without missing responses to this item, we excluded 68 (2.5%) who failed to comply. Of these 68, 15 also met the long string criterion for exclusion. Those failing the attention check also tended to give a higher number of identical responses to the RSS (median = 13) than those who passed (median = 5; Hedges' *g* = 1.8; Kendall's τ scaled to *r* = 0.20 [77]).

We used the *forestplot* package [78] to visualize comparisons of effect size estimates and confidence intervals across all samples and the total sample. In the overall sample with 95% confidence based on a negative binomial regression model [79], we would expect the mean number of identical responses to be between 2.0 and 2.8 times larger among people who fail this attention check (Figure 1a). Conversely, the odds of a participant failing the attention check increase by 19%–28% for every unit increase in the number of identical responses based on a logistic regression model with 95% confidence (Figure 1b) [80]. These relationships support the convergent validity of these criteria for identifying IER.

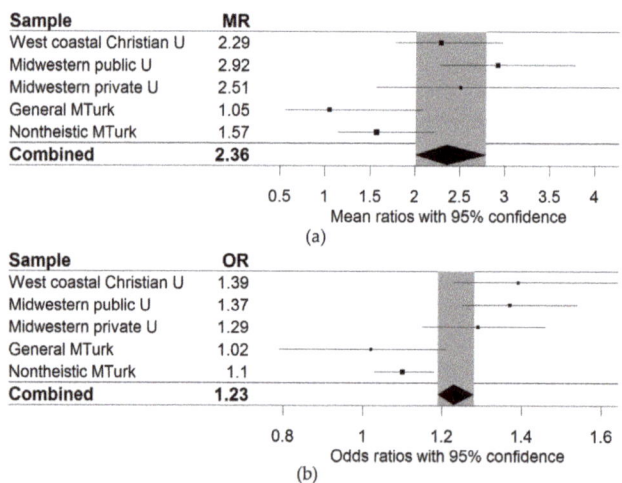

Figure 1. (a) Forest plot of ratios of mean equal responses if attention check is failed *vs.* passed; (b) Forest plot of odds ratios for attention check failure per equal response. Combined *N* = 2697; MR = mean ratio; OR = odds ratio; U = university.

However, the general MTurk sample had fewer, rarer failures (*n* = 5 of 1158 or 0.4%) than the nontheistic MTurk sample and the private Midwestern university (*ns* = 21 of 638 or 3.4%, and 8 of 288 or 2.9%, respectively; Fisher's exact test of independence *p* < 0.001). The latter pair of samples also had rarer failures than the west coastal Christian and public Midwestern universities (*ns* = 11 of 211 or 5.5%, and 23 of 401 or 6.1%, respectively; Fisher's exact test of independence *p* = 0.128; for all five samples, Fisher's exact test of independence *p* < 0.001). The relationship between attention check failure and number of identical responses also strengthened in the university samples (see Figure 1a,b; for interaction of attention and sample in negative binomial model, likelihood ratio $\chi^2_{(4)} = 13.7, p = 0.008$). This suggests greater awareness of attention checking items among MTurk workers, and demonstrates the value of using both independent screening criteria to exclude a greater portion of invalid data.

The exclusion criteria jointly reduced the total sample size to $N = 5705$ (97.3%). They reduced the west coastal Christian university's sample to $n = 1069$ (97.0%), the Midwestern public university's sample to 1870 (96.1%), the Midwestern private university's sample to 1006 (98.7%), the general MTurk sample to 1149 (99.2%), and the nontheistic MTurk sample to 611 (95.8%).

3.2. Exploratory Factor Analyses of the RSS

We began our reanalysis of the latent structure of the RSS by performing exploratory factor analyses of the items. These analyses provided a purely empirical basis for judging whether the items' covariance structure would naturally support the original six-factor measurement model, and if this would change when extracting a general factor. Using the *psych* package [81], we estimated polychoric correlations for all pairs of RSS items separately in each of our five samples. We then performed exploratory factor analysis of each sample's polychoric correlation matrix using minres (ordinary, unweighted least squares) estimation to extract six factors, which we rotated using the oblimin oblique criterion. These analyses produced good fit statistics for the west coastal Christian and Midwestern public university samples (Tucker–Lewis Indices (TLIs) = 0.96 and 0.97, root mean square errors of approximation (RMSEAs) = 0.05, *df*-corrected root mean square residuals (RMSRs) = 0.01–0.02), acceptable fit for the Midwestern private university and unscreened MTurk samples (TLIs = 0.92 and 0.94, RMSEAs = 0.08 and 0.07, RMSRs = 0.02), and very poor fit for the nontheistic MTurk sample (TLI = 0.20, RMSEA = 0.36, RMSRs = 0.04).

In this last case, symptoms of over-factoring manifested. Items belonging to the Divine and Demonic subscales loaded together on the first factor, with Demonic items loading more weakly (Demonic $\lambda_1 = 0.46$–0.59; Divine $\lambda_1 = 0.66$–0.90). Demonic items also loaded on the sixth factor ($\lambda_6 = 0.41$–0.53), as did item 13 from the Interpersonal subscale ("felt angry at organized religion"), which loaded negatively ($\lambda_6 = -0.46$; on the Interpersonal factor, $\lambda_3 = 0.79$). This suggests nontheistic people may differentiate less between divine and demonic agents as targets for attributions of any R/S struggles they experience with respect to supernatural entities. Extracting only five factors offered little improvement in the fit statistics (TLI = 0.25, RMSEA = 0.35, *df*-corrected RMSR = 0.04), but produced a factor pattern with reasonably simple structure (all primary λs $\geqslant 0.63$, all secondary λs $\leqslant 0.30$), in which Divine and Demonic items shared the first factor.

As in Exline and colleagues [19], the first eigenvalue of the RSS items greatly exceeded the others in all samples. Its magnitude ranged from 12 to 14, exceeding the next largest by 8–11, or factors of 3–5. This predominant general factor and strong factor correlations (median = 0.41 across samples) imply a plausible bifactor structure [23].

Exploratory bifactor analyses using Schmid and Leiman's [82] transformation of the initial six-factor solutions supported the presence of a general factor in all five samples. For loadings on the general factors across samples, median $\lambda_{general} = 0.59$–0.70; all $\lambda_{general} > 0.32$, except item 13 in the nontheistic MTurk sample ($\lambda_{general} = 0.19$). Ratios of general factors' eigenvalues to group factors' largest eigenvalues = 3–5. Median percentages of general variance in each item = 46%–62%. These results suggest that the RSS items' common covariance (*i.e.*, excluding unique residual variances) split relatively evenly between the general factor and all group factors.

3.3. Confirmatory Factor Analyses of the RSS

We fit all structural equation models (SEMs) to polychoric correlations using ULSMV estimation in the *lavaan* package [83]. We note a few exceptions to these estimation methods below. All χ^2, CFI, and RMSEA fit statistics used variance-scaling and mean-adjusting corrections [39]. We calculated ω reliabilities for factors using the *semTools* package [84]. This formula, presented by Green and Yang [85] as $\rho_{X\bar{X}}$, does not assume equal loadings across any factor's indicators, and it uses the observed (not model-implied) total covariance to estimate reliability conservatively.

3.3.1. Original Measurement Model

We tested the original RSS measurement model [19] for measurement invariance across all five samples. Constraining the loadings, thresholds, residuals, and latent variances and covariances to have equal estimates across samples resulted in an optimal blend of model parsimony and replicability across samples and good fidelity to the empirical covariance structure ($\chi^2_{(1,976)}$ = 4790, CFI = 0.96, RMSEA = 0.04, weighted root mean square residual (WRMR) = 6.12; Figure 2). Estimating thresholds, residuals, and latent variances and covariances independently in each sample did not improve the model's fit statistics enough to justify the loss of parsimony (metric *vs.* configural ΔCFI = 0.002, strict *vs.* metric ΔCFI = −0.006, constrained variances *vs.* metric ΔCFI = −0.005, covariances *vs.* metric ΔCFI = −0.007), but latent means differed significantly across samples (constrained means *vs.* strong invariance ΔCFI = −0.069; Table 5). Reliability also varied across samples and factors (Table 6).

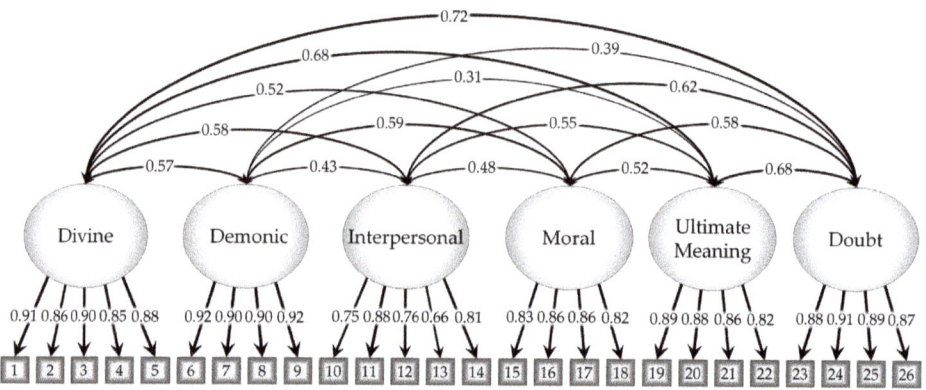

Figure 2. Original measurement model of the RSS. Squares represent items. Ovals represent latent factors. Line weights correspond to their path coefficients, which are standardized. See Table 5 for latent means and variances. Thresholds and residuals are omitted.

Table 5. Latent means (and variances) for RSS factors across samples and measurement models.

Sample	Model	Divine	Demonic	Interpersonal	Moral	Ultimate Meaning	Doubt	General
WCC	Original	1.0 (4.5)	2.5 (5.7)	0.6 (1.3)	0.9 (2.2)	−0.3 (4.0)	0.3 (3.5)	—
	Restricted	−15.2 (1.2)	−10.6 (4.1)	−6.3 (0.6)	−8.0 (1.0)	−13.8 (1.7)	−13.8 (1.1)	16.3 (3.3)
	Unrestricted	0.4 (4.5)	0.4 (3.3)	0.3 (1.0)	−0.2 (1.3)	−0.3 (5.7)	−0.1 (4.0)	0.6 (0.2)
MWU	Original	0.5	0.9	0.3	0.1	0.0	0.1	—
	Restricted	−3.0	−1.9	−1.2	−1.9	−2.9	−2.9	3.5
	Unrestricted	0.4	0.4	0.2	−0.2	0.0	0.0	0.1
MWR	Original	0.0	0.0	0.0	0.0	0.0	0.0	—
	Restricted	0.0	0.0	0.0	0.0	0.0	0.0	0.0
	Unrestricted	0.0	0.0	0.0	0.0	0.0	0.0	0.0
GMT	Original	0.2	0.6	0.4	−0.6	−0.0	−0.3	—
	Restricted	7.1	6.2	3.2	3.3	5.7	5.7	−6.9
	Unrestricted	0.4	1.4	0.4	−0.1	−0.1	−0.2	−0.2
NMT	Original	0.1	−0.8	0.5	−0.8	0.4	−0.3	—
	Restricted	13.8	10.4	6.2	6.8	11.8	11.5	−13.7
	Unrestricted	0.6	1.1	0.6	0.2	0.4	−0.0	−0.5

Note: WCC = west coastal Christian university; MWU = Midwestern public university; MWR = Midwestern private university; GMT = general MTurk; NMT = nontheistic MTurk. The MWR sample's means served as a comparative baseline. All models used strict, latent variance, and latent covariance constraints across samples. Therefore, the WCC variance estimates apply to all samples.

Table 6. Reliability coefficient ω for RSS factors across samples.

Sample	Divine	Demonic	Interpersonal	Moral	Ultimate Meaning	Doubt	General
WCC	0.83	0.89	0.83	0.82	0.77	0.69	0.90
MWU	0.95	10.02	0.87	0.88	0.78	0.78	10.01
MWR	0.85	0.89	0.77	0.84	0.76	0.73	0.89
GMT	0.78	0.86	0.78	0.82	0.75	0.68	0.98
NMT	0.75	0.85	0.77	0.78	0.74	0.68	0.81

Note: WCC = west coastal Christian university; MWU = Midwestern public university; MWR = Midwestern private university; GMT = general MTurk; NMT = nontheistic MTurk. Calculations used the original measurement model, except for the general factor, which used the restricted model.

Ultimately, fit statistics compared well with Exline and colleagues' [19] original results for the RSS. Their use of ML estimation without polychoric correlations did not prevent an accurate, positive conclusion regarding the validity of the RSS. The strict invariance of the RSS across these populations indicates that calculating latent scores from averages of responses should not have introduced substantially unequal biases in their analyses of correlations with other variables.

3.3.2. Restricted Bifactor Measurement Model

A restricted bifactor model of the RSS maintained good fit statistics with the same measurement invariance constraints ($\chi^2_{(1,961)}$ = 5277, CFI = 0.96, RMSEA = 0.04; WRMR = 6.55; Figure 3). Surprisingly, each invariance constraint improved model fit (metric *vs.* configural invariance ΔCFI = 0.002[3], strict *vs.* metric ΔCFI = 0.007, constrained variances *vs.* metric ΔCFI = 0.023). All items loaded fairly strongly on both the general factor ($\lambda_{general}$ = 0.46–0.78) and their respective group factors (λs = 0.43–0.78). These loadings sufficed to estimate all factors well, which supports both the multidimensional and unidimensional frameworks for the RSS. Reliabilities differed from the original model by less than 0.03, and the general factor's reliability also varied across samples (Table 6).

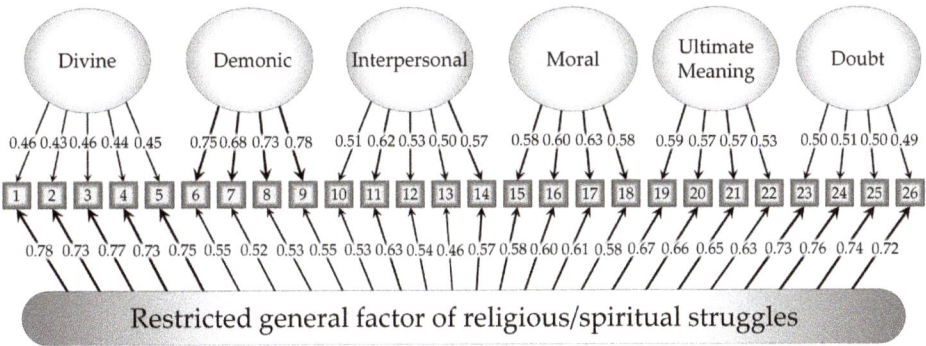

Figure 3. Restricted bifactor measurement model of the RSS. Squares represent items. Ovals represent latent factors. Line weights correspond to their path coefficients, which are standardized. See Table 5 for latent means and variances. Thresholds and residuals are omitted.

In most items, the general factor explained a slightly larger amount of covariance than the group factors. However, this model appeared to fit marginally worse than the original model due to the constrained group factor covariances. The general factor represented an explanation for these covariances, but did not allow any two factors to covary more with each other than with all other factors.

---

3   We used WLSMV estimation for this test of metric invariance because ULSMV could not produce scaled fit statistics for the configural model.

For instance, by sharing one general factor, the relatively unique Demonic items ($\lambda_{general}$ = 0.52–0.55, λ_{group} = 0.68–0.78, all first-order factor rs = 0.31–0.59) may have attenuated loadings for relatively similar Divine and Doubt items ($\lambda_{general}$ = 0.72–0.78, λ_{group} = 0.43–0.51, factor r = 0.72). Therefore, next we tested a bifactor model with free covariances among group factors and an orthogonal general factor.

3.3.3. Unrestricted Bifactor Measurement Model

This model produced the best fit statistics of all RSS CFAs ($\chi^2_{(1,946)}$ = 4126, CFI = 0.97, RMSEA = 0.03, WRMR = 5.49; Figure 4). It continued to perform well in measurement invariance testing, achieving strict measurement invariance (metric *vs.* configural invariance ΔCFI = −0.002,[4] strict *vs.* metric ΔCFI = −0.002) with invariant latent factor covariances and variances (constrained covariances *vs.* metric invariance ΔCFI = −0.006; variances *vs.* metric ΔCFI = −0.008). This model's ω reliabilities did not differ from the other models' values by more than 0.04.

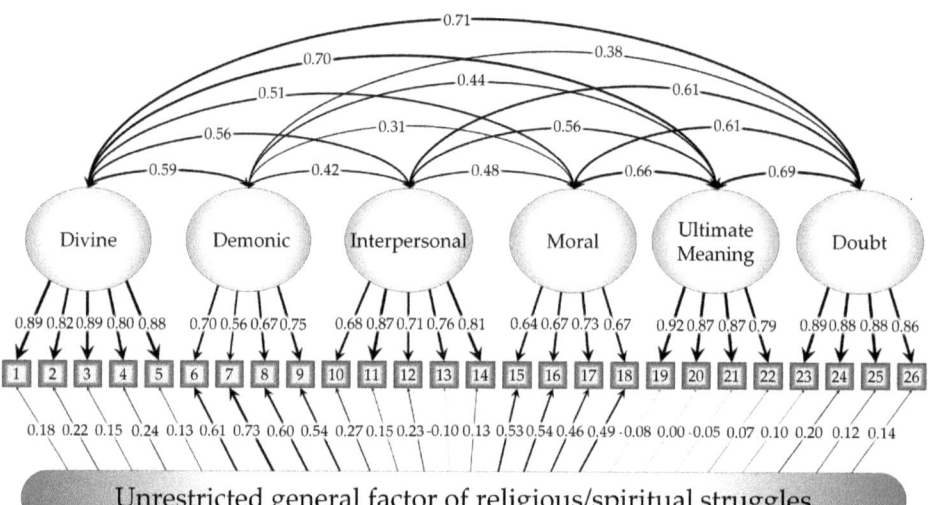

Figure 4. Unrestricted bifactor model of the RSS. Squares represent items. Ovals represent latent factors. Line weights correspond to their path coefficients, which are standardized. Loadings with dashed grey lines differed insignificantly from zero (*p* > 0.08). See Table 5 for latent means and variances. Thresholds and residuals are omitted.

Group factor correlations strongly resembled those from the original model without a general factor ($|\Delta r|$ = 0.01–0.03), except for the correlations among Demonic, Moral, and Ultimate Meaning struggles. Correlations with Ultimate Meaning struggle increased for both Demonic (Δr = 0.13) and Moral struggles (Δr = 0.14). The Demonic-Moral correlation lost almost half its strength (Δr = 0.28), presumably because these factors' common covariance transferred to the general factor. Loadings on the Moral and Demonic group factors also decreased ($\Delta\lambda_{Moral}$ = −0.13–−0.19; $\Delta\lambda_{Demonic}$ = −0.17–−0.34); others changed very little in either direction ($\Delta\lambda_{group}$ = −0.10–0.07). This supports the comparability of this model's group factor structure to the original structure, as do extremely high correlations between corresponding factors' regression scores (rs = 0.980–0.999, except

---

4   We used unscaled CFIs for this test of metric invariance because neither ULSMV nor WLSMV could compute scaled fit statistics for the configural model. Cheung and Rensvold [44] did not specify whether their criteria for measurement invariance apply equally to scaled or unscaled fit statistics.

Demonic $r = 0.723$, and Moral $r = 0.861$). We believe the lower loadings and convergent factor score correlations for the Demonic and Moral factors resulted from the general factor absorbing relatively large portions of the covariance in these factors' indicators.

Initially the unrestricted general factor did not facilitate a clear psychological interpretation. The general factor of the restricted bifactor model more clearly represented a common latent factor of R/S struggle constructed specifically to explain correlations among different kinds of R/S struggles and render their group factors independent. The general factor of the unrestricted bifactor model clearly did not have the same effect, because the strong group factor covariances from the original model remained mostly unaltered. Furthermore, items loaded much more weakly on this general factor than on the restricted model's general factor. Only Demonic items loaded strongly on the general factor ($\lambda_{general} = 0.54$–0.73), and Moral items loaded moderately ($\lambda_{general} = 0.46$–0.54); all other items had weak or insignificant loadings ($\lambda_{general} = -0.10$–$0.27$). To avoid building further results on sampling error and to maintain a focus on replication of theory-driven results, we chose not to trim insignificant loadings, but that option seems open to future replications. Regardless, this general factor related disproportionately to Demonic and Moral items, not unlike religiousness in Exline and colleagues' initial study of the RSS [19].

Following these efforts to optimize the RSS measurement model, we returned to the question of whether a bifactor structure would alter the RSS group factors' relationships with religiousness and distress. Incorporating these related constructs into the SEM would also create an opportunity to learn more about the psychologically ambiguous general factor. Hence we turn next to SEMs of the RSS, religiousness, and distress.

3.4. Structural Equation Models with Religiousness and Distress

3.4.1. Exclusion criteria, Measurement Invariance, and Latent Distributional Differences

Before including our measures of religiousness and distress, we screened their data in preparation for measurement invariance testing. Despite the aforementioned advantages of ULSMV estimation, using it in *lavaan* necessitated listwise deletion of incomplete response sets.[5] We tested measurement invariance for each measure separately, but only used data from participants with complete responses on all measures used here so that results would better reflect the degree of measurement invariance attainable for the SEM that included all measures. Therefore, analyses in this section exclude the nontheistic MTurk sample entirely, because its participants did not receive the Perceived Stress Scale (PSS) [67] nor the religious belief salience measure (RBS) [61], and only 42 completed the religious participation (RP) measure [9].

Only the Big Five Inventory (BFI) [69] contained a sufficient number of items (some reverse-coded) to check for long strings of invariant responding. Of the original 5863 participants who responded to the RSS, an absolute minimum of three participants gave identical responses to 38 out of 44 BFI items. As with the RSS, we excluded 140 participants (2.4%) with more than 38 identical responses, though only 69 of these participants met all other criteria. Altogether, these criteria further reduced the west coastal Christian university's sample size by 159 ($n = 910$), the Midwestern public university's by 321 (1549), the Midwestern private university's by 172 (834), and the general MTurk sample size by 136 (1013), resulting in a final sample of $N = 4306$ (75.5% of valid RSS data or 73.4% of the original sample).Unidimensional measurement model CFAs achieved good fit statistics for RBS, RP, and anxiety, but only acceptable fit for neuroticism, perceived stress, and depression (Table 7). Strict equality constraints improved fit for all factor models except depression, which achieved metric invariance. Latent variances did not vary significantly for depression (ΔCFI $= -0.001$ *vs.* metric-invariant model), anxiety ($\Delta = -0.005$ *vs.* strict model), and RBS (ΔCFI $= -0.001$ *vs.* strict), but varied significantly across

---

5   Mplus can use ULSMV with pairwise complete data.

samples for other factors, as did latent means for all factors (Table 8). The strictly invariant model of depression fit significantly worse than the metric-invariant model; nonetheless, we used it to estimate latent mean differences with a minimum of avoidable bias while avoiding modifications.

Table 7. Measurement model fit, invariance, and reliability statistics for religiousness and distress.

	Religiousness			Distress		
Statistic	Belief Salience	Participation	Depression	Anxiety	Neuroticism	Perceived Stress
CFI	1.00	0.99	0.90	0.99	0.97	0.92
RMSEA	0.01	0.05	0.09	0.05	0.06	0.09
WRMR	2.49	6.38	7.18	2.98	4.66	7.52
Metric ΔCFI	0.000	0.001	0.028	0.005	0.015	0.056
Strict ΔCFI	0.000	0.022	−0.013	0.005	0.016	0.084
Reliability ω	0.96–0.98	0.50–0.82	0.77–0.91	0.86–0.91	0.77–0.89	0.75–0.91

Note: Fit and reliability statistics apply to strictly invariant models; "Strict ΔCFI" compares strictly invariant models' CFIs to metric models'; "Metric ΔCFI" compares metric models' CFIs to configural models'; Reliabilities varied by sample, only once below 0.73 for the west coastal Christian university.

Table 8. Latent means (and variances) for religiousness and distress factors across samples.

	Religiousness			Distress		
Sample	Belief Salience	Participation	Depression	Anxiety	Neuroticism	Perceived Stress
WCC	5.2 (5.7)	2.4 (0.6)	0.1 (0.4)	0.2 (2.3)	−0.1 (0.4)	0.2 (0.8)
MWU	0.9 (8.1)	0.5 (1.4)	0.1 (0.5)	0.3 (2.6)	0.1 (0.4)	0.1 (0.7)
MWR	0.0 (10.4)	0.0 (1.7)	0.0 (0.5)	0.0 (2.3)	0.0 (0.4)	0.0 (0.5)
GMT	0.5 (21.7)	0.3 (2.2)	−0.3 (0.9)	−0.3 (4.2)	−0.2 (0.8)	−0.4 (1.5)

Note: WCC = west coastal Christian university; MWU = Midwestern public university; MWR = Midwestern private university; GMT = general MTurk; The MWR sample's means served as a comparative baseline. All models used strict invariance constraints across samples.

The west coastal Christian university had much higher latent means for religiousness, as expected. Only this sample produced a particularly low reliability estimate for religious participation; all other reliabilities exceeded 0.73. The general MTurk sample did not show any signs of over-representing nonreligious populations, despite evidence of this in other studies [58]. However, the MTurk sample had slightly lower distress means, and more variance in all latent factors. We suspect that these differences may reflect the sample's greater diversity of education, occupation, and (greater) age.

3.4.2. Latent Correlations

The following sections present results from large multi-group SEMs that analyzed the latent correlations among R/S struggles, religiousness, and distress. These correlations varied across samples. However, invariance tests ensured consistency of factor measurement across samples.

The first of these sections establishes a theoretical baseline for these latent correlations as estimated using the original measurement model of the RSS with only six correlated first-order factors and *simple structure* (*i.e.*, one loading per item). Subsequent sections present and compare corresponding correlations derived from similar SEMs using a restricted (*i.e.*, orthogonal group factors) bifactor measurement model for the RSS first, and then using an unrestricted bifactor measurement model with correlated group factors. These comparisons across four populations and three SEMs permitted thorough consideration of whether R/S struggles might relate strongly enough to religiousness or distress to threaten their discriminant validity if one models R/S struggles with either one or many dimensions.

Without establishing measurement invariance directly across these models, we can only assume that all latent factors correspond approximately across models. This seems defensible for all factors with unchanged measurement models, but the six psychological constructs originally represented by the RSS factors may not correspond so closely to the group factors in the bifactor measurement models, and the general factors surely must change when restricting *versus* freely estimating group factor correlations. We consider the effects of these changes across models on latent correlations, but avoid exact statistical comparisons in light of possible measurement variance transferring from deliberate changes in the RSS measurement model to indirect changes in other factors' models.

Original RSS Measurement Model

We first estimated an SEM with the original measurement models for the RSS and all measures of religiousness and distress, allowing all latent factors to covary freely. This model fit adequately ($\chi^2_{(10,436)}$ = 23,974, CFI = 0.91, RMSEA = 0.04, WRMR = 4.20) and maintained strict measurement invariance across samples (strict *vs.* metric invariance ΔCFI = −0.007, metric *vs.* configural ΔCFI = 0.004).

Across the Midwestern public and private university and general MTurk samples, as in the original sample [19], strong positive relationships arose between the Demonic struggle factor and the religiousness factors (both RBS and RP; *r*s = 0.53–0.61; Table 9). Moderate relationships arose between the Moral struggle factor and religiousness (*r*s = 0.32–0.46). Other struggles exhibited weaker correlations with religiousness, all either positive or insignificantly negative (*r*s = −0.07–0.27), except Ultimate Meaning struggle (*r*s = −0.18–0.08).

The west coastal Christian university sample presented exceptions to each of the above. Here, the two religiousness factors related more negatively to all struggles. In this sample, RBS and RP only related positively to Demonic struggle, but much less than in the other samples (*r*s = 0.10 and 0.17, respectively), and insignificantly to Moral struggle (both *r*s = −0.05). Other struggles related negatively and moderately overall (*r*s = −0.19−−0.42), setting aside a more weakly negative correlation between Interpersonal struggle and RP (*r* = −0.09).

The RSS factors' latent correlations with all distress factors emerged as uniformly positive and more stable across samples than with religiousness. Ultimate Meaning struggle generally related the most strongly to distress (*r*s = 0.41–0.64), followed by Divine struggle (*r*s = 0.33–0.56). Other struggles related more moderately (*r*s = 0.10–0.42), except Interpersonal struggle and depression in the west coastal Christian university sample (*r* = 0.52).

Restricted Bifactor RSS Measurement Model

Next, we estimated this SEM with the restricted bifactor measurement model substituted for the original RSS model. This yielded acceptable fit statistics ($\chi^2_{(10,440)}$ = 24,284, CFI = 0.91, RMSEA = 0.04, WRMR = 4.31), but also produced invalidly large correlations ($|r| > 1$) between religiousness factors and all R/S struggle factors. Using diagonally weighted least squares instead of unweighted least squares did not resolve this problem. Using maximum likelihood (ML) estimation on polychoric correlations produced non-convergence errors, as it tends to [36]. However, treating the data as continuous for the purpose of ML estimation allowed the model to converge with interpretable parameter estimates.

Table 9. Latent correlations between factors of the RSS and factors of religiousness and distress.

RSS Factor	Measurement Model	Religiousness		Distress			
		Belief Salience	Participation	Depression	Anxiety	Neuroticism	Perceived Stress
Divine	Original	−0.35/0.00/0.24/0.17	−0.19/0.10/0.24/0.15	0.56/0.45/0.46/0.46	0.49/0.42/0.44/0.44	0.44/0.33/0.38/0.35	0.50/0.43/0.42/0.51
	Restricted	−0.13/−0.14/−0.13/−0.02	−0.07/−0.18/−0.34/−0.03	0.25/0.11/0.16/0.12	0.24/0.14/0.04/0.04	0.20/0.09/0.11/0.06	0.35/0.14/0.16/0.18
	Unrestricted	−0.40/−0.17/0.05/0.06	−0.24/−0.08/0.06/0.04	0.57/0.46/0.44/0.46	0.50/0.41/0.41/0.43	0.45/0.36/0.39/0.35	0.50/0.44/0.39/0.50
Demonic	Original	0.10/0.53/0.57/0.59	0.17/0.58/0.60/0.61	0.35/0.30/0.28/0.21	0.33/0.26/0.30/0.25	0.21/0.10/0.16/0.16	0.31/0.23/0.22/0.22
	Restricted	0.18/0.28/0.18/0.27	0.24/0.36/0.20/0.37	0.14/0.09/0.09/0.09	0.15/0.07/0.03/0.08	0.09/−0.03/−0.00/0.10	0.17/0.03/0.02/0.06
	Unrestricted	−0.10/0.10/0.02/0.34	−0.01/0.16/0.10/0.34	0.41/0.38/0.29/0.22	0.39/0.28/0.24/0.25	0.29/0.22/0.22/0.20	0.37/0.31/0.15/0.22
Inter-personal	Original	−0.23/−0.04/0.13/−0.07	−0.09/0.14/0.27/0.02	0.52/0.33/0.33/0.35	0.42/0.28/0.30/0.34	0.31/0.22/0.26/0.25	0.35/0.22/0.26/0.28
	Restricted	−0.06/−0.15/−0.21/−0.14	−0.00/−0.07/−0.20/−0.07	0.29/0.07/0.11/0.14	0.15/0.07/−0.06/0.09	0.08/0.01/0.05/0.10	0.17/−0.02/0.05/0.09
	Unrestricted	−0.27/−0.16/−0.05/−0.17	−0.13/0.01/0.10/−0.10	0.53/0.33/0.30/0.34	0.43/0.27/0.26/0.32	0.33/0.24/0.26/0.26	0.36/0.22/0.22/0.27
Moral	Original	−0.05/0.38/0.46/0.33	−0.05/0.34/0.42/0.32	0.36/0.30/0.34/0.35	0.31/0.29/0.34/0.36	0.23/0.19/0.32/0.26	0.31/0.26/0.36/0.36
	Restricted	0.06/0.26/0.25/0.20	0.02/0.09/0.02/0.16	0.18/0.06/0.14/0.14	0.13/0.12/0.06/0.09	0.08/0.05/0.14/0.10	0.20/0.08/0.21/0.19
	Unrestricted	−0.19/−0.01/−0.03/0.02	−0.18/−0.06/−0.06/−0.02	0.40/0.34/0.34/0.39	0.34/0.29/0.28/0.37	0.27/0.29/0.39/0.32	0.34/0.32/0.34/0.38
Ultimate Meaning	Original	−0.42/−0.18/0.06/−0.18	−0.25/−0.05/0.08/−0.18	0.60/0.54/0.56/0.64	0.47/0.42/0.47/0.55	0.48/0.41/0.55/0.54	0.45/0.46/0.48/0.59
	Restricted	−0.23/−0.32/−0.25/−0.31	−0.15/−0.26/−0.31/−0.31	0.42/0.36/0.44/0.54	0.23/0.25/0.21/0.35	0.31/0.24/0.35/0.44	0.31/0.27/0.31/0.44
	Unrestricted	−0.42/−0.18/0.05/−0.19	−0.25/−0.06/0.08/−0.18	0.60/0.54/0.56/0.65	0.46/0.42/0.47/0.56	0.48/0.41/0.55/0.54	0.44/0.46/0.48/0.59
Doubt	Original	−0.34/−0.01/0.26/0.16	−0.20/0.06/0.20/0.07	0.42/0.31/0.32/0.32	0.36/0.30/0.32/0.35	0.37/0.28/0.36/0.29	0.33/0.26/0.32/0.33
	Restricted	−0.15/−0.16/−0.03/0.05	−0.04/−0.21/−0.34/−0.05	0.15/−0.03/0.01/−0.02	0.12/0.02/−0.07/−0.01	0.20/0.03/0.07/0.08	0.20/−0.06/0.04/0.01
	Unrestricted	−0.39/−0.15/0.09/0.05	−0.24/−0.08/0.05/−0.04	0.43/0.31/0.30/0.31	0.36/0.28/0.29/0.33	0.39/0.30/0.36/0.29	0.33/0.27/0.29/0.32
General	Restricted	−0.26/0.10/0.32/0.19	−0.17/0.22/0.51/0.19	0.39/0.40/0.34/0.36	0.33/0.32/0.40/0.39	0.26/0.28/0.28/0.25	0.26/0.36/0.30/0.36
	Unrestricted	0.41/0.67/0.74/0.50	0.38/0.69/0.71/0.53	−0.05/0.04/0.13/0.08	−0.04/0.09/0.19/0.11	−0.11/−0.08/0.03/0.02	−0.06/0.00/0.16/0.09

Note: Slashes divide correlations by sample in the following order: west coastal Christian university/Midwestern public university/Midwestern private university/general MTurk. SEMs using the original and unrestricted bifactor measurement models for the RSS used strict measurement invariance constraints. The restricted bifactor RSS SEM used partial metric invariance constraints.

ML estimation produced a very poor CFI = 0.66 in spite of other fairly good fit statistics ($\chi^2_{(9,570)}$ = 16,510, RMSEA = 0.03, standardized root mean square residual (SRMR) = 0.06). We chose not to evaluate these fit statistics according to absolute thresholds for acceptability of fit, given evidence of downward bias in fit statistics when using maximum likelihood estimation on ordinal data from several simulation studies [24,26,30–37]. In light of other indications of adequate fit for the same model using ULSMV estimation or other RSS measurement models, as well as support from measurement model CFAs of each questionnaire considered separately, we assumed acceptable model specification, and only evaluated fit statistics relatively for this model across levels of invariance. It only achieved partial metric invariance (ΔCFI < 0.01) after allowing loadings for two items to remain freely estimated.[6] We report the following parameter estimates from this SEM, but urge caution in comparing them directly to other models' estimates and in interpreting them as true population parameters. Relative to estimates produced with polychoric correlations and ULSMV estimation, ML estimates suffer more bias in the form of attenuated loadings and covariances.

The general factor of the RSS correlated inconsistently with the two religiousness factors across samples. It correlated most strongly and positively with RBS and RP in the Midwestern private university sample (rs = 0.32 and 0.51, respectively), more weakly in the Midwestern public university and general MTurk samples (rs = 0.10–0.22), and negatively in the west coastal Christian university sample (rs = −0.26 and −0.17). Religiousness correlations with the RSS group factors appeared more stable across samples, but shifted toward more negative values like the correlations in the west coastal Christian university sample with the original RSS measurement model. Correlations only remained moderately positive at most across samples for Demonic (rs = 0.18–0.36) and Moral struggles (rs = 0.02–0.26), but ranged from moderately negative to insignificant for other struggles (rs = −0.34–0.05).

As with the original RSS measurement model, the RSS group factors' relationships with the distress factors varied less across samples, and all correlations remained positive or insignificant. Moderate correlations with distress factors manifested for the general RSS factor (rs = 0.25–0.40) and Ultimate Meaning struggle (rs = 0.21–0.54). Two moderate correlations also appeared in the west coastal Christian university sample between Divine struggle and perceived stress (r = 0.35) and between Interpersonal struggle and depression (r = 0.29). Overall, other R/S struggle factors correlated weakly or insignificantly with distress (rs = −0.07–0.25).

Unrestricted Bifactor RSS Measurement Model

Third, we estimated the SEM using the bifactor model of the RSS with correlated group factors and the conventional measurement models for RBS and RP, neuroticism, the PSS, anxiety, and the CES-D. This SEM achieved marginally better fit statistics than the SEM with the original RSS measurement model ($\chi^2_{(10,380)}$ = 22,534, CFI = 0.92, RMSEA = 0.03; WRMR = 3.98) and again maintained strict invariance acceptably (strict *vs.* metric invariance ΔCFI = −0.006).[7]

---

6 The fourth CES-D item and the 13th RSS item (an interpersonal struggle item) as it loaded on the restricted general factor required freely estimated loadings. These loadings varied more across samples than all others in the configural model (standardized s^2_λ = 0.03 and 0.02, respectively). Scaling corrections worsened these models' fit statistics dramatically (ΔCFI = −0.218 with partial metric invariance). Without these corrections, these models did not indicate a significant lack of full metric invariance (full metric *vs.* configural invariance ΔCFI = −0.005).

7 The configural model failed to calculate scaled fit statistics and robust standard errors, and produced inadmissible parameter estimates in the west coastal Christian university sample. A single-group version with that sample showed no such problems, but failed to converge with the Midwestern public university data using ULSMV or WLSMV estimation. Using ML without polychoric correlations, this model converged with no problems (other than a poor CFI statistic), and the multi-group version established metric invariance (ΔCFI = −0.005 *vs.* configural). Again, scaled fit statistics gave marginally more, technically significant cause for concern (ΔCFI = −0.011). We deemed this concern negligible, since this same minor difference in outcomes as in the restricted bifactor RSS SEM only necessitated free estimation of two loadings across that model's groups. Furthermore, the unscaled fit statistics for the WLSMV-estimated multi-group models also indicated metric invariance (ΔCFI = −0.002 *vs.* configural), and no inadmissible parameters resulted from the strictly invariant model using ULSMV estimation, which fit acceptably.

Loadings on the general factor of the RSS changed slightly from those estimated in CFA of its measurement model alone. Loadings strengthened for Moral struggle items ($\lambda_{general}$ = 0.49–0.61), the second Demonic item (about evil temptation; $\lambda_{general}$ = 0.82), and some Interpersonal ($\lambda_{general}$ = −0.12–0.38) and other Demonic items ($\lambda_{general}$ = 0.60–0.68). All other loadings weakened ($\lambda_{general}$ = −0.06–0.29).

The unrestricted general factor of the RSS correlated much more positively with factors of religiousness than in the restricted bifactor RSS SEM. However, these correlations remained inconsistent (with a similar pattern of inconsistency) across samples. RBS and RP correlated with the RSS' general factor positively and most strongly in the Midwestern private and public university samples (rs = 0.67–0.74), followed by the general MTurk sample (rs = 0.50 and 0.53), with only moderately positive correlations in the west coastal Christian university sample (rs = 0.41 and 0.38).

As in the SEM using the original RSS measurement model, religiousness correlated more negatively to the RSS group factors in the west coastal Christian university sample (rs = −0.27–−0.01), especially RBS with Divine, Ultimate Meaning, and Doubt struggles (rs = −0.42–−0.39). Across the other three samples, weak or insignificant correlations had mixed valences (rs = −0.19–0.16), except for moderately positive correlations with Demonic struggle in the general MTurk sample (both rs = 0.34). Overall, this reduction in the correlations of religiousness with RSS group factors, particularly Demonic and Moral struggle, suggested that the general factor had absorbed much of the RSS factors' positive covariance with religiousness, improving its already sufficient discriminant validity.

Correlations with distress changed very little relative to the SEM with the original RSS measurement model. As in this SEM, all RSS group factors' correlations with all distress factors remained consistently positive. Again, Ultimate Meaning struggle correlated most (rs = 0.41–0.65), followed by Divine struggle (rs = 0.35–0.50). Other struggles also correlated with distress positively and moderately (rs = 0.20–0.43), with two exceptions. On the high end, Interpersonal struggle correlated strongly with depression in the west coastal Christian university sample (r = 0.53); on the low end, Demonic struggle correlated insignificantly with perceived stress in the Midwestern private university sample (r = 0.15). The general factor only correlated significantly with anxiety in the Midwestern private university sample (r = 0.19; all other rs = −0.11–0.16). These results establish fairly consistent, positive relationships with distress that vary among different kinds of R/S struggle.

4. Discussion

This study sought to update the measurement model for the Religious and Spiritual Struggles Scale (RSS) [19] and replicate it across five distinct samples, with special attention devoted to the effects of modern SEM methodology and bifactor structures on the RSS factors' relationships with religiousness and distress. We wished to thoroughly test the latent structure of the RSS for stability and applicability across adult populations with varying degrees of religiousness, and to scrutinize its discriminant validity as a unique set of constructs.

4.1. Measurement Validation

Results seem very encouraging for the measurement characteristics of the RSS. Its fit statistics have improved with these methodological updates since Exline and colleagues' [19] initial analyses using normal-theory maximum likelihood estimation. Model parameters remained mostly as described there, and cohered well to the intended structure of the measure.

Strict measurement invariance held across two regions of the USA, across one relatively religious sample and one relatively nonreligious sample, and across other demographic differences between university students and the MTurk community. Strict invariance exhibits the robustness of this measure against typical demographic variation within the USA. This result also absolves Exline and colleagues' study of any confound between comparisons of correlations across samples and biasing due to calculating factor scores by averaging item response ranks. Exploratory factor analysis of the nontheistic MTurk sample raised interesting questions about structural discriminant validity within supernatural struggles (Divine and Demonic) among nonbelievers, but confirmatory factor analysis suggested that these questions can await other nontheistic samples without urgency.

The restricted bifactor model lent new support to the relatively untested unidimensional scoring approach for the RSS, while taking nothing away from the multidimensional approach that Exline and colleagues [19] supported more directly. Its mutually strong loading pairs and equivalently good fit statistics upheld the validity of all factors in question, both narrow and broad. Thus the nature of R/S struggles appears at once both complex and coherent, unified and diverse. Its multifaceted and potentially hierarchical nature bode well for research applications at all levels of depth and detail, whether assessing types of R/S struggle discretely or holistically. For modern research powered by SEM, the unrestricted bifactor model offers minor improvements on the already good fit of the original measurement model. It did not alter the internal structure of the original RSS factors substantially, though Demonic and Moral struggles seemed much more independent of each other and slightly more related to Ultimate Meaning struggle.

4.2. Religiousness, Distress, and Discriminant Validity

Further research seems warranted particularly for the unrestricted bifactor model with correlated group factors. Adding this general factor to the original model improved its fit statistics consistently and seemed to improve discriminant validity with religiousness overall. However, what kind of construct this general factor represents—whether mere method error or something more psychologically meaningful—remains debatable, as does the question of whether the group factors have changed in this model *versus* the original. Loadings and factor score correlations suggest they have not changed, but latent correlations with religiousness indicate some subtle changes. The general factor correlates very strongly with religiousness, especially among our Midwestern university populations. We did not expect correlations to differ across populations in the USA, but our evidence of several differences in correlations with religiousness also warrants further study.

The comparative stability of moderate correlations with distress speaks to the importance of addressing R/S struggles in the course of efforts to improve human experience in general, whether by reducing suffering or promoting growth. Implications here seem quite clear: R/S struggles often accompany negative emotions, but vary independently for the most part, and may play an important role in the course of coping with life's challenges. This holds true regardless of how one measures distress or how one uses the RSS. Bifactor modeling did not show strong effects on the RSS group factors' correlations with distress. Essentially no changes occurred with the unrestricted bifactor model. The restricted bifactor model may have transferred some positive covariance to its general factor, reducing correlations slightly between distress and the RSS group factors.

To some extent these results lend the restricted and unrestricted bifactor models of the RSS to slightly different applications. If discriminant validity with distress presents a special concern, the restricted bifactor model may help reduce correlations with the Ultimate Meaning and Divine struggle factors. If discriminant validity with religiousness matters more in a given application, the unrestricted bifactor model may improve the Demonic and Moral struggle factors' independence.

No other factors gave cause for so much as mild concern about external discriminant validity throughout our analyses, except arguably the unrestricted general factor of the RSS, which correlated quite strongly with religiousness in the Midwestern university samples. Given weaker evidence of this correlation in the other samples and somewhat inconsistent performance with religiousness across populations, we cannot conclude that this general factor clearly represents a facet of religiousness itself. Nonetheless, we predict that the unrestricted bifactor model of the RSS would decrease group factor correlations with religiousness to varying degrees in new samples, as this pattern occurred consistently across all our samples.

If the RSS' unrestricted general factor does not represent a novel construct, it improves the independence of its original constructs. Perhaps its relationship with religiousness implies a transition in the content of R/S struggles between levels of religious involvement and embeddedness. Demonic and Moral struggles seem more compatible with an ideological investment in Christian doctrinal orthodoxy than other R/S struggles, whereas Divine, Interpersonal, Ultimate Meaning, and Doubt struggles seem somewhat more controversial or unorthodox, though not rarer. If the unrestricted general factor represents a common contribution of religiousness to Demonic and Moral struggles, this might allow SEM to isolate these struggles' more domain-specific variance, thus avoiding the need for separate measures of religiousness for statistical control.

Conversely, if the unrestricted general factor differs irreducibly from religiousness, it may represent a valuably distinct aspect of R/S experience. If this construct contributes to Demonic and Moral struggles independently of religiousness, further insights on its nature might aid prediction, explanation, or intervention as methods for these purposes continue to develop. Longitudinal research would enable a test of independent prediction over time and other tests of construct validity.

Cross-cultural research would more stringently test the measurement invariance of the RSS in general and the unrestricted general factor in particular. If the unrestricted general factor's loadings depend heavily on these American cultural and largely Christian religious contexts, the latent factor might amount to little more than uninterpretable nuisance covariance. However, if its structure proves more robustly universal, this result would support its meaningfulness as a psychological entity. Intermediate results might suggest interesting possibilities as well. For instance, if Demonic item loadings vary across cultures according to their religious affiliations or spiritual beliefs, but Moral item loadings and the general factor's correlation with religiousness remain consistent, this might imply that only Demonic struggle depends on varying religious beliefs across cultures. If the Demonic factor correlations also support this conclusion when using the original measurement model, but the unrestricted bifactor model continues to produce a more independent Demonic factor across cultures, then that latter factor might represent the more universal form of Demonic struggle that depends less on religious context. Analogous possibilities also exist for Moral struggles.

4.3. Methodological Observations

These results suggest that researchers should devote more careful consideration to the comparison of religiously mixed populations to populations with specific religious affiliations. Concerns about the heterogeneity of Internet worker populations seem comparatively minimal. Our close comparisons between university samples and MTurk samples (even one with selective sampling) reinforce the already well-established viability of MTurk populations for psychological research. The west coastal Christian university sample proved to be the least comparable sample—even less like the other university samples than the general MTurk sample. We cannot rule out other differences in the west coastal Christian sample as potential causes of differences in their results, but given much less evidence of differences in the general MTurk sample despite its very different distributions of age, education, and location, religion seems the most plausible cause of variance.

Some challenges arose concerning SEM estimator convergence and invalidly large latent correlations when employing bifactor models, especially in larger, multi-group SEMs. Our ability to circumvent these problems using different estimators, equality constraints across groups, and by avoiding the use of polychoric correlations in the restricted bifactor SEM, suggest the need for a better understanding of how these choices affect convergence rates. Bifactor models with polychoric correlations particularly seemed to increase the incidence of improper correlation estimates.

Using multi-group SEM to estimate latent correlations among many factors presents probably the largest burden of complexity and computational labor[8] as compared to calculations of conventional correlations among scores that treat responses as continuous numerical data and average them. Results

---

[8] Our largest SEM took over a day to converge using the newest Intel processor overclocked to 4.5 GHz. (*Lavaan* currently uses only one core per SEM.) Using maximum likelihood estimation without polychoric correlations reduced processing time drastically, as did using simpler SEMs or pooling data into one sample, but our interests prohibited these shortcuts.

did not reveal any clear threats to the simpler scoring methods of classical test theory as applied to these measures; in fact, the strong, relatively even loadings and strict invariance of the simple structure SEM indicated ideal conditions for these methods. Nonetheless, validation via our more demanding methods should precede the use of more basic methods in general, and provided us maximally rigorous, exact tests and exceptionally strong evidence of replicability across populations. Moreover, though the restricted bifactor CFA effectively validated the use of a total score for all RSS items [23], a total score would not divide items' covariance into group factor variance and general factor variance; it would conflate these two influences despite their theoretical independence. Only through SEM could we gain the insights described here regarding the different sets of correlations of the RSS' group and general factors with religiousness and distress.

4.4. Limitations and Future Directions

Our multi-group SEMs ventured outside well-researched applications of measurement invariance testing. We do not know whether Cheung and Rensvold's [44] guidelines for acceptable changes in fit statistics across levels of invariance apply in measurement invariance tests of such complex SEMs across four samples, especially using estimators for ordinal data and scaled fit statistics. Direct tests of partial invariance across different measurement models of the same factors would also help determine to what extent estimating an unrestricted general factor changes the identity of the group factors relative to a model without bifactor structure. These issues necessitate more advanced simulation studies and measurement invariance testing methods than we could find.

We deliberately limited the complexity of our latent factor measurement modeling strategies to test simple structures and basic bifactor structures for the RSS only. Future analyses should extend this multi-sample framework to explore modification indices and attempt to replicate any subtle improvements these might identify. For instance, the unrestricted bifactor model of the RSS suggests one could trim many insignificant loadings. Very strong latent correlations between the two religiousness factors and among the four distress factors would permit simpler representations of their external relationships via general factors. We considered bifactor structures for these measures as well, but we do not report them here.

Longitudinal research would help to address the remaining questions of whether these factors maintain stability over time or change together in the ways one would expect from their correlations. Longitudinal data might also offer limited gains in the capacity for causal inference, but only true experimentation could serve this need directly. Innovative, ethically sensitive manipulations of religiousness, R/S struggle, and distress could prove most valuable for resolving the ambiguity of causal directions involved in these relationships.

Behavioral data or observer reports from relationally close others could reduce our vulnerability to biases in self-reports such as acquiescence, self-enhancement, and extreme responding. These alternative measurement methods would enhance our basis for judging discriminant validity and the degree of relatedness among our constructs of interest. If collected in tandem with these self-report measures, they could further test measurement validity as well.

In light of global variations in culture and R/S experiences and beliefs, this research could greatly benefit from cross-cultural replication. Our conclusions depend entirely on a sample of predominantly white Christians from the USA. Others have noted that as a western, educated, industrialized, rich, and democratic population (WEIRD) [86], the USA may represent the global population poorly in many senses. Future work should consider both the context of different belief systems such as nontheistic, polytheistic, or animistic religions, and the influences of regional norms on expressions of religious beliefs and negative emotions. Furthermore, less socially or cognitively complex populations test the limits of discriminant validity for closely related constructs, which may lose their independence, as Saucier [87] demonstrated with personality structure across culture. Similarly, complexity of latent structure may increase with age. Preliminary results from analyses of retrospectively reported R/S struggles in childhood and adolescence support this hypothesis [88]. Therefore, future sampling efforts should also seek participants from younger and older age groups.

Other available opportunities for measurement invariance testing remain unexplored in our samples. Our MTurk samples included a wide range of ages, and all samples may have enough men to test invariance by gender. Ethnic and R/S subsamples have small enough sizes to threaten power for invariance tests across these groups, but some of our more thoroughly invariant samples may permit pooling across populations for certain purposes. Ongoing data collection efforts will also expand some of these samples over time. Future analyses should avoid pooling the west coastal Christian university's data with other samples when testing relationships between the RSS factors and religiousness, given the uniquely more negative relationships we observed for this sample. Denominational differences among Christians may pose another untested explanation for the uniqueness of this sample's correlations relative to the other largely Christian samples. Evidence of denominational differences in the relationships between religiousness and well-being [89] and between religious coping and adjustment to major surgery [90] also implies that relationships between the RSS factors and distress may vary across denominations. Preliminary evidence of other demographic differences in RSS factor scores suggests that other influences abound [91]. This line of research has many potential nuances left to consider.

5. Conclusions

The Religious and Spiritual Struggles Scale (RSS) [19] effectively measures its six varieties of R/S struggle as well as a more general factor of total R/S struggle. The RSS shows no signs of measurement bias across five demographically and religiously diverse populations in the USA, though the latent constructs it measures differ in distribution. R/S struggles vary mostly independently of religiousness and distress; these factors correlate with R/S struggles to unequal degrees, but never so strongly as to threaten their discriminant validity. An unrestricted bifactor model of the RSS shows mixed potential to reduce the original subscales' correlations with religiousness and gain deeper insights on the nature of these relationships, which seem clearest with Demonic and Moral struggles. Ultimate Meaning and Divine struggles stand out as the strongest connections to distress. A restricted bifactor model may help to partition these relationships into weaker, struggle-specific relationships and a more general relationship with R/S struggle as an abstract gestalt.

Acknowledgments: We wish to express our gratitude to the John Templeton Foundation for funding this research (Grant #36094). We did not receive funds for covering the costs to publish in open access.

Author Contributions: Nick Stauner conceived and designed the analyses and wrote the manuscript. Julie J. Exline, Joshua B. Grubbs, Kenneth I. Pargament, David F. Bradley and Alex Uzdavines conceived and designed the surveys and directed data collection and management. Julie J. Exline, Joshua B. Grubbs and Kenneth I. Pargament contributed edits following the manuscript's preparation, and David F. Bradley contributed during its revisions. Alex Uzdavines contributed methodological advice and support on measurement invariance testing.

Conflicts of Interest: The authors declare no conflict of interest. The founding sponsors had no role in the design of the study; in the collection, analyses, or interpretation of data; in the writing of the manuscript, and in the decision to publish the results.

Abbreviations

The following abbreviations are used in this manuscript:

BFI	Big Five Inventory [69]
CES-D	Center for Epidemiological Studies—Depression scale [62]
CFA	confirmatory factor analysis
CFI	comparative fit index
CI	confidence interval
GMT	general MTurk

ML	maximum likelihood
MTurk	Amazon Mechanical Turk
MWU	Midwestern public university
MWR	Midwestern private university
NMT	nontheistic MTurk
PSS	Perceived Stress Scale [67]
R/S	religious and spiritual
RSS	Religious and Spiritual Struggles Scale [19]
RBS	religious belief salience [61]
RP	religious participation [9]
RMSEA	root mean square error of approximation
RMSR	*df*-corrected root mean square residual
SEM	structural equation model
TLI	Tucker–Lewis index
ULSMV	unweighted least squares with mean and variance adjustments
WLSMV	diagonally weighted least squares with mean and variance adjustments
WRMR	weighted root mean square residual
WCC	west coastal Christian university

References

1. Julie J. Exline. "Religious and spiritual struggles." In *APA Handbook of Psychology, Religion, and Spirituality: Context, Theory, and Research*. Edited by Kenneth I. Pargament, Julie J. Exline and James W. Jones. Washington: American Psychological Association, 2013, vol. 1, pp. 459–75.

2. Kenneth I. Pargament, Nichole A. Murray-Swank, Gina M. Magyar, and Gene G. Ano. "Spiritual struggle: A phenomenon of interest to psychology and religion." In *Judeo-Christian Perspectives on Psychology*. Edited by William R. Miller and Harold D. Delaney. Washington: American Psychological Association, 2005.

3. Julie J. Exline, Crystal L. Park, Joshua M. Smyth, and Michael P. Carey. "Anger toward God: Social-cognitive predictors, prevalence, and links with adjustment to bereavement and cancer." *Journal of Personality and Social Psychology* 100 (2011): 129–48. [CrossRef] [PubMed]

4. Hisham Abu-Raiya, Kenneth I. Pargament, Neal Krause, and Gail Ironson. "Robust links between religious/spiritual struggles, psychological distress, and well-being in a national sample of American adults." *American Journal of Orthopsychiatry* 85 (2015): 565–75. [CrossRef] [PubMed]

5. Julie J. Exline, and Eric D. Rose. "Religious and spiritual struggles." In *Handbook of the Psychology of Religion and Spirituality*, 2nd ed. Edited by Raymond F. Paloutzian and Crystal L. Park. New York: Guilford, 2013, pp. 380–98.

6. Aaron Murray-Swank, and Nichole A. Murray-Swank. "Spiritual and religious problems: Integrating theory and clinical practice." In *APA Handbook of Psychology, Religion, and Spirituality: An Applied Psychology of Religion and Spirituality*. Edited by Kenneth I. Pargament, Annette Mahoney and Edward P. Shafranske. Washington: American Psychological Association, 2013, vol. 2, pp. 421–37.

7. Kenneth I. Pargament. *Spiritually Integrated Psychotherapy: Understanding and Addressing the Sacred*. New York: Guilford, 2007.

8. Nick Stauner, Julie J. Exline, and Kenneth I. Pargament. "Religious and spiritual struggles as concerns for health and well-being." *Horizonte* 14 (2016): 48–75. [CrossRef]

9. Julie J. Exline, Ann M. Yali, and William C. Sanderson. "Guilt, discord, and alienation: The role of religious strain in depression and suicidality." *Journal of Clinical Psychology* 56 (2000): 1481–96. [CrossRef]

10. Crystal L. Park. "Religion and meaning." In *Handbook of the Psychology of Religion and Spirituality*. Edited by Raymond F. Paloutzian and Crystal L. Park. New York: Guilford, 2013.

11. Kenneth I. Pargament. *The Psychology of Religion and Coping: Theory, Practice, and Research*. New York: Guilford, 1997.

12. J. Irene Harris, Christopher R. Erbes, Brian E. Engdahl, Henry Ogden, Raymond H. A. Olson, Ann Marie M. Winskowski, Kelsey Campion, and Saari Mataas. "Religious distress and coping with stressful life events: A longitudinal study." *Journal of Clinical Psychology* 68 (2012): 1276–86. [CrossRef] [PubMed]

13. Kenneth I. Pargament, Harold G. Koenig, Nalini Tarakeshwar, and June Hahn. "Religious struggle as a predictor of mortality among medically ill elderly patients: A two-year longitudinal study." *Archives of Internal Medicine* 161 (2001): 1881–85. [CrossRef] [PubMed]

14. Steven Pirutinsky, David H. Rosmarin, Kenneth I. Pargament, and Elizabeth Midlarsky. "Does negative religious coping accompany, precede, or follow depression among Orthodox Jews?" *Journal of Affective Disorders* 132 (2011): 401–5. [CrossRef] [PubMed]

15. Kelly M. Trevino, Michael J. Balboni, Angelika A. Zollfrank, Tracy A. Balboni, and Holly G. Prigerson. "Negative religious coping as a correlate of suicidal ideation in patients with advanced cancer." *Psychooncology* 23 (2014): 936–45. [CrossRef] [PubMed]

16. Hisham Abu-Raiya, and Kenneth I. Pargament. "Religious coping among diverse religions: Commonalities and divergences." *Psychology of Religion and Spirituality* 7 (2015): 24–33. [CrossRef]

17. Kenneth I. Pargament, Kavita M. Desai, and Kelly M. McConnell. "Spirituality: A pathways to posttraumatic growth or decline?" In *Handbook of Posttraumatic Growth: Research and Practice*. Edited by Lawrence G. Calhoun and Richard G. Tedeschi. Mahwah: Lawrence Erlbaum, 2006, pp. 121–37.

18. Tracey E. Robert, and Virginia A. Kelly, eds. *Critical Incidents in Integrating Spirituality into Counseling*. Alexandria: American Counseling Association, 2014.

19. Julie J. Exline, Kenneth I. Pargament, Joshua B. Grubbs, and Ann M. Yali. "The Religious and Spiritual Struggles scale: Development and initial validation." *Psychology of Religion and Spirituality* 6 (2014): 208–22. [CrossRef]

20. Christopher G. Ellison, and Jinwoo Lee. "Spiritual struggles and psychological distress: Is there a dark side of religion?" *Social Indicators Research* 98 (2010): 501–17. [CrossRef]

21. George Fitchett, Patricia E. Murphy, Jo Kim, James L. Gibbons, Jacqueline R. Cameron, and Judy A. Davis. "Religious struggle: Prevalence, correlates and mental health risks in diabetic, congestive heart failure, and oncology patients." *International Journal of Psychiatry in Medicine* 34 (2004): 179–96. [CrossRef] [PubMed]

22. Kelly M. McConnell, Kenneth I. Pargament, Christopher G. Ellison, and Kevin J. Flannelly. "Examining the links between spiritual struggles and symptoms of psychopathology in a national sample." *Journal of Clinical Psychology* 62 (2006): 1469–84. [CrossRef] [PubMed]

23. Steven P. Reise, Tyler M. Moore, and Mark G. Haviland. "Bifactor models and rotations: Exploring the extent to which multidimensional data yield univocal scale scores." *Journal of Personality Assessment* 92 (2010): 544–59. [CrossRef] [PubMed]

24. Francisco P. Holgado Tello, Salvador Chacón Moscoso, Isabel Barbero García, and Enrique Vila Abad. "Polychoric *versus* Pearson correlations in exploratory and confirmatory factor analysis of ordinal variables." *Quality and Quantity, the International Journal of Methodology* 44 (2010): 153–66. [CrossRef]

25. Ana M. Quiroga. "Studies of the polychoric correlation and other correlation measures for ordinal variables." Ph.D. Thesis, Uppsala University, Uppsala, Sweden, 1992.

26. David B. Flora, and Patrick J. Curran. "An empirical evaluation of alternative methods of estimation for confirmatory factor analysis with ordinal data." *Psychological Methods* 9 (2004): 466–91. [CrossRef] [PubMed]

27. Kenneth A. Bollen, and Kenney H. Barb. "Pearson's *r* and coarsely categorized measures." *American Sociological Review* 46 (1981): 232–39. [CrossRef]

28. Maxine S. Stern. "The Effect of Grouping on the Correlation Coefficient." Paper presented at the Annual Meeting of the American Sociological Association, Denver, CO, USA, 1971.

29. Peter B. Wylie. "Effects of coarse grouping and skewed marginal distributions on the Pearson product moment correlation coefficient." *Educational and Psychological Measurement* 36 (1976): 1–7. [CrossRef]

30. Emin Babakus, Carl E. Ferguson, Jr., and Karl G. Jöreskog. "The sensitivity of confirmatory maximum likelihood factor analysis to violations of measurement scale and distributional assumptions." *Journal of Marketing Research* 24 (1987): 222–28. [CrossRef]

31. Conor V. Dolan. "Factor analysis of variables with 2, 3, 5 and 7 response categories: A comparison of categorical variable estimators using simulated data." *British Journal of Mathematical and Statistical Psychology* 47 (1994): 309–26. [CrossRef]

32. Edward E. Rigdon, and Carl E. Ferguson, Jr. "The performance of the polychoric correlation coefficient and selected fitting functions in confirmatory factor analysis with ordinal data." *Journal of Marketing Research* 28 (1991): 491–97. [CrossRef]

33. Diana Mîndrilă. "Maximum likelihood (ML) and diagonally weighted least squares (DWLS) estimation procedures: A comparison of estimation bias with ordinal and multivariate non-normal data." *International Journal of Digital Society* 1 (2010): 60–66. [CrossRef]
34. Wei C. Wang, and Everarda G. Cunningham. "Comparison of alternative estimation methods in confirmatory factor analyses of the general health questionnaire." *Psychological Reports* 97 (2005): 3–10. [CrossRef] [PubMed]
35. Andre Beauducel, and Philipp Y. Herzberg. "On the performance of maximum likelihood *versus* means and variance adjusted weighted least squares estimation in CFA." *Structural Equation Modeling: A Multidisciplinary Journal* 13 (2006): 186–203. [CrossRef]
36. Nick Stauner. "Estimators for Structural Equation Modeling of Nonnormal Likert Scale Data." Poster presented at the Convention of the American Psychological Association, Toronto, ON, Canada, August 2015. Available online: http://www.slideshare.net/NickStauner/estimators-for-structural-equation-models-of-likert-scale-data-57210233 (accessed on 2 June 2016).
37. Pui-Wa Lei. "Evaluating estimation methods for ordinal data in structural equation modeling." *Quality and Quantity* 43 (2009): 495–507. [CrossRef]
38. Bengt Muthén. "A general structural equation model with dichotomous, ordered categorical and continuous latent variable indicators." *Psychometrika* 49 (1984): 115–32. [CrossRef]
39. Albert Satorra, and Peter M. Bentler. "Corrections to test statistics and standard errors in covariance structure analysis." In *Latent Variables Analysis: Applications for Development Research*. Edited by Alexander von Eye and Clifford C. Clogg. Thousand Oaks: Sage Publications, 1994.
40. Mijke Rhemtulla, Patricia É. Brosseau-Liard, and Victoria Savalei. "When can categorical variables be treated as continuous? A comparison of robust continuous and categorical SEM estimation methods under suboptimal conditions." *Psychological Methods* 17 (2012): 354–73. [CrossRef] [PubMed]
41. Fan Yang-Wallentin, Karl G. Jöreskog, and Hao Luo. "Confirmatory factor analysis of ordinal variables with misspecified models." *Structural Equation Modeling: A Multidisciplinary Journal* 17 (2010): 392–423. [CrossRef]
42. Carlos G. Forero, Alberto Maydeu-Olivares, and David Gallardo-Pujol. "Factor analysis with ordinal indicators: A Monte Carlo study comparing DWLS and ULS estimation." *Structural Equation Modeling: A Multidisciplinary Journal* 16 (2009): 625–41. [CrossRef]
43. Robert J. Vandenberg, and Charles E. Lance. "A review and synthesis of the measurement invariance literature: Suggestions, practices, and recommendations for organizational research." *Organizational Research Methods* 3 (2000): 4–70. [CrossRef]
44. Gordon W. Cheung, and Roger B. Rensvold. "Evaluating goodness-of-fit indexes for testing measurement invariance." *Structural Equation Modeling: A Multidisciplinary Journal* 9 (2002): 233–55. [CrossRef]
45. Daniel K. Mroczek, Eileen K. Graham, Joshua P. Rutsohn, Nicholas A. Turiano, Emily Bastarache, Lorien G. Elleman, and 13 study representatives from the IALSA Network. "Using Multi-Study Coordinated Analysis to Enhance Replicability: An Example Using Personality, Smoking, and Mortality Risk with 12 Longitudinal Data Sets." Paper presented at the 4th Biannual Conference of the Association for Research in Personality, St. Louis, MO, USA, 11–13 June 2015.
46. Patrick J. Curran, and Andrea M. Hussong. "Integrative data analysis: The simultaneous analysis of multiple data sets." *Psychological Methods* 14 (2009): 81–100. [CrossRef] [PubMed]
47. Scott M. Hofer, and Andrea M. Piccinin. "Integrative data analysis through coordination of measurement and analysis protocol across independent longitudinal studies." *Psychological Methods* 14 (2009): 150–64. [CrossRef] [PubMed]
48. Geoff Cumming. "The new statistics: Why and how." *Psychological Science* 25 (2014): 7–29. [CrossRef] [PubMed]
49. Michael Buhrmester, Tracy Kwang, and Samuel D. Gosling. "Amazon's Mechanical Turk: A new source of inexpensive, yet high-quality, data?" *Perspectives on Psychological Science* 6 (2011): 3–6. [CrossRef] [PubMed]
50. Samuel D. Gosling, Simine Vazire, Sanjay Srivastava, and Oliver P. John. "Should we trust web-based studies? A comparative analysis of six preconceptions about internet questionnaires." *American Psychologist* 59 (2004): 93–104. [CrossRef] [PubMed]
51. Winter Mason, and Siddharth Suri. "Conducting behavioral research on Amazon's Mechanical Turk." *Behavior Research Methods* 44 (2012): 1–23. [CrossRef] [PubMed]

52. Linda J. Skitka, and Edward G. Sargis. "The Internet as psychological laboratory." *Annual Review of Psychology* 57 (2006): 529–55. [CrossRef] [PubMed]

53. Danielle N. Shapiro, Jesse Chandler, and Pam A. Mueller. "Using Mechanical Turk to study clinical populations." *Clinical Psychological Science* 1 (2013): 213–20. [CrossRef]

54. Joseph K. Goodman, Cynthia E. Cryder, and Amar Cheema. "Data collection in a flat world: The strengths and weaknesses of Mechanical Turk samples." *Journal of Behavioral Decision Making* 26 (2013): 213–24. [CrossRef]

55. Gabriele Paolacci, and Jesse Chandler. "Inside the Turk: Understanding Mechanical Turk as a participant pool." *Current Directions in Psychological Science* 23 (2014): 184–88. [CrossRef]

56. Gabriele Paolacci, Jesse Chandler, and Panagiotis G. Ipeirotis. "Running experiments on Amazon Mechanical Turk." *Judgment and Decision Making* 5 (2010): 411–19.

57. Jon Sprouse. "A validation of Amazon Mechanical Turk for the collection of acceptability judgments in linguistic theory." *Behavior Research Methods* 43 (2011): 155–67. [CrossRef] [PubMed]

58. Andrew R. Lewis, Paul A. Djupe, Stephen T. Mockabee, and Joshua Su-Ya Wu. "The (Non) Religion of Mechanical Turk Workers." *Journal for the Scientific Study of Religion* 54 (2015): 419–28. [CrossRef]

59. Benjamin T. Wood, Everett L. Worthington, Jr., Julie J. Exline, Ann M. Yali, Jamie D. Aten, and Mark R. McMinn. "Development, refinement, and psychometric properties of the Attitudes Toward God Scale (ATGS-9)." *Psychology of Religion and Spirituality* 2 (2010): 148–67. [CrossRef]

60. Julie J. Exline, Kenneth I. Pargament, Todd W. Hall, and Valencia A. Harriott. "Predictors of growth from spiritual struggle among Christian undergraduates: Religious coping and perceptions of helpful action by God are both important." *Journal of Positive Psychology* (forthcoming).

61. Bruce E. Blaine, and Jennifer Crocker. "Religiousness, race, and psychological well-being: Exploring social psychological moderators." *Personality and Social Psychology Bulletin* 21 (1995): 1031–41. [CrossRef]

62. Elena M. Andresen, Judith A. Malmgren, William B. Carter, and Donald L. Patrick. "Screening for depression in well older adults: Evaluation of a short form of the CES-D." *American Journal of Preventive Medicine* 10 (1994): 77–84. [PubMed]

63. Michael Irwin, Kamal H. Artin, and Michael N. Oxman. "Screening for depression in the older adult: Criterion validity of the 10-item Center for Epidemiological Studies Depression Scale (CES-D)." *Archives of Internal Medicine* 159 (1999): 1701–4. [CrossRef] [PubMed]

64. Wendy Zhang, Nadia O'Brien, Jamie I. Forrest, Kate A. Salters, Thomas L. Patterson, Julio S. G. Montaner, Robert S. Hogg, and Viviane D. Lima. "Validating a shortened depression scale (10 item CES-D) among HIV-positive people in British Columbia, Canada." *PLoS ONE* 7 (2012): e40793. [CrossRef] [PubMed]

65. Robert L. Spitzer, Kurt Kroenke, Janet B. W. Williams, and Bernd Löwe. "A brief measure for assessing generalized anxiety disorder: The GAD-7." *Archives of Internal Medicine* 166 (2006): 1092–97. [CrossRef] [PubMed]

66. Bernd Löwe, Oliver Decker, Stefanie Müller, Elmar Brähler, Dieter Schellberg, Wolfgang Herzog, and Philipp Y. Herzberg. "Validation and standardization of the Generalized Anxiety Disorder Screener (GAD-7) in the general population." *Medical Care* 46 (2008): 266–74. [CrossRef] [PubMed]

67. Sheldon Cohen, Tom Kamarck, and Robin Mermelstein. "A global measure of perceived stress." *Journal of Health and Social Behavior* 24 (1983): 386–96. [CrossRef]

68. Jonathan W. Roberti, Lisa N. Harrington, and Eric A. Storch. "Further psychometric support for the 10-item version of the perceived stress scale." *Journal of College Counseling* 9 (2006): 135–47. [CrossRef]

69. Oliver P. John, Eileen M. Donahue, and Robert L. Kentle. *The Big Five Inventory: Versions 4a and 54.* Berkeley: Institute of Personality and Social Research, University of California, 1991.

70. Robert R. McCrae, and Paul T. Costa, Jr. "A five-factor theory of personality." In *Handbook of Personality: Theory and Research*, 2nd ed. Edited by Lawrence A. Pervin and Oliver P. John. New York: Guilford Press, 1999.

71. John M. Hettema, Carol A. Prescott, and Kenneth S. Kendler. "Genetic and environmental sources of covariation between generalized anxiety disorder and neuroticism." *American Journal of Psychiatry* 161 (2004): 1581–87. [CrossRef] [PubMed]

72. Christopher J. Soto, and Oliver P. John. "Ten facet scales for the Big Five Inventory: Convergence with NEO PI-R facets, self-peer agreement, and discriminant validity." *Journal of Research in Personality* 43 (2009): 84–90. [CrossRef]

73. R. Core Team. "R: A Language and Environment for Statistical Computing." *R Foundation for Statistical Computing*, 2015. Available online: http://www.R-project.org/ (accessed on 2 June 2016).

74. Jason L. Huang, Paul G. Curran, Jessica Keeney, Elizabeth M. Poposki, and Richard P. DeShon. "Detecting and deterring insufficient effort responding to surveys." *Journal of Business and Psychology* 27 (2012): 99–114. [CrossRef]

75. Justin A. DeSimone, Peter D. Harms, and Alice J. DeSimone. "Best practice recommendations for data screening." *Journal of Organizational Behavior* 36 (2015): 171–81. [CrossRef]

76. John A. Johnson. "Ascertaining the validity of individual protocols from web-based personality inventories." *Journal of Research in Personality* 39 (2005): 103–29. [CrossRef]

77. Andrew R. Gilpin. "Table for conversion of Kendall's Tau to Spearman's Rho within the context measures of magnitude of effect for meta-analysis." *Educational and Psychological Measurement* 53 (1993): 87–92. [CrossRef]

78. Max Gordon, and Thomas Lumley. "Forestplot: Advanced Forest Plot Using 'Grid' Graphics (Version 1.3)." 2015. Available online: http://CRAN.R-project.org/package=forestplot (accessed on 2 June 2016).

79. Fiona McElduff, Mario Cortina-Borja, Shun-Kai Chan, and Angie Wade. "When *t*-tests or Wilcoxon-Mann-Whitney tests won't do." *Advances in Physiology Education* 34 (2010): 128–33. [CrossRef] [PubMed]

80. Statistical Consulting Group. "FAQ: How do I Interpret Odds Ratios in Logistic Regression?" Available online: http://www.ats.ucla.edu/stat/mult_pkg/faq/general/odds_ratio.htm (accessed on 14 July 2015).

81. William Revelle. "Psych: Procedures for Personality and Psychological Research." 2015. Available online: http://CRAN.R-project.org/package=psych (accessed on 2 June 2016).

82. John Schmid, and John M. Leiman. "The development of hierarchical factor solutions." *Psychometrika* 22 (1957): 53–61. [CrossRef]

83. Yves Rosseel. "lavaan: An R package for structural equation modeling." *Journal of Statistical Software* 48 (2012): 1–36. [CrossRef]

84. semTools Contributors. "semTools: Useful Tools for Structural Equation Modeling (R Package Version 0.4–11)." 2016. Available online: http://cran.r-project.org/package=semTools (accessed on 2 June 2016).

85. Samuel B. Green, and Yanyun Yang. "Reliability of summed item scores using structural equation modeling: An alternative to coefficient alpha." *Psychometrika* 74 (2009): 155–67. [CrossRef]

86. Joseph Henrich, Steven J. Heine, and Ara Norenzayan. "Most people are not WEIRD." *Nature* 466 (2010): 29. [CrossRef] [PubMed]

87. Gerard Saucier. "The Big Two as a common-denominator model of personality-attribute structure." In *Strong Cross-Cultural Tests of Personality Models*. Paper presented at the 4th Biennial Conference of the Association for Research in Personality, St. Louis, MO, USA, 11–13 June 2015.

88. Steffany J. Homolka, and Julie J. Exline. "Measuring Adolescent Religious and Spiritual Struggles: A Retrospective Pilot Study." Paper presented at the Society for Research in Child Development's Religion and Spirituality Pre-Conference, Philadelphia, PA, USA, 18 March 2015, and at the 123rd annual APA Convention, Toronto, ON, Canada, 6–9 August 2013.

89. Andrew P. Tix, and Patricia A. Frazier. "Mediation and moderation of the relationship between intrinsic religiousness and mental health." *Personality and Social Psychology Bulletin* 31 (2005): 295–306. [CrossRef] [PubMed]

90. Andrew P. Tix, and Patricia A. Frazier. "The use of religious coping during stressful life events: Main effects, moderation, and mediation." *Journal of Consulting and Clinical Psychology* 66 (1998): 411–22. [CrossRef] [PubMed]

91. Nick Stauner, Julie J. Exline, and Kenneth I. Pargament. "The demographics of religious and spiritual struggles in the USA." In *Belief and Nonbelief are Complex: Longitudinal, Demographical, and Cognitive Perspectives*. Paper presented at the Convention of the Society for the Scientific Study of Religion, Newport Beach, CA, USA, 23–25 October 2015.

 *religions*

Article

The NERSH International Collaboration on Values, Spirituality and Religion in Medicine: Development of Questionnaire, Description of Data Pool, and Overview of Pool Publications

Niels Christian Hvidt [1,*], Alex Kappel Kørup [1,2], Farr A. Curlin [3], Klaus Baumann [4], Eckhard Frick [5,6], Jens Søndergaard [1], Jesper Bo Nielsen [1], René dePont Christensen [1], Ryan Lawrence [7], Giancarlo Lucchetti [8], Parameshwaran Ramakrishnan [9,10], Azimatul Karimah [11], Andreas Schulze [12], Inga Wermuth [12], Esther Schouten [12], René Hefti [13,14], Eunmi Lee [4], Nada A. AlYousefi [15], Christian Balslev van Randwijk [1], Can Kuseyri [12], Tryphon Mukwayakala [12], Miriam Wey [16], Micha Eglin [16], Tobias Opsahl [1] and Arndt Büssing [17]

1   Research Unit of General Practice, Institute of Public Health, University of Southern Denmark, Odense C 5000, Denmark; akorup@health.sdu.dk (A.K.K.); jsoendergaard@health.sdu.dk (J.S.); jbnielsen@health.sdu.dk (J.B.N.); rechristensen@health.sdu.dk (R.P.C.); crandwijk@health.sdu.dk (C.B.v.R.); toops14@student.sdu.dk (T.O.)
2   Department of Mental Health Kolding-Vejle, Vejle 7100, Denmark
3   Trent Center for Bioethics, Humanities, and History of Medicine, Duke University, Durham NC 27613, USA; farr.curlin@duke.edu
4   Caritas Science and Christian Social Work, Faculty of Theology, Freiburg University, Freiburg im Breisgau 79098, Germany; klaus.baumann@theol.uni-freiburg.de (K.B.); stella22800@gmail.com (E.L.)
5   Research Centre Spiritual Care, Department of Psychosomatic Medicine and Psychotherapy, The University Hospital Klinikum rechts der Isar, Langerstr. 3, Munich 81675, Germany; Eckhard.Frick@tum.de
6   Munich School of Philosophy, Kaulbachstr. 31, Munich 80539, Germany
7   Department of Psychiatry, Columbia University Medical Center, New York, NY 10032, USA; rel2137@columbia.edu
8   Department of Medicine, Federal University of Juiz de Fora, Avenida Eugênio de Nascimento s/n-Aeroporto, Juiz de Fora 36038330, MG, Brazil; g.lucchetti@yahoo.com.br
9   Harvard Divinity School, Harvard University, Cambridge, MA 02138, USA; par469@mail.harvard.edu
10 AdiBhat Foundation, New Delhi 110048, India
11 Department of Psychiatry, Universitas Airlangga, Surabaya, East Java 60115, Indonesia; azimatul.karimah@fk.unair.ac.id
12 Medical Faculty, Ludwig Maximilian University of Munich, München 81377, Germany; andreas.schulze@med.uni-muenchen.de (A.S.); inga.wermuth@med.uni-muenchen.de (I.W.); esther.schouten@med.uni-muenchen.de (E.S.); cankuseyri91@gmail.com (C.K.); Tryphon.Tryphon.Kisamba@campus.lmu.de (T.M.)
13 Medical Faculty, University of Bern, Bern 3012, Switzerland
14 Research Institute for Spirituality and Health (RISH), Langenthal 4900, Switzerland; rene.hefti@rish.ch
15 College of Medicine, King Saud University (KSU), Riyadh 11461, Saudi Arabia; nalyousefi@ksu.edu.sa
16 Medical Faculty, University of Basel, Basel 4003, Switzerland; miriam.wey@stud.unibas.ch (M.W.); micha.eglin@stud.unibas.ch (M.E.)
17 Institute of Integrative Medicine, Faculty of Medicine, Witten/Herdecke University, Gerhard-Kienle-Weg 4, Herdecke D-58313, Germany; Arndt.Buessing@uni-wh.de
*   Correspondence: nchvidt@health.sdu.dk; Tel.: +45-6550-4325

Academic Editor: Paweł Marian Socha
Received: 18 May 2016; Accepted: 26 July 2016; Published: 23 August 2016

Abstract: Modern healthcare research has only in recent years investigated the impact of health care workers' religious and other moral values on medical practice, interaction with patients, and ethically complex decision-making. Thus far, no international data exist on the way such values vary across different countries. We therefore established the NERSH International Collaboration on Values in Medicine with datasets on physician religious characteristics and values based on the same survey instrument. The present article provides (a) an overview of the development of the original and optimized survey instruments, (b) an overview of the content of the NERSH data pool at this stage and (c) a brief review of insights gained from articles published with the questionnaire. The questionnaire was developed in 2002, after extensive pretesting in the United States and subsequently translated from English into other languages using forward-backward translations with Face Validations. In 2013, representatives of several national research groups came together and worked at optimizing the survey instrument for future use on the basis of the existing datasets. Research groups were identified through personal contacts with researchers requesting to use the instrument, as well as through two literature searches. Data were assembled in Stata and synchronized for their comparability using a matched intersection design based on the items in the original questionnaire. With a few optimizations and added modules appropriate for cultures more secular than that of the United States, the survey instrument holds promise as a tool for future comparative analyses. The pool at this stage consists of data from eleven studies conducted by research teams in nine different countries over six continents with responses from more than 6000 health professionals. Inspection of data between groups suggests large differences in religious and other moral values across nations and cultures, and that these values account for differences in health professional's clinical practices.

Keywords: religion and health; spirituality; physician values; communication; medical ethics

---

1. Introduction

This article describes the development, contents, and first cross national comparisons based on an international research tool, first developed in 2002 and executed in 2003 with subsequent publications [1–10], translated into seven languages [11–28] and optimized in 2013. The data document the impact of Health Professionals' (HPs') religious and secular beliefs and values on the clinical encounter.

Research publications on the relationship between religion, spirituality and health have increased significantly over recent years. This is evident by simple searches on Medline using the search words *Religion* (understood as the communal convictions and practices believers engage in as they search for the sacred) and especially *Spirituality* (mostly referring to the interior life individuals experience in their search for the sacred, not ruling out fellowship with other believers), and a number of journals have been dedicated to the study of the relationship between Spirituality and Health. Various articles have been dedicated to the conceptualization of religion, spirituality and faith (abbreviated R/S in this article) [29–31].

Historically, most religions include substantial reflection on the nexus of spirituality, health and suffering. This holds for Christianity as well. Thus, Amanda Porterfield describes how Christianity historically focused on disease through spiritual resources and practices, but also through altruistically motivated care for sufferers, which contributed significantly to the growth of Christianity in Roman times and throughout Western history. Indeed, modern health care has historical roots in the Christian vision of active charity that in Western Monasteries saw significant scientific and organizational anchoring [32].

Still today, many countries know nurses as *sisters* (a title for nuns) and numerous hospitals are still attached to and draw inspiration from monastic orders. A recent *Lancet Series on Faith-Based Health Care* focused on how faith institutions continue to have tremendous importance in third world countries [33]. In modern times, a stronger emphasis on scientific approaches to medicine has led to relatively little appreciation of religion within institutionalized health care. In part this has reflected broader critiques of religion in the works of positivists such as Auguste Comte and among clinicians such as Sigmund Freud, who saw religion as "universal compulsory neurosis", "infantile helplessness" and "regression to primary narcissism" [34,35]. Within health care, R/S orientations and resources of patients often have been relegated to the private sphere, although substantial research indicates that when sick, people are most likely to care about existential, spiritual and religious questions [36].

Not surprisingly, then, modern healthcare research has only seen limited interest in the impact of HPs' personal values and their impact on the medical practice, the interaction with patients, and ethically complex decision-making. To date no scientific reviews have been published on the impact of spirituality on medical practice.

Things have started to change with Farr Curlin and colleagues developing the survey Religion and Spirituality in Medicine: Physicians' Perspectives (RSMPP 2002) in 2002. After administering this questionnaire to a representative sample of more than 1100 US physicians, the researchers published a series of papers describing their findings [1–10]. After translation into other languages, the RSMPP has so far led to the publication of ten other research articles [11–20] and eight theses [21–28]. Curlin and colleagues went on to develop other questionnaires focusing on specific aspects of health care, leading to more than 32 further publications [37–66]. However, other researchers introduced various changes to the original questionnaire which complicated comparisons across different studies. Therefore, we established the *NERSH International Collaboration on Values in Medicine* to discuss these different versions and finally to consent the "core" elements of the questionnaire battery, and to add further items or to specify some phrasings.

The *NERSH collaboration on Values in Medicine* is hosted by the Board of the *Network for Research in Spirituality and Health* (NERSH—www.nersh.org). In 2011, the Board members met at the founding seminar of *Internationale Gesellschaft für Gesundheit und Spiritualität* (www.iggs-online.org) in Munich and later as members of the editorial board of *Spiritual Care—Zeitschrift für Spiritualität in den Gesundheitsberufen (Journal of Spirituality in Health Care*—http://www.degruyter.com/view/j/spircare) and who had collaborated variously in the *Scandinavian Network for Faith and Health* (www.faith-health.org), and the *European Network of Research on Religion, Spirituality and Health* (http://www.fisg.ch). Baumann, Büssing and Hvidt were subsequently granted fellowships as an Interdisciplinary Research Group (IRG) at the German *Freiburg Institute for Advanced Studies* (FRIAS) from October 2012 to March 2014 with the aim of improving research based attention to spiritual needs and challenges of patients (esp. with chronic diseases), relatives and HPs who care for them [67–69]. Like Eckhard Frick, they had started independently to conduct research involving the RSMPP in translated form [22–26] or other similar instruments for the measurement of HP values [70]. The shared interests came together at FRIAS.

Farr Curlin's study was the first of its kind [1], and soon the NERSH founders discovered a lacuna in the international research community: Until now, no large-scale international comparisons exist to describe how HP values vary across different nations and cultures and how that potentially affects their professional life. Therefore, the *NERSH International Collaboration on Values in Medicine* was established with datasets on physician values from the research teams that used the RSMPP, covering eleven studies conducted by research teams in nine different countries over six continents. The present article is the first publication from this collaboration. It provides (1) an overview of the development of the original and optimized survey instruments; (2) an overview of the content of the NERSH data pool at this stage; (3) a brief overview of insights gained from individual articles published with the questionnaire until now.

2. Methods and Materials

2.1. Development of the RSMPP

The NERSH questionnaire mainly builds on the RSMPP questionnaire developed by Curlin et al. in 2002. It includes a number of sections:

- *Physician perspectives on religion/spirituality (R/S) and health* containing 50 items. The items were written by Curlin and colleagues after thorough review of relevant literature and data gathered from qualitative pilot interviews. Items were subsequently revised for clarity and cogency through multiple expert panel reviews [2].
- *Religious Characteristics* consisting of 21 questions based on existing religiosity measures: 3A Religious affiliation, 3B Intrinsic religiosity, 3C Frequency of religious service attendance, 3D Beliefs, 3E Spirituality vs. Religiosity, 3F Religious Coping [1], and
- *Demographics* containing 18 items.

Development of the RSMPP has been described in detail in prior publication [1].

2.2. International Translations and Validations of the RSMPP

International research teams translated the RSMPP using mainly forward-backward translations with Face Validations in the following years [11–28].

At Freiburg, Germany in December 2008–January 2009, Eunmi Lee and Klaus Baumann translated the primary parts of the RSMPP and added a few items they deemed appropriate for their setting. In Denmark Christian Balslev van Randwijk and Niels Christian Hvidt translated it into Danish in 2010 [28] with a few necessary adaptations to the Danish context. At Munich, Germany in 2010, Inga Wermuth and Andreas Schulze translated the RSMPP in its entirety, likewise; a few alterations were inspired by the Danish adaptations. Both slightly different German translations are now harmonized in one German version available at the NERSH.org—Tool-box. Nada A. AlYousefi translated it into Arabic in 2009, Giancarlo Lucchetti into Portuguese in 2010, Tryphon Mukwayakala into French in 2012, and Can Kuseyri into Turkish in 2015. In 2014, Eunmi Lee translated the Freiburg version into Korean.

2.3. Development of the NERSH Instrument

The establishment of the NERSH International Collaboration on Values in Medicine collaboration and the optimized NERSH instrument involved (1) two expert round table meetings six months apart at FRIAS with use of Nominal Group Technique (NGT) voting consensus procedure on items; and (2) internal reliability analyses (Cronbach's Alpha) with some parts of the questionnaire.

2.3.1. Expert Round Table Meetings with NGT

The first meeting took place from 20–22 February 2013 and the second from 30 September to 1 October 2013.

US team representatives had sent beforehand a list of items that they had previously employed in questionnaires and worked particularly well, and that they deemed appropriate to include in the NERSH questionnaire. These were presented to participants beforehand and were part of a proposed updated (new) NERSH instrument.

Second, an adapted form of Nominal Group Technique (NGT) [71,72], a qualitative research method which enables researchers to gather information and opinions from experts was used. Initially, all items were reviewed in a round table discussion so that the purpose and functionality of all items were clearly present to all experts, recalling the use they had made of the items in their individual experience with the RSMPP. Then, all attending experts (n = 14) scored all items on a scale of zero (low appreciation) to three (high appreciation). Results were noted down on a flipchart and later transferred to a word document containing all items. Items that received an overall score lower than ten were excluded from the updated questionnaire.

It became clear that the original RSMPP included items from Koenig et al.'s *DUREL (Duke Religiosity Index)* five-item measure but had left out one item that was now reinserted. Furthermore, items the Freiburg group had benefited from using were added. Three scales by Büssing, appropriate for analyses in more secular culture (ASP [73,74] and SpREUK-15 [75,76]) were proposed as additional modules for future research. More items that were identified during the NGT-process as thematically related were grouped in leading to fewer overall questionnaire batteries (see Section 2.4 below).

Finally, it was decided to create a new acronym for the instrument, the future joint data pool and the collaboration itself as the RSMPP acronym was found difficult to remember and a new acronym was needed to indicate that the instrument was truly improved and the joint pool and collaboration constituted new initiatives.

2.3.2. Internal Reliability

On the basis of datasets obtained by then (Balslev, Curlin, Lee, Mukwaiakala, Wermuth), Büssing performed internal reliability analyses (Cronbach's Alpha) with the aim of looking for topics in the questionnaire that had some quality with respect to internal congruence, also in view of identifying items that could be eliminated. However, as the basic questionnaire was primarily intended to collect opinions (survey), and not to measure and quantify specific attitudes, convictions and behaviors, only some topics were identified as being suitable as scales (see Appendix A).

The respective topics will be revalidated in future studies using the updated NERSH questionnaire.

2.3.3. Face Validation

Both the English and translated German versions of the NERSH questionnaire were tested for comprehension and clarity through Face Validation, interviewing HPs that had filled in the questionnaire. Adjustments were made both to the original English and the German version.

2.4. Characteristics of NERSH Questionnaire

The revised NERSH questionnaire now consists of the same sections as the original RSMPP but in different sequence and with some more items: (1) Demographics (10 items vs. originally 14 items); (2) Evaluation of Patient Values (19 items vs. 22 items); (3) Evaluation of HP's Values (16 items vs. 12 items) with proposed added modules appropriate for research in secular cultures: ASP, SpREUK (see NERSH questionnaire in English and German, including version with highlighted differences between the RSMPP and the NERSH questionnaire in Supplementary Materials S1–S3). The reason why the updated and complemented NERSH questionnaire counts fewer items is that more items have now been grouped in thematically congruent batteries following the NGT rounds as mentioned above under Section 2.3.1.

Until now the NERSH questionnaire has been translated into German and Portuguese in 2015 with data available in the NERSH pool only in German until now.

2.5. Identification of Eligible Datasets for Inclusion in NERSH International Data Pool on Values in Medicine

Research groups that had used the RSMPP and updated NERSH questionnaire were identified in three ways:

2.5.1. Personal Contacts

Farr Curlin kept record of researchers who had requested permission to use the RSMPP and shared that information with the NERSH board.

2.5.2. Citation Search

In March 2016 Hvidt and Kørup conducted a citation search in Web of Science of articles that quoted any of the original articles published on the RSMPP (Appendix B). It led to a total of 316 hits. References were screened in the Review program Covidence by the second author. A total of 292 were identified as irrelevant, 24 scanned for possible relevance, and two studies emerged of which Curlin had no knowledge, one from Brazil, the other from Saudi Arabia. They had both used parts of Curlin's questionnaire, mainly the sections on physician evaluation of spirituality among patients [12,13]. Hvidt contacted the authors who agreed to participate.

2.5.3. Systematic Search

In order to make sure that no studies had been overlooked, Hvidt and Kørup conducted a literature search in Medline, Embase, PsychInfo, Web of Science and Google Scholar. In Medline, for instance, the search string was the following: ((questionn * or survey * or cross-section * or national sample *) and (religious or religio * or spiritual * or religiosity)) adj3 (professional * or physician * or psychiatris * or doctor * or staff * or ((nurs * or medic *) adj3 professor *))).mp. [mp = title, abstract, original title, name of substance word, subject heading word, keyword heading word, protocol supplementary concept word, rare disease supplementary concept word, unique identifier]. See the detailed search strings for the other databases in Appendix C.

The search yielded 1572 hits. Hvidt and Kørup each reviewed half of these references for eligibility. The search did not identify any further studies that had used the RSMPP for data collection.

2.6. Description of Pool of Data Harvested with Versions of the RSMPP and the NERSH Instruments

Data are collected in STATA and synchronized for their comparability using a matched intersection design based on the items in the original RSMPP questionnaire. Data are stored on a secure Stata Server at the Research Unit of General Practice at the University of Southern Denmark and can be made available to all upon request.

The international pool from the NERSH collaboration at the present (April 2016) consists of data from eleven studies conducted by research teams in nine different countries over six continents (see map—Figure 1 and overview of the International NERSH Data Pool in Appendix D). All datasets are based on the original RSMPP questionnaire developed by Farr Curlin in 2002, including 48 items on "Religion and Spirituality in Medicine", and although minor alterations have been made by some of the researchers in order to optimize the tool for local settings, the primary items are included in all datasets.

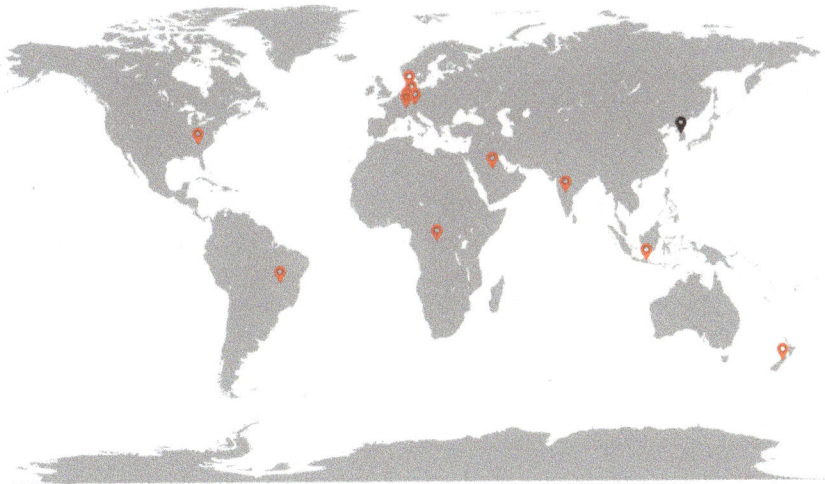

Figure 1. Map showing the countries where the NERSH data has been collected. Red pins are samples included in the NERSH pool to date, grey pins are samples soon to be included in the pool.

In Curlin's first data collection the RSMPP questionnaires was sent to a random sample of 2000 practicing U.S. Physicians with a response rate of 63%.

The first data collection using a translated version of the RSMPP was done by AlYousefi in 2009–2010. The Indonesian sample by Karimah was collected in 2010, and the Indian version was collected from 2010 to 2012 by Ramakrishnan. The Danish version was translated in 2009 but data was first collected in the years 2011–2012. Meanwhile in Freiburg, Germany, Baumann et al. collected their data using the German translation in 2008 (Pilot) and nationwide in 2011. The New Zealand, Congo and Brazil datasets were all collected entirely during 2012. Later, the nation-wide German sample by Wermuth et al. was collected over two years from 2013 to 2014. During 2014 a German sample related to transplantation medicine was performed as well as the Austrian sample of hospital workers in Salzburg. Last to be collected into the pool in 2016 were the Turkish sample of physicians working in Germany and the Swiss Sample of practitioners working outside the hospital. Data from a recent data collection from South Korea will be added in the near future.

Currently, some datasets are still in process of completion and will be added in the near future; this preliminary description thus focuses on the raw data collected from the individual research units. Additional statistics and combined statistics of the NERSH pool including reliability measures of previous suggested subscales in the original questionnaire by Lucchetti (2015) will be published in a future article once the pool has been completely established.

The NERSH data was thus collected between 2002 and 2016, and includes a total of 6137 individuals (3318 females and 2611 males plus one transgender and 207 unknown). Mean age in the studies varies from 28.4 (27.0–29.8) among the Brazilian nurse students and 29.2 (CI95% 28.4–29.9) in the Indonesian sample to 49.0 (CI95% 48.5–49.5) found in the sample of 1144 American physicians. The Danish study of 911 physicians has a mean age of 48.9 (48.0–49.8) with a bimodal distribution. The study from New Zealand only measured age in deciles, but 64.7% of the individuals lie in the range of 40 to 59 years of age, which is similar to the Danish and American study.

The pool contains 4019 physicians, 1028 nurses, 77 psychologists/psychotherapists and 1013 of other or unknown occupation. Response rates range from as low as 18% (116 responses out of 642 questionnaires sent in New Zealand) to 95% (Brazil) and 99% (Indonesia)—the latter two secured due to tight follow-up including personal meetings and encouragements to complete the forms.

The current description of the data is based on the individual contributions from NERSH collaborators. At the time of writing the data pool is still undergoing synchronization. The process of synchronization and a detailed quantitative description of the data pool will soon be published in another article by Kørup et al.

3. Results

3.1. Chronological Overview of Existing Studies Using the Original RSMPP

The first publication based on the RSMPP questionnaire was published in 2005 and centred on "Religious characteristics of U.S. physicians" [1]. The objective was to provide a description of U.S. physicians' religious characteristics compared to those of the U.S. population. Curlin found that compared to the general population, physicians in the US were less likely to say they try to carry their religious beliefs over into all their dealings with life (58% vs. 73%) and twice as likely to say they cope with life crises without relying on God (61% vs. 29%). At the same time, 55% of physicians reported that religious beliefs influence their medical practice. Curlin proposed that these findings suggested the need for attention to the way religious commitments shape clinical engagements.

The second publication from 2006 reported "The association of physicians' religious characteristics with their attitudes and self-reported behaviors regarding religion and spirituality in the clinical encounter" [2]. The vast majority of physicians agree that it is acceptable to address R/S issues if the patients bring it up, but are more reluctant to inquire about patient's R/S (45% agree), talk about their own beliefs (14% say never, 43% say only when the patient brings it up) and pray with the patient (17% say never, 43% only when patients bring it up). Religious physicians are more likely to address R/S issues in the clinical encounter across all of these measures.

The third article raised the question: "Do religious physicians disproportionately care for the underserved?" [3] Those physicians who were highly spiritual, who agreed that their religious beliefs influenced their practice of medicine, or who were raised in a family emphasizing needs of the poor were significantly more likely to report practice among the undeserved; those who were more religious were more likely to view their medical practice as a calling, but they were not more likely to practice among the undeserved.

The fourth article had an ethical focus. It was titled "Religion, conscience, and controversial clinical practices" and was published with the *New England Journal of Medicine* [4]. The article centers on the ethical rights and obligations of physicians regarding the provision of treatment to which they morally object; 63% of physicians believe it to be acceptable to disclose moral objections to patients, 86% believe that physicians are obligated to present all options to patients, and 71% agree they are obligated to refer to physicians who do not object.

The fifth article centered on differences in how psychiatrist and other physicians evaluate the R/S of their patients: "The relationship between psychiatry and religion among U.S. physicians" [5]. Psychiatrists recognize the positive influence of R/S on health but are more likely than other physicians to consider R/S being sometimes a source of patient suffering through negative emotions (82% vs. 44%), and are more likely to encounter R/S issues in their clinical setting (92% vs. 74%). Likewise, psychiatrists are more comfortable than their non-psychiatrist colleagues in addressing R/S issues with their patients.

The sixth article likewise had a particular focus on psychiatry: "The relationship between psychiatry and religion among U.S. physicians." The article documents that psychiatrists are less religious on a number of measures, although compared to other physicians they were more likely to be Jewish (29% vs. 13%) [6]. Non-psychiatrist physicians who were religious were more likely to refer patients to clergy members and religious counselors and less willing to refer them to psychologists and psychiatrists, leading to the conclusion that "historic tensions between religion and psychiatry continue to shape the care patients receive for mental health concerns".

The seventh article centered on "Physicians' observations and interpretations of the influence of religion and spirituality on health" and how such interpretations depend on physician's own R/S [7]. Sixty-three percent believed R/S influenced health of patients, 76% believed it could help patients cope with disease, give them a peaceful state of mind (75%) and provide emotional and practical help via the religious community (55%). More religious physicians were more likely to report observing positive religious health influences.

The eighth article focused on ethical dilemmas of terminal care and in particular to what degree physicians have "religious and other objections to physician-assisted suicide, terminal sedation, and withdrawal of life support." [8]. Sixty-nine percent object to the first, 18% to the second and 5% to the third practice, and objections were more pronounced among highly religious and Asian physicians, as well as among those who have more experience caring for the dying. These findings suggest that care for patients at the end of life may depend on value differences among physicians.

The ninth article (by Stern et al.) using Curlin's 2003 data focused on "Jewish physicians' beliefs and practices regarding religion/spirituality in the clinical encounter." [9]. On each of four dimensions of physician beliefs and practices regarding R/S in clinical practice, Jewish physicians ascribed less importance to the effect of R/S on health and lesser role for physicians in addressing R/S in the clinical encounter. Stern et al. found that these differences were mediated by lower R/S among Jewish physicians as well as R/S practice level and demographics, once again pointing to how R/S—here focusing on affiliation—impacts clinically-relevant beliefs.

Finally, in the tenth publication, "Physicians in the USA: Attendance, beliefs and patient interactions Franzen used the same 2003 dataset to investigate the association of Physicians' R/S attendance and beliefs with patient interactions, in particular religious support in the clinical encounter, asking what characteristics are related to inclusion or avoidance [10]. Franzen finds that R/S orientation, more than religious attendance, predicts the inclusion of R/S topics. Furthermore, Franzen found that some physician specialties have more R/S physicians than others, suggesting again that clinical interaction on R/S issues is not distributed evenly in the health care system.

In conclusion, the US studies from the RSMPP suggest that values, spirituality and religiosity impact multiple areas of health care in multiple ways.

3.2. Chronological Overview of Articles Using Translations of the RSMPP

The first article based on translations of the RSMPP was published in 2011 by Lee at al. on the basis of pilot study data collection in Freiburg, Germany and centered on "The meaning of religion/spirituality in psychiatry from staff's perspective" [11]. The survey was answered by 197 (response rate 44%) at the department of psychiatry and psychotherapy of the Freiburg University Hospital in 2009. Although 95% of the respondent considered R/S as an important patient coping strategy, they did not integrate R/S practices in their therapies, mainly due to lack of time and training as well as the fear of offending patients.

The second article written by Tomasso et al. focused on the "Knowledge and attitudes of nursing professors and students from Brazil concerning the interface between spirituality, religiosity and health" [12]. It was answered by 30 nursing professors and 118 students. 95% of participants were religiously affiliated. Similarly to the aforementioned German sample, 96% believed R/S influences patients' health. Seventy-seven percent wished to address R/S issues, but only 36% felt prepared to do so, mainly due to lack of time, fear of imposing personal beliefs and offending patients

The third article was published in 2012 by Al-Yousefi and reported "Observations of Muslim physicians regarding the influence of religion on health and their clinical approach" [13]. It was written based on data from 225 Muslim physicians working in a tertiary care hospital in Saudi Arabia. As in the aforementioned studies, 91% agreed that R/S had a positive influence on health. However, 62% believed R/S could lead patients to refuse recommended medical therapy, much higher than the 2% of physicians in Curlin's 2005 study that found R/S led patients to refuse, delay or stop medically indicated therapy. Over 50% of physicians never queried about R/S issues. Family physicians were the most likely to initiate R/S discussion, and—not surprisingly—physicians with high R/S were more likely to share own religious views. The main barriers to addressing R/S were the same as in the aforementioned studies.

The fourth article was published 2013 by Lee and Baumann on the now nationwide psychiatric staff sample and reports "German psychiatrists' observation and interpretation of religiosity/spirituality" in regard to their therapies" [14]. The data shows that German psychiatrists consider R/S influences on patients' mental health to be positive and important. It also indicates that the R/S orientation of the psychiatrists themselves significantly influences this appreciation and their attitude toward R/S in the clinical setting.

The fifth article was published in 2013 by Ramakrishnan et al. on "Perspectives of Indian traditional and allopathic professionals on religion/spirituality and its role in medicine: Basis for developing an integrative medicine program" [15]. Data was collected in five TCAM and two allopathic tertiary care medical institutes in India. Both groups (75%/85%) of practitioners believed that spiritual focus increases with illness, 58% of both groups reported that patients receive support from their religious communities and 87% of TCAM (traditional complementary and alternative medicine prescriber) and 73% of conventional medical doctors (termed "allopaths") considered spiritual healing a beneficial complement to allopathic medicine. Only 11% of allopaths and 40% of TCAMs had received training in R/S, however 82% of TCAM and 63% of allopaths considered integration of spirituality an important element of the health care system.

The sixth article from 2014 was based on the same dataset and focused on "Indian health care professionals' attitude towards spiritual healing and its role in alleviating stigma of psychiatric services" [16]. It gauged TCAM and allopathic practitioners' perspectives on patients' R/S needs in mental health services. Just below half of both groups believed that their patients approach R/S or TCAM practitioners for mental illness treatment; 91% of TCAM and 70% of allopaths were satisfied with R/S healers. 91% of TCAM and 73% of allopaths believe mental health stigma could be minimized by integration with spiritual care services.

The seventh article, also from 2014, involved a combination of the aforementioned dataset with data collected in Indonesia by Karimah et al. in a cross-cultural comparison on "Religious/spiritual characteristics of Indian and Indonesian physicians and their acceptance of spirituality in health care" [17]. The researchers investigated differences in Indian and Indonesian physicians' R/S characteristics and found Indonesian physicians to score higher on a range of R/S measures than their Indian colleagues. They also gauged different attitudes toward integration of TCAM with the modern health care system. As expected, they found Indonesian physicians (that are known for their integration of traditional medicine with modern medicine) to be more in favor of such integration than Indian physicians; the more spiritually inclined physicians, TCAM physicians in particular, were most comfortable attending to patients' spiritual needs.

The eighth article, by Lee et al. from 2014, building on the aforementioned nationwide German dataset, first published 2013 is titled: "Religiosity/spirituality and mental health: Psychiatric staff's attitudes and behaviors. It shows the tension and ambivalences of mental health staff between their readiness to integrate R/S aspects into treatment—basically considered as appropriate to be dealt with in therapies—and their attitudes and claims of professional neutrality [18].

In the ninth article, again from the Freiburg, Germany group, Lee et al. (2015) asked "How do psychiatric staffs approach religiosity/spirituality in clinical practice? Differing perceptions among psychiatric staff members and clinical chaplains" [19] and continued the research focus of their main study but also included responses from clinical chaplains and their mutual perceptions. In general, psychiatric staff members (psychiatrist, psychologists and nurses) saw themselves as "prepared and open to dealing with religiosity/spirituality in therapeutic settings". However, the perception of Chaplains differs significantly from the staff's own self-rating, leading the authors to suggest additional dialogue between the two groups of professionals with daily presence in the mental health care system. In 2014–2015, Lee and Baumann initiated a study in South Korean hospitals with psychiatric wards. Data have been collected and are going to be analyzed.

The tenth article was by Lucchetti et al., titled "Spirituality, religiosity, and health: a comparison of physicians' attitudes in Brazil, India, and Indonesia" [20]. It compared the aforementioned datasets from Brazil, India and Indonesia and found Indonesian doctors to be the most religious, Brazilian doctors to be most convinced that R/S influences health; Indonesian and Brazilian doctors were both more convinced than Indian physicians that it was appropriate to discuss R/S with patients. The authors conclude from these and other differences that "Ethnicity and culture can have an important influence on how spirituality is approached in medical practice. S/R curricula that train physicians how to address spirituality in clinical practice must take these differences into account."

As mentioned, eight doctoral theses were or are being published on the basis of translations of the RSMPP [21–28]. Their topics cover many of the topics addressed above, but their populations are often unique as in Kuseyri's sample of Turkish physicians living in Germany [23], Mukwayakala's study of physicians in Congo [24], Schouten's nationwide study of HPs in perinatal medicine [25], and Randwijk's study of highly secular Danish physicians [26].

The same conclusion emerges from the overview of the international publications from the RSMPP: Values, spirituality and religiosity impact health care in multiple ways, regardless of national and cultural settings.

3.3. Glimpse of Trends in the NERSH Data Pool of Physician Values

Preliminary analyses indicate large cross-national differences illustrated with a sample of items (see Table 1). Ninety-six percent of the 122 Indonesian physicians answered that they believe in a life after death, whereas only 20% of the Danish physicians share this belief. More than half of the American and Austrian physicians believe in life after death.

Table 1. Differences in percent of important sample items of the NERSHS Data Pool.

	Indonesia	Brazil	Austria	USA	Denmark	Congo
Do you believe there is a life after death? (%) Yes	95.9%	23.7%	64.3%	58.5%	20.3%	-
My whole approach to life is based on my religion (%) Agree or Strongly Agree	92.6%	36.1%	-	41.1%	10.6%	51.8%
When r/s topics come up in conversation, I pray with the patient (%) Never	39.5%	7.2%	71.4%	43.7%	90.5%	28.6%
When r/s topics come up in the conversation, I respectfully share my own religious ideas and experiences (%) Never	11.4%	6.2%	32.1%	25.2%	55.2%	0.0%
In general is it appropriate or inappropriate for a physician to discuss religious/spiritual issues when a patient brings them up? (%) Always appropriate + Usually appropriate	90.2%	99.0%	96.0%	92.2%	83.3%	67.0%

When physicians were asked if they agreed or strongly agreed with the statement that their whole approach to life is based on their religion, 93% of the Indonesian sample agree with this, whereas only 11% of the Danish physicians agree. In cases where religious or spiritual topics arise in the clinical setting 91% of Danish physicians would never pray with the patient, while in Brazil only 7% answered that they would never pray with the patient. Likewise, 55% of Danish physicians would never share their own religious ideas and experiences, while only 6% of the Brazilian doctors and none of the physicians from Congo selected that answer.

More than 9 out of 10 of the physicians from Indonesia, Brazil, Austria and USA find it appropriate for physicians to discuss religious or spiritual issues when a patient brings them up in the clinical setting (Item marked either Always appropriate or Usually appropriate). For Denmark, this proportion is 83% and for Congo this is surprisingly low at 67%. The German samples cover specific groups of physicians with specific results for these groups.

As mentioned we are currently working on another article for a more in-depth quantitative description of the data pool including an overview of the distribution of participant occupation and religious affiliation across the included countries.

4. Summary

The NERSH survey instrument has been found to work well across cultures, and with a few optimizations and additions targeting secular cultures, it holds promise as a tool for future comparative analyses. Data are comparable and individual publications until now as well as initial analyses of the joint data pool suggest that large differences do exist across nations and cultures.

The articles published from versions of the RSMPP and data collected with the RSMPP and updated NERSH instruments already suggest three important initial insights:

1. In the eyes of HPs, R/S is an important element of the life of patients. R/S may help patients cope with their disease and may positively influence their health. However, HPs also report various barriers for engaging their patients on R/S themes. These are mainly centred on lack of training, lack of time and fear of offending patients or imposing own beliefs on them.
2. The idea that health care is a value neutral sphere, mainly driven by a scientifically neutral and "objective" approach, is challenged by research. HP values (both R/S and atheistic) are subjective, personal, and deep. They have a profound influence on communication with patients, in particular when it comes to existential and R/S issues, controversial issues in Health Care, and understanding of one's own professional identity.
3. Just as HPs' personal values impact health care (communication, ethics and professional identity), so are the same values highly impacted by culture. This is clear in the enormous differences in R/S when comparing for instance Denmark with Brazil and the impact these differences have on HPs evaluation of patient R/S. This insight might help HPs to adopt a humble attitude

while reflecting on the context of their own values, which may lead to improved attention to the particular values and needs of patients, be they atheist or R/S. Such reflecting may improve critical ethical reflection, increase respect for both religious and agnostic worldviews and improve communication with patients in their search for resources for dealing with their illness.

5. Invitation for Researchers to Join and Availability of Questionnaire

The development of the NERSH International Collaboration on Values in Medicine is considered an ongoing process. Researchers who wish to publish research papers on the existing NERSH data are invited to contact the NERSH board and propose what article they would like to publish on the data, with a proposed title and abstract. Researchers who contributed with original data have first priority, but apart from that article ideas are allocated to potential first authors in the order that the ideas are presented to the board.

Likewise, we invite researchers to use the updated NERSH Questionnaire to complement the existing NERSH Pool with data from their respective data. In particular, data is needed from the Slavic cultures. A written NERSH Agreement has been drafted for those who wish to participate in the NERSH International Collaboration on Values in Medicine. It stipulates the rights of all participants to be invited as co-authors on articles that employ data they contributed, and allows the NERSH collaborators the rights to propose articles and to use the data accordingly, as long as the NERSH board is in agreement. Another identical Agreement exists that further stipulates the rights to use the NERSH Questionnaire and contribute data as mentioned above. All who contribute to the pool co-authoring this article have signed this Agreement. Users of the NERSH questionnaire are requested to code their data according to the NERSH Physician Values Coding Manual, available on the Toolbox of www.nersh.org.

6. Limitations

The NERSH collaboration depends on the rigor of each research team involved and shares the limitations reported by each individual research article to which we refer [1–28]. Not all sample sizes and response rates are equally good which may impact generalizability of findings.

Comparability of data for future joint NERSH articles will be challenged by the fact that some themes are inquired upon with different numbers of items, response categories, and formulations, that may even have different meanings in different cultural contexts. How we address these challenges and potential limitations in the existing dataset will be one of the issues of the next upcoming article of the NERSH collaboration. As mentioned in the present article, one of the primary incentives of the development of the optimized NERSH questionnaire was precisely to address some of these limitations in future data collections.

Finally, the NERSH database could benefit from future data collections from cultures under-represented or not represented at all, such as the Slavic countries in order to reflect a higher degree of global representability.

Supplementary Materials: The optimized NERSH instrument is available in the supplementary material under www.mdpi.com/2077-1444/7/8/107/s1 in English for physicians (Figure S1) and all HPs (Figure S2) as well as German for physicians (Figure S3) and all HPs (Figure S4); we provide a version in which differences between the original RSMPP and the updated NERSH have been noted in the margin (Figure S5). The final versions S1, S2, S3, and S4 are available as well on the Toolbox menu of www.nersh.org. Researchers wishing to use the NERSH questionnaire are invited to contact the first author and NERSH coordinator Niels Christian Hvidt.

Acknowledgments: We wish to thank the Freiburg Institute for Advanced Studies (FRIAS) for financial, institutional and practical support for the NERSH initiation. The original RSMPP was supported by The Robert Wood Johnson Foundation and The Greenwall Foundation The Danish study received funding from I.M. Dæhnfeldt Foundation, from The Danish College of General Practitioners as well as from the Faculty of Health Sciences, University of Southern Denmark. The Freiburg study received a starting grant by the innovative research fund of Albert-Ludwig-University Freiburg, Germany; we are grateful to Mathias Berger MD, Ulrich Voderholzer MD and Anne Zahn MD (who coauthored some of the Freiburg articles) for their support and cooperation. The Indonesian study received funding from the AdiBhat foundation; we are greatful to

Kuntaman Kuntaman, MD, PhD, for coordinating the study between India and Indonesia and participating on paper writing. The Brazilian group expresses gratitude to Claudia Tomasso RN, Gabriela Romano MD and Alessandra Lucchetti MD (who coauthored some of the Brazilian articles) for their support and cooperation. The Indian study was made possible by the generosity in time, personal and financial support of HELP and AdiBhat Foundations in USA and India, respectively. The HELP Foundation is a nonprofit organization in Omaha, NE, USA, serving the underprivileged population with its community-based urgent care clinics. AdiBhat is a nonprofit organization founded in New Delhi to develop spirituality as a medical subject. The Indonesia study received funding as well from the AdiBhat Foundation. Kuntaman Kuntaman, MD, PhD, is acknowledged for coordinating the study between India and Indonesia and participating on paper writing.

Author Contributions:

Niels Christian Hvidt, wrote the article, conceived, designed, performed the experiments for the local data collections, he was involved with, co-founder and coordinator of the NERSH-Network;

Alex Kappel Kørup, managed the joint NERSH-database, analyzed the data, contributed to the writing of the article;

Farr A. Curlin, conceived, designed, performed the experiments for the original data collection RSMPP questionnaire and data collection, contributed to the writing of the article;

Klaus Baumann, conceived, designed, performed the experiments for the local data collection, he was involved with, co-founder of the NERSH-Network;

Eckhard Frick, conceived, designed, performed the experiments for the local data collection, he was involved with, co-founder of the NERSH-Network;

Jens Søndergaard, hosting of NERSH-database, research oversight;

Jesper Bo Nielsen, hosting of NERSH-database, research oversight;

René dePont Christensen, statistical oversight on final NERSH-database;

Ryan Lawrence, conceived, designed, performed the experiments for the local data collection, he was involved with;

Giancarlo Lucchetti, conceived, designed, performed the experiments for the local data collection, he was involved with;

Parameshwaran Ramakrishnan, conceived, designed, performed the experiments for the local data collection, he was involved with;

Azimatul Karimah, conceived, designed, performed the experiments for the local data collection, she was involved with;

Andreas Schulze, conceived, designed, performed the experiments for the local data collection, he was involved with;

Inga Wermuth, conceived, designed, performed the experiments for the local data collection, she was involved with;

Esther Schouten, conceived, designed, performed the experiments for the local data collection, she was involved with;

René Hefti, conceived, designed, performed the experiments for the local data collection, he was involved with;

Eunmi Lee, conceived, designed, performed the experiments for the local data collection, she was involved with;

Nada A. AlYousefi, conceived, designed, performed the experiments for the local data collection, she was involved with;

Christian Balslev van Randwijk, conceived, designed, performed the experiments for the local data collection, he was involved with;

Can Kuseyri, conceived, designed, performed the experiments for the local data collection, he was involved with;

Tryphon Mukwayakala, conceived, designed, performed the experiments for the local data collection, he was involved with;

Miriam Wey, conceived, designed, performed the experiments for the local data collection, she was involved with;

Micha Eglin, conceived, designed, performed the experiments for the local data collection, she was involved with;

Tobias Opsahl, contributed to materials;

Arndt Büssing, analysed the data, contributed to the writing of the paper, co-founder of the NERSH-Network.

Conflicts of Interest: The authors declare no conflict of interest.

Abbreviations

The following abbreviations are used in this manuscript:

ASP	Aspects of Spirituality
DUREL	Duke Religiosity Index
FRIAS	Freiburg Institute for Advanced Studies
HPs	Health Professionals

IRG	Interdisciplinary Research Group
NERSH	Network for Research in Spirituality and Health
NGT	Nominal Group Technique
R/S	R/s understood as a unit of both, although they conceptually and phenomenologically have different traits
RSMPP	Questionnaire Religion and Spirituality in Medicine: Physicians' Perspectives
SpREUK	Spiritual and Religious Attitudes in Dealing with Illness
TCAM	Traditional Complementary and Alternative Medicine

Appendix A

Item Complexes

- Item complex #20: Positive experience of r/s in the clinical practice (i.e., helps patients to cope with and endure illness and suffering; causes guilt, anxiety, or other negative emotions that lead to increased patient suffering; gives patients a positive, hopeful state of mind; leads patients to refuse, delay, or stop medically indicated therapy; helps to prevent severe consequences of disease, etc.). Cronbach's alphas ranged from 0.60 to 0.79 between the four samples. This indicates that the putative scale is of questionable to acceptable internal validity. Therefore, we added additional items as used in the Freiburg sample that had the best internal reliability with a 6-item version of the scale (i.e., adding: patients receive emotional or practical support from their religious community; religiosity/spirituality in general influences the health of patients/relatives positively; is strengthened or deepened through the experience of illness).
- Item complex # 21: Inquiry about religious/spiritual issues in specific situations (i.e., When a patient presents with a minor illness or injury; faces a frightening diagnosis or crisis; faces the end of life; suffers from anxiety or depression; comes for a history and physical; faces an ethical quandary). This topic was addressed in four datasets; Cronbach's alpha ranged from 0.83 to 0.90 which indicates a good to very good internal reliability of this putative scale.
- Item complex #22: Frequency of specific responses when religious/spiritual issues come up in discussions with patients (i.e., listen carefully and empathetically; try to change the subject in a tactful way; encourage patients in their own religious/spiritual beliefs and practices; respectfully share my own religious ideas and experiences; pray with the patient). This topic was addressed in five datasets, but was found to be of questionable to acceptable internal validity (Cronbach's alpha ranged from 0.61 to 0.74).
- Item complex #28: Controversial Issues in Medicine (i.e., Physician assisted suicide; Sedation to unconsciousness in dying patients; Withdrawal of artificial life support; Abortion for congenital abnormalities; Abortion for failed contraception; Prescription of birth control to teenagers between the age of 14 and 16 if their parents do not approve). This topic was addressed in four datasets, and was found to be of questionable to acceptable internal validity (Cronbach's alpha ranged from 0.62 to 0.78).

Appendix B Citation Search in Web of Science

Table B1. Overview of Citation Search in Web of Science.

ID	Term(s)	Results
1	Religious characteristics of US physicians–A national survey [1]	1
2	Citing articles	85

ID	Term(s)	Results
1	The association of physicians' religious characteristics with their attitudes and self-reported behaviors regarding religion and spirituality in the clinical encounter [2]	1
2	Citing articles	59

ID	Term(s)	Results
1	Do religious physicians disproportionately care for the underserved? [3]	1
2	Citing articles	15

ID	Term(s)	Results
1	Religion, conscience, and controversial clinical practices AND Curlin [4]	1
2	Citing articles	131

ID	Term(s)	Results
1	Religion, spirituality, and medicine: Psychiatrists' and other physicians' differing observations, interpretations, and clinical approaches [5]	1
2	Citing articles	46

ID	Term(s)	Results
1	The relationship between psychiatry and religion among US physicians [6]	1
2	Citing articles	32

ID	Term(s)	Results
1	Physicians' observations and interpretations of the influence of religion and spirituality on health [7]	1
2	Citing articles	43

ID	Term(s)	Results
1	To die, to sleep: US physicians' religious and other objections to physician-assisted suicide, terminal sedation, and withdrawal of life support [8]	1
2	Citing articles	34

Appendix C Literature Search

Table C1. Overview.

Database	Interface	Date of Search
Google Scholar	Internet	12-04-16
Web of Science	Internet	13-04-16
Embase	Ovid	12-04-16
Medline	Ovid	13-04-16
PsychInfo	Ovid	13-04-16

Table C2. Google Scholar.

ID	Term(s)	Results
1	"Religion and Spirituality in Medicine: Physicians' Perspectives"	8

Table C3. Web of Science.

ID	Term(s)	Results
1	TOPIC:(((questionn * OR survey * OR cross-section * OR national sample *) AND (religious OR religio * OR spiritual * OR religiosity) near/3 (professional * OR physician * OR psychiatris * OR doctor * OR staff * OR ((nurs * or medic *) near/3 (professor *)))))	308
2	Refined by: LANGUAGES: (ENGLISH OR DANISH OR SPANISH OR FRENCH OR GERMAN) Timespan: All years. Search language = Auto	305

Table C4. Embase (Embase + Embase Classic).

ID	Term(s)	Results
1	(((questionn * or survey * or cross-section * or national sample *) and (religious or religio * or spiritual * or religiosity)) adj3 (professional * or physician * or psychiatris * or doctor * or staff * or ((nurs * or medic *) adj3 professor *))).mp. [mp = title, abstract, heading word, drug trade name, original title, device manufacturer, drug manufacturer, device trade name, keyword]	1431
2	limit 1 to (danish or english or french or german or italian or norwegian or spanish or swedish)	1400

Table C5. Medline.

ID	Term(s)	Results
1	((questionn * or survey * or cross-section * or national sample *) and (religious or religio * or spiritual * or religiosity)) adj3 (professional * or physician * or psychiatris * or doctor * or staff * or ((nurs * or medic *) adj3 professor *))).mp. [mp = title, abstract, original title, name of substance word, subject heading word, keyword heading word, protocol supplementary concept word, rare disease supplementary concept word, unique identifier]	1021
2	limit 1 to (danish or english or french or german or italian or norwegian or spanish or swedish)	998

Table C6. PsychInfo.

ID	Term(s)	Results
1	(((questionn * or survey * or cross-section * or national sample *) and (religious or religio * or spiritual * or religiosity)) adj3 (professional * or physician * or psychiatris * or doctor * or staff * or ((nurs * or medic *) adj3 professor *))).mp. [mp = title, abstract, heading word, table of contents, key concepts, original title, tests & measures]	829
2	limit 1 to (danish or english or french or german or italian or norwegian or spanish or swedish)	804

Appendix D

Table D1. Overview of the International NERSH Data Pool.

Country	Location	Sampling Year(s)	Occupation	n	Specialties	n	%	Religious Affiliation (%)	n	%	n_total	RR*	Gender	n	%	Mean Age (CI95%)
USA	Nationwide	2002	All physicians		Anesthesiology	39	3.4	None	80	7.0	1144	63%	Male	842	73.6	49.0 (48.5-49.5)
					General Pract	17	1.5	Atheist	19	1.7			Female	300	26.2	
					Neuro	18	1.6	Agnostic	18	1.6			n/a	2	0.2	
					OB/GYN	80	7.0	Buddhist	13	1.1						
					Optho	18	1.6	Hindu	54	4.7						
					Pathology	20	1.7	Jewish	181	15.8						
					Peds – General	87	7.6	Mormon	17	1.5						
					Physiatry	16	1.4	Muslim	33	2.9						
					Psych	100	8.7	Protestants	428	37.4						
					Ped Subspec.	60	5.2	Catholic	244	21.3						
					Gen Med	129	11.3	Orthodox	22	1.9						
					FP	158	13.8	Other	18	1.6						
					EM	15	1.3	Unanswered	17	1.5						
					Dermatology	11	1.0									
					Med Subspec.	231	20.2									
					Radiology	25	2.2									
					Unanswered	2	0.2									
					General Surgery	23	2.0									
					Surg Subsp.	77	6.7									
					Other	18	1.6									
Germany	Freiburg, University clinic	2008-2009	Mixed psychiatric staff		Physicians	18	21.1	Protestants	30	34.9	87	44%	Male	38	43.2	41.5
					Psychologists and psychotherapists	11	12.9	Catholics	28	32.5			Female	49	56.8	
					Nursing staff	39	44.7	No affiliation	23	26.5						
					Other psychiatric staff	18	21.2									
Saudi Arabia	Riyadh, King Abdul-Aziz Medical City	2009-2010	All physicians		Family medicine	73	32.4	Muslim	225	100	225	64%	Male	128	56.9	36.6 (35.4-37.6)
					Internal med. and subspec.	38	16.9						Female	97	43.1	
					OB/GYN	31	13.8									
					Pediatrics	21	9.3									
					Surgical subspec.	30	13.3									
					Emergency med.	9	4									
					Oncology and palliative care	19	8.4									
					ICU and anaesthesia	4	1.8									

Table D1. *Cont.*

Country	Location	Sampling Year(s)	Occupation	n	Specialties	n	%	Religious Affiliation (%)	n	%	n$_{total}$	RR*	Gender	n	%	Mean Age (CI95%)
Indonesia	Dr. Soetomo General Hospital, Surabaya, East Java	2010	All physicians		Anatomy	1	0.8	None	2	1.6	122	99%	Male	55	45.1	29.2 (28.4–29.9)
					Microbiology	1	2.5	Other	7	5.7			Female	65	53.3	
					Pathology	3	1.6	Hindu	2	1.6			n/a	2	1.6	
					Forensic	1	0.88	Christian	7	5.7						
					Ophtalmology	10	8.2	Muslim	104	85.2						
					ENT	1	0.8									
					Pediatric	2	1.6									
					General medicine	23	18.9									
					Surgery	14	11.5									
					OBG	7	5.7									
					Psychiatry/neurology	17	13.9									
					Radiology	8	6.6									
					Anesthesiology	8	6.6									
					Psychotherapist	1	0.8									
					Unanswered	14	11.5									
Brazil	São Paulo	2010	Teachers	30	Nursing			**Teachers**			148	99%	Male	15	10.1	Teachers 41.4 (38.6–44.2)
			Students	118				Catholics	25	16.7			Female	133	89.9	Students 28.4 (27.0–29.8)
								Spiritists	20	13.3						
								Evangelical	20	13.3						
								Students								
								Catholics, 30.8%	46	30.8						
								Evangelicals, 11.1%	16	11.1						
								None or others	22	14.8						
Germany, Freiburg	Nationwide. Departments of psychiatry and psychotherapy in university clinics + faith based clinics.	2010–2011	Psychiatrist	121	All psychiatry			No affiliation	88	21.8	404	24%	Male	145	35.9	39.9 (38.8–41)
			Psychotherapist	16				Catholic	115	28.5			Female	252	62.4	
			Other therapeut	25				Protestant	128	31.7			n/a	7	1.7	
			Psychologist	32				Free Church	10	2.5						
			Nurse or assistant	160				Orthodox	1	0.2						
			Other	32				Muslim	5	1.2						
								Buddhist	7	1.7						
								Agnostic/Atheist	34	8.4						
								Other	9	2.2						

Religions **2016**, *7*, 107

Table D1. *Cont.*

Country	Location	Sampling Year(s)	Occupation	n	Specialties	n	%	Religious Affiliation (%)	n	%	n_total	RR*	Gender	n	%	Mean Age (CI95%)
India	Selected hospitals	2010–2012	TCAM		Anatomy	8	2	None or others	11	3.7	394	50%	Male	148	37.6	31.6 (30.5–32.8)
			-Physicians	192	Physiology	15	3.8	Hindu	257	65.2			Female	230	58.4	
			-Nurses	79	Biochemistry	5	1.3	Christian	54	13.7			n/a	16	4	
			-Residents	0	Pharmacology	23	5.8	Muslim	58	14.7						
			-Interns	48	Microbiology	4	1									
			-Students	0	Pathology	7	1.8									
			-All-Therapists	36	Forensic	6	1.5									
			-Non-clinical physicians	0	Opthalmology	1	0.3									
			-Unknown	13	ENT	11	2.8									
			Allopaths	16	PSM	12	3.0									
			-Physicians	201	Gen medicine	49	12.4									
			-Nurses	54	Surgery	4	1.0									
			-Residents	29	OBG	16	4.0									
			-Interns	44	Psychiatry+neuro	57	14.5									
			-Students	0	Pediatrics	26	6.6									
			-All-Therapists	33	Radiology	0	0									
			-Non-clinical physicians	0	Anesthesiology	18	4.6									
			-Unknown	35	Psychotherapist	16	4.1									
				6	Physical medicine and rehab +spec.	18	4.6									
Denmark	Nationwide, selection criteria?	2011–2012	All physicians		General practitioner	261	28.6	Missing 8 (0.9)	8	0.9	911	61%	Male	524	57.5	48.9 (48.0–49.8)
					Mixed hospital physicians	650	71.4	Do not wish to answer	4	0.4			Female	387	42.5	
								No affiliation	183	20.1						
								Other	20	2.2						
								Buddhist	2	0.2						
								Hindu	1	0.1						
								Muslim	6	0.7						
								The Orthodox Church	11	1.2						
								Roman Catholic Church	29	3.2						
								Danish National Church	647	71.0						
								Other	4	0.4						
New Zealand	Psychiatry	2012	Psychiatrists	91	All psychiatry			No affiliation	53	45.7	116	18%	Male	73	62.9	Agegroups (n)
			Non specialists	25				Christian	42	36.2			Female	39	33.6	20-29 4
								Buddhist	3	2.6			Trans-gender	1	0.9	30-39 19
								Hindu	4	3.4			n/a	3	2.6	40-49 32
								Other	4	3.4						50-59 43
								Object to answer	3	2.6						60-69 14
								Unanswered	7	6.0						70+ 3

Table D1. *Cont.*

Country	Location	Sampling Year(s)	Occupation	n	Specialties	n	%	Religious Affiliation (%)	n	%	n_total	RR*	Gender	n	%	Mean Age (CI95%)
Brazil	Marília - Marília University Hospital	2012	Physicians	81	Internal Med.	146	75.3	None	9	7.4	194	95%	Male	145	74.7	37.7 (36.1–39.3)
			Residents	113	Pediatricians	12	6.2	Other	0	0			Female	49	25.3	
					Surgeons/surgical physicians	26	13.4	Hindu	0	0						
					Ob/GYN	10	5.2	Christian	166	94.9						
								Muslim	0	0						
Congo R.D.	University Hospital of Kinshasa	2012	Mixed hospital physicians		No data			No affiliation	12	11	112	82%	Male	84	75	35 (33.5–36.8)
								Roman Catholics	43	38			Female	28	25	
								Orthodox Christians	1	1						
								Protestant Christians	22	10						
								Others	34	30						
Germany, Munich	Nationwide Perinatal	2013–2014	Physicians	482	Perinatal hospital professionals			Does not apply	115	7	1,637	82%	Male	192	11.7	39.1 (38.6–39.6)
			Midwife	257				No response	15	0.9			Female	1312	80.1	
			Nurses	529				None	409	25.0			n/a	133	8.1	
			Psychologist	18				Roman	639	39.0						
			Others	351				Orthodox	8	0.5						
								Protestant (without Free-Church)	409	25.0						
								Other Christian denominations								
								Islam	21	1.3						
								Jewish	13	0.8						
								Buddhist	1	0.1						
								Other	6	0.4						
								non-Christian denominations	1	0.1						
Germany, Munich	Transplantation medicine	2014	Physician	48	Internal med.	3	1.6				187	64%	Male	53	28.3	34.6 (32.9–36.3)
			Nurse	127	Intensive care	88	47.1						Female	134	71.7	
			Other	12	Surgery	38	20.3									
					Neurology	7	3.7									
					Anesthesiology	19	10.2									
					Other	32	17.1									
Austria, Salzburg	Brothers of Mercy hospital	2014	Physician	28	Internal medicine	54	23	Not religious	29	13	231	52%	Male	54	23	39.3 (37.7–41.0)
			Nursing care	114	Surgery	37	16	Catholic	143	62			Female	133	58	
			Other	29	Anesthetics	12	5	Protestant	8	3			n/a	44	19	
			Unanswered	60	Others	62	27	Others	6	8						
					Unanswered	66	29	Unanswered,	45	19						

Table D1. *Cont.*

Country	Location	Sampling Year(s)	Occupation	n	Specialties	n	%	Religious Affiliation (%)	n	%	n_total	RR*	Gender	n	%	Mean Age (CI95%)
Switzerland	Region of Bale and Aarau	2015–2016	All physicians, practicing outside the hospital		General practitioner	104	100	Christian	80	76.2	104	75%	Male	73	70.5	53.8 (51.9–55.7)
								Jewish	2	1.9			Female	31	29.5	
								Islam	2	1.9						
								No affiliation	19	18.1						
								Unanswered	2	1.9						
Germany, Munich	Turkish physicians	2016	All physicians		Psychiatry + psychotherapists	9	7.4	Muslim	79	65.3	121	22%	Male	42	34.8	33.2 (31.7–34.7)
					Anesthetics	1	0.8	No affiliation	21	17.4			Female	79	65.3	
					Orthopedics	4	3.3	Exited a religious community	1	0.8						
					Intensive care	3	2.5	Roman catholic	1	0.8						
					OB/GYN	5	4.1	Other	1	0.8						
					Internal medicine	16	13.2	Unanswered	18	14.9						
					Surgery	17	14									
					Neurology	10	8.3									
					Pediatric	9	7.4									
					Other 28	28	23.1									
					Unanswered	19	15.7									

Note: * = Response Rat.

References

1. Curlin, Farr A., John D. Lantos, Chad J. Roach, Sarah A. Sellergren, and Marshall H. Chin. "Religious Characteristics of U.S. Physicians: A National Survey." *Journal of General Internal Medicine* 20 (2005): 629–34. [CrossRef] [PubMed]
2. Curlin, Farr A., Marshall H. Chin, Sarah A. Sellergren, Chad J. Roach, and John D. Lantos. "The Association of Physicians' Religious Characteristics with Their Attitudes and Self-Reported Behaviors Regarding Religion and Spirituality in the Clinical Encounter." *Medical Care* 44 (2006): 446–53. [CrossRef] [PubMed]
3. Curlin, Farr A., Lydia S. Dugdale, John D. Lantos, and Marshall H. Chin. "Do religious physicians disproportionately care for the underserved? " *The Annals of Family Medicine* 5 (2007): 353–60. [CrossRef] [PubMed]
4. Curlin, Farr A., Ryan E. Lawrence, Marshall H. Chin, and John D. Lantos. "Religion, Conscience, and Controversial Clinical Practices." *New England Journal of Medicine* 356 (2007): 593–600. [CrossRef] [PubMed]
5. Curlin, Farr A., Ryan E. Lawrence, Shaun Odell, Marshall H. Chin, John D. Lantos, Harold G. Koenig, and Keith G. Meador. "Religion, Spirituality, and Medicine: Psychiatrists' and Other Physicians' Differing Observations, Interpretations, and Clinical Approaches." *American Journal of Psychiatry* 164 (2007): 1825–31. [CrossRef] [PubMed]
6. Curlin, Farr A., Shaun V. Odell, Ryan E. Lawrence, Marshall H. Chin, John D. Lantos, Keith G. Meador, and Harold G. Koenig. "The Relationship between Psychiatry and Religion among U.S. Physicians." *Psychiatric Services* 58 (2007): 1193–208. [CrossRef] [PubMed]
7. Curlin, Farr A., Sarah A. Sellergren, John D. Lantos, and Marshall H. Chin. "Physicians' Observations and Interpretations of the Influence of Religion and Spirituality on Health." *Archives of Internal Medicine* 167 (2007): 649–54. [CrossRef] [PubMed]
8. Curlin, Farr A., Chinyere Nwodim, Jennifer L. Vance, Marshall H. Chin, and John D. Lantos. "To Die, to Sleep: Us Physicians' Religious and Other Objections to Physician-Assisted Suicide, Terminal Sedation, and Withdrawal of Life Support." *American Journal of Hospice and Palliative Medicine* 25 (2008): 112–20. [CrossRef] [PubMed]
9. Stern, Robert M., Kenneth A. Rasinski, and Farr A. Curlin. "Jewish Physicians' Beliefs and Practices Regarding Religion/Spirituality in the Clinical Encounter." *Journal of Religion and Health* 50 (2011): 806–17. [CrossRef] [PubMed]
10. Franzen, Aaron B. "Physicians in the USA: Attendance, Beliefs and Patient Interactions." *Journal of Religion and Health* 54 (2015): 1886–900. [CrossRef] [PubMed]
11. Baumann, Klaus, Eunmi Lee, and Anne Zahn. "'Religion in Psychiatry and Psychotherapy?' A Pilot Study: The Meaning of Religiosity/Spirituality from Staff's Perspective in Psychiatry and Psychotherapy." *Religions* 2 (2011): 525–35.
12. Tomasso, Claudia de Souza, Ideraldo Luiz Beltrame, and Giancarlo Lucchetti. "Knowledge and Attitudes of Nursing Professors and Students Concerning the Interface between Spirituality, Religiosity and Health." *Revista Latino-Americana De Enfermagem* 19 (2011): 1205–13. [CrossRef]
13. Al-Yousefi, Nada A. "Observations of Muslim Physicians Regarding the Influence of Religion on Health and Their Clinical Approach." *Journal of Religion and Health* 51 (2012): 269–80. [CrossRef] [PubMed]
14. Lee, Eunmi, and Klaus Baumann. "German Psychiatrists' Observation and Interpretation of Religiosity/Spirituality." *Evidence-Based Complementary and Alternative Medicine* 2013 (2013): article 280168. [CrossRef] [PubMed]
15. Ramakrishnan, P., A. Dias, A. Rane, A. Shukla, S. Lakshmi, B. K. Ansari, R. S. Ramaswamy, A. R. Reddy, A. Tribulato, A. K. Agarwal, and et al. "Perspectives of Indian Traditional and Allopathic Professionals on Religion/Spirituality and Its Role in Medicine: Basis for Developing an Integrative Medicine Program." *Journal of Religion and Health* 53 (2013): 1161–75. [CrossRef] [PubMed]
16. Ramakrishnan, P., A. Rane, A. Dias, J. Bhat, A. Shukla, S. Lakshmi, B. K. Ansari, R. S. Ramaswamy, R. A. Reddy, A. Tribulato, and et al. "Indian Health Care Professionals' Attitude Towards Spiritual Healing and Its Role in Alleviating Stigma of Psychiatric Services." *Journal of Religion and Health* 53 (2014): 1800–14. [CrossRef] [PubMed]

17. Ramakrishnan, P., A. Karimah, K. Kuntaman, A. Shukla, B. K. Ansari, P. H. Rao, M. Ahmed, A. Tribulato, A. K. Agarwal, H. G. Koenig, and et al. "Religious/Spiritual Characteristics of Indian and Indonesian Physicians and Their Acceptance of Spirituality in Health Care: A Cross-Cultural Comparison." *Journal of Religion and Health* 54 (2014): 649–63. [CrossRef] [PubMed]

18. Lee, Eunmi, Anne Zahn, and Klaus Baumann. "Religiosity/Spirituality and Mental Health: Psychiatric Staff's Attitudes and Behaviors." *Open Journal of Social Sciences* 2 (2014): 7. [CrossRef]

19. Lee, Eunmi, Anne Zahn, and Klaus Baumann. "How Do Psychiatric Staffs Approach Religiosity/Spirituality in Clinical Practice? Differing Perceptions among Psychiatric Staff Members and Clinical Chaplains." *Religions* 6 (2015): 930–47. [CrossRef]

20. Lucchetti, Giancarlo, Parameshwaran Ramakrishnan, Azimatul Karimah, Gabriela R. Oliveira, Amit Dias, Anil Rane, A. Shukla, S. Lakshmi, B. K. Ansari, R. S. Ramaswamy, and et al. "Spirituality, Religiosity, and Health: A Comparison of Physicians' Attitudes in Brazil, India, and Indonesia." *International Journal of Behavioral Medicine* 23 (2016): 63–70. [CrossRef] [PubMed]

21. Butcher, Wyatt. "Spirituality, Religion and Psychiatric Practice in New Zealand: A Survey of Psychiatrists in New Zealand." 2013. Available online: https://ourarchive.otago.ac.nz/handle/10523/242/browse?value=Butcher%2C+Wyatt+Hillary&type=author (accessed on 5 April 2016).

22. Lee, Eunmi. *Religiosität Bzw. Spiritualität in Psychiatrie Und Psychotherapie. Ihre Bedeutung Für Psychiatrisches Wirken Aus Der Sicht Des Psychiatrischen Personals Anhand Einer Bundesweiten Personalbefragung.* Studien Zur Theologie Und Praxis Der Caritas Und Sozialen Pastoral, 28. Würzburg: Echter, 2014.

23. Kuseyri, Can. "Spiritualität Türkischstämmiger Ärzte in Deutschland." MD Thesis (German Dr.med.), Ludwig Maximilian University, 2016, forthcoming. Available online: http://www.nersh.org (accessed on 6 August 2016).

24. Mukwayakala-Kisamba, Tryphon. "Spiritualität Bei Ärzten Im Kongo." MD Thesis (German Dr.med.), Ludwig Maximilian University, 2016, forthcoming. Available online: http://www.nersh.org (accessed on 6 August 2016).

25. Schouten, Esther. "Spiritualität in Der Perinatologie." MD Thesis (German Dr.med.), Ludwig Maximilian University, 2016, forthcoming. Available online: http://www.nersh.org (accessed on 6 August 2016).

26. Van Randwijk, Christian Balslev. "Faith and Values of Danish Physicians." Ph.D. Dissertation, University of Southern Denmark, 2016, forthcoming. Available online: http://www.nersh.org (accessed on 6 August 2016).

27. Eglin, Micha. "Religious Beliefs and Patient Observation in Swiss General Practitioners." MD Thesis (Swiss Dr.Med.), University of Basel, 2016. forthcoming. Available online: http://www.nersh.org (accessed on 6 August 2016).

28. Wey, Miriam. "Religious Beliefs and Medical Practice in Swiss General Practitioners." MD Thesis (Swiss Dr.Med.), University of Basel, 2016. forthcoming. Available online: http://www.nersh.org (accessed on 6 August 2016).

29. Hall, Daniel E., Harold G. Koenig, and Keith G. Meador. "Conceptualizing 'Religion'." *Perspectives in Biology and Medicine* 47 (2004): 386–401. [CrossRef] [PubMed]

30. Hill, Peter C., Kenneth Pargament II, Ralph W. Hood, Jr., Michael E. McCullough, James P. Swyers, David B. Larson, and Brian J. Zinnbauer. "Conceptualizing Religion and Spirituality: Points of Commonality, Points of Departure." *Journal for the Theory of Social Behaviour* 30 (2000): 51–77. [CrossRef]

31. La Cour, Peter, and Niels Christian Hvidt. "Research on Meaning-Making and Health in Secular Society: Secular, Spiritual and Religious Existential Orientations." *Social Science & Medicine* 71 (2010): 1292–99. [CrossRef] [PubMed]

32. Porterfield, Amanda. *Healing in the History of Christianity.* New York: Oxford University Press, 2005.

33. "Lancet Series on Faith-Based Health Care." Available online: http://www.thelancet.com/series/faith-based-health-care (accessed on 6 April 2016).

34. Freud, Sigmund. *Civilizations and Its Discontents.* New York: W. W. Norton, 1959.

35. Baumann, Klaus. "The Birth of Human Sciences, Especially Psychology." In *L'uomo Moderno E La Chiesa—Atti Del Congresso (Analecta Gregoriana, 317).* Edited by Paul Gilbert. Rome: Gregorian & Biblical Press, 2012, pp. 391–408.

36. Koenig, Harold G., Dana E. King, and Verna Benner Carson. *Handbook of Religion and Health,* 2nd ed. Oxford and New York: Oxford University Press, 2012.

37. Lawrence, Ryan E., and Farr A. Curlin. "Physicians' Beliefs About Conscience in Medicine: A National Survey." *Academic Medicine* 84 (2009): 1276–82. [CrossRef] [PubMed]
38. Lawrence, Ryan E., and Farr A. Curlin. "Autonomy, Religion and Clinical Decisions: Findings from a National Physician Survey." *Journal of Medical Ethics* 35 (2009): 214–18. [CrossRef] [PubMed]
39. Lawrence, Ryan E., Kenneth A. Rasinski, John D. Yoon, and Farr A. Curlin. "Obstetrician-Gynecologist Physicians' Beliefs About Emergency Contraception: A National Survey." *Contraception* 82 (2010): 324–30. [CrossRef] [PubMed]
40. Lawrence, Ryan E., Kenneth A. Rasinski, John D. Yoon, and Farr A. Curlin. "Obstetrician-Gynecologists' Beliefs About Assisted Reproductive Technologies." *Obstetrics & Gynecology* 116 (2010): 127–35. [CrossRef] [PubMed]
41. Stulberg, Debra B., Ryan E. Lawrence, Jason Shattuck, and Farr A. Curlin. "Religious Hospitals and Primary Care Physicians: Conflicts over Policies for Patient Care." *Journal of General Internal Medicine* 25 (2010): 725–30. [CrossRef] [PubMed]
42. Yoon, John D., Kenneth A. Rasinski, and Farr A. Curlin. "Conflict and Emotional Exhaustion in Obstetrician-Gynaecologists: A National Survey." *Journal of Medical Ethics* 36 (2010): 731–35. [CrossRef] [PubMed]
43. Yoon, John D., Kenneth A. Rasinski, and Farr A. Curlin. "Moral Controversy, Directive Counsel, and the Doctor's Role: Findings from a National Survey of Obstetrician-Gynecologists." *Academic Medicine* 85 (2010): 1475–81. [CrossRef] [PubMed]
44. Lawrence, Ryan E., Kenneth A. Rasinski, John D. Yoon, and Farr A. Curlin. "Adolescents, Contraception and Confidentiality: A National Survey of Obstetrician-Gynecologists." *Contraception* 84 (2011): 259–65. [CrossRef] [PubMed]
45. Lawrence, Ryan E., Kenneth A. Rasinski, John D. Yoon, and Farr A. Curlin. "Obstetrician-Gynecologists' Beliefs About Safe-Sex and Abstinence Counseling." *International Journal of Gynecology & Obstetrics* 114 (2011): 281–85. [CrossRef] [PubMed]
46. Lawrence, Ryan E., Kenneth A. Rasinski, John D. Yoon, and Farr A. Curlin. "Obstetrician-Gynecologists' Views on Contraception and Natural Family Planning: A National Survey." *American Journal of Obstetrics and Gynecology* 204 (2011): 124.e1–e7. [CrossRef] [PubMed]
47. Lawrence, R. E., K. A. Rasinski, J. D. Yoon, and F. A. Curlin. "Factors Influencing Physicians' Advice About Female Sterilization in USA: A National Survey." *Human Reproduction* 26 (2011): 106–11. [CrossRef] [PubMed]
48. Rasinski, Kenneth A., Youssef G. Kalad, John D. Yoon, and Farr A. Curlin. "An Assessment of Us Physicians' Training in Religion, Spirituality, and Medicine." *Medical Teacher* 33 (2011): 944–45. [CrossRef] [PubMed]
49. Rasinski, Kenneth A., John D. Yoon, Youssef G. Kalad, and Farr A. Curlin. "Obstetrician-Gynaecologists' Opinions About Conscientious Refusal of a Request for Abortion: Results from a National Vignette Experiment." *Journal of Medical Ethics* 37 (2011): 711–14. [CrossRef] [PubMed]
50. Stulberg, Debra B., Annie M. Dude, Irma Dahlquist, and Farr A. Curlin. "Abortion Provision among Practicing Obstetrician-Gynecologists." *Obstetrics & Gynecology* 118 (2011): 609–14. [CrossRef] [PubMed]
51. Lawrence, Ryan E., Kenneth A. Rasinski, John D. Yoon, Harold G. Koenig, Keith G. Meador, and Farr A. Curlin. "Physicians' Beliefs About Faith-Based Treatments for Alcoholism." *Psychiatric Services* 63 (2012): 597–604. [CrossRef] [PubMed]
52. Lawrence, R. E., K. A. Rasinski, J. D. Yoon, K. G. Meador, H. G. Koenig, and F. A. Curlin. "Primary Care Physicians' and Psychiatrists' Approaches to Treating Mild Depression." *Acta Psychiatrica Scandinavica* 126 (2012): 385–92. [CrossRef] [PubMed]
53. Rasinski, Kenneth A., Ryan E. Lawrence, John D. Yoon, and Farr A. Curlin. "A Sense of Calling and Primary Care Physicians' Satisfaction in Treating Smoking, Alcoholism, and Obesity." *Archives of Internal Medicine* 172 (2012): 1423–24. [CrossRef] [PubMed]
54. Stulberg, Debra B., Annie M. Dude, Irma Dahlquist, and Farr A. Curlin. "Obstetrician-Gynecologists, Religious Institutions, and Conflicts Regarding Patient-Care Policies." *American Journal of Obstetrics & Gynecology* 207 (2012): 73e1–e5. [CrossRef] [PubMed]
55. Lawrence, Ryan E., Kenneth A. Rasinski, John D. Yoon, and Farr A. Curlin. "Religion and Anxiety Treatments in Primary Care Patients." *Anxiety Stress Coping* 26 (2013): 526–38. [CrossRef] [PubMed]

56. Lawrence, Ryan E., Kenneth A. Rasinski, John D. Yoon, and Farr A. Curlin. "Religion and Beliefs About Treating Medically Unexplained Symptoms: A Survey of Primary Care Physicians and Psychiatrists." *The International Journal of Psychiatry in Medicine* 45 (2013): 31–44. [CrossRef] [PubMed]

57. Lawrence, Ryan E., Kenneth A. Rasinski, John D. Yoon, and Farr A. Curlin. "Physicians' Beliefs About the Nature of Addiction: A Survey of Primary Care Physicians and Psychiatrists." *The American Journal on Addictions* 22 (2013): 255–60. [CrossRef] [PubMed]

58. Putman, M. S., and F. A. Curlin. "Authors' Reply to Dirksen et al." *Journal of Pain and Symptom Management* 45 (2013): e2–e3. [CrossRef] [PubMed]

59. Putman, Michael S., John D. Yoon, Kenneth A. Rasinski, and Farr A. Curlin. "Intentional Sedation to Unconsciousness at the End of Life: Findings from a National Physician Survey." *Journal of Pain and Symptom Management* 46 (2013): 326–34. [CrossRef] [PubMed]

60. Wolenberg, Kelly M., John D. Yoon, Kenneth A. Rasinski, and Farr A. Curlin. "Religion and United States Physicians' Opinions and Self-Predicted Practices Concerning Artificial Nutrition and Hydration." *Journal of Religion and Health* 52 (2013): 1051–65. [CrossRef] [PubMed]

61. Lawrence, Ryan E., Kenneth A. Rasinski, John D. Yoon, and Farr A. Curlin. "Physician Race and Treatment Preferences for Depression, Anxiety, and Medically Unexplained Symptoms." *Ethnicity & Health* 20 (2015): 354–64. [CrossRef] [PubMed]

62. Lawrence, Ryan E., Kenneth A. Rasinski, John D. Yoon, and Farr A. Curlin. "Primary Care Physicians' and Psychiatrists' Willingness to Refer to Religious Mental Health Providers." *International Journal of Social Psychiatry* 60 (2014): 627–36. [CrossRef] [PubMed]

63. Putman, Michael S., John D. Yoon, Kenneth A. Rasinski, and Farr A. Curlin. "Directive Counsel and Morally Controversial Medical Decision-Making: Findings from Two National Surveys of Primary Care Physicians." *Journal of General Internal Medicine* 29 (2014): 335–40. [CrossRef] [PubMed]

64. Lawrence, Ryan E., Kenneth A. Rasinski, John D. Yoon, and Farr A. Curlin. "Psychiatrists' and Primary Care Physicians' Beliefs About Overtreatment of Depression and Anxiety." *The Journal of Nervous and Mental Disease* 203 (2015): 120–25. [CrossRef] [PubMed]

65. Ravella, Krishna C., Farr A. Curlin, and John D. Yoon. "Medical School Ranking and Medical Student Vocational Identity." *Teaching and Learning in Medicine* 27 (2015): 123–29. [CrossRef] [PubMed]

66. Yoon, John D., Jiwon H. Shin, Andy L. Nian, and Farr A. Curlin. "Religion, Sense of Calling, and the Practice of Medicine: Findings from a National Survey of Primary Care Physicians and Psychiatrists." *Southern Medical Journal* 108 (2015): 189–95. [CrossRef] [PubMed]

67. Baumann, Klaus, Arndt Büssing, and Niels Chrsitian Hvidt. "Geisteswissenschaftliches Kolloquium Klaus Baumann (Freiburg)/Arndt Büssing (Witten/Herdecke)/Niels Hvidt (Odense): Empirische Forschung Über Religiöse Und Spirituelle Aspekte Bei Patientinnen Und Ärztinnen." *Freiburg Institute for Advanced Studies.* Available online: https://www.frias.uni-freiburg.de/en/events/humanities-and-social-sciences-colloquium/ geisteswissenschaftliches-kolloquium-klaus-baumann-freiburg-arndt-bussing-witten-herdecke-niels-hvidt- odense-empirische-forschung-uber-religiose-und-spirituelle-aspekte-bei-patientinnen-und-arztinnen (accessed on 6 April 2016).

68. Büssing, Arndt, Klaus Baumann, Niels Christian Hvidt, Harold G. Koenig, Christina M. Puchalski, and John Swinton. "Spirituality and Health. Editorial." *Evidence-Based Complementary and Alternative Medicine* 2014 (2014): article 682817. [CrossRef] [PubMed]

69. Büssing, A., A. T. Hirdes, K. Baumann, Niels Christian Hvidt, and P. Heusser. "Aspects of Spirituality in Medical Doctors and Their Relation to Specific Views of Illness and Dealing with Their Patients' Individual Situation." *Evidence-Based Complementary and Alternative Medicine* 2013 (2013): article 734392. [CrossRef] [PubMed]

70. Voltmer, Edgar, Arndt Büssing, HaroldG Koenig, and Faten Al Zaben. "Religiosity/Spirituality of German Doctors in Private Practice and Likelihood of Addressing R/S Issues with Patients." *Journal of Religion and Health* 53 (2013): 1741–52. [CrossRef] [PubMed]

71. Delbecq, Andre L., Andrew H. Van de Ven, and David H. Gustafson. *Group Techniques for Program Planning: A Guide to Nominal Group and Delphi Processes.* Glenview: Scott Foresman, 1975.

72. Jones, Jeremy, and Duncan Hunter. "Consensus Methods for Medical and Health Services Research." *British Medical Journal* 311 (1995): 376–80. [CrossRef] [PubMed]

73. Büssing, Arndt, Thomas Ostermann, and Peter F. Matthiessen. "Distinct Expressions of Vital Spirituality 'the Asp Questionnaire as an Explorative Research Tool'." *Journal of Religion and Health* 46 (2007): 267–86. [CrossRef]
74. Büssing, A, D. R. Recchia, J. Surzykiewicz, and K. Baumann. "Ausdrucksformen Der Spiritualität Bei Schülern Und Jungen Erwachsenen." *Spiritual Care*, forthcoming.
75. Bussing, Arndt, Thomas Ostermann, and Peter Matthiessen. "Role of Religion and Spirituality in Medical Patients: Confirmatory Results with the Spreuk Questionnaire." *Health and Quality of Life Outcomes* 3 (2005): 10. [CrossRef] [PubMed]
76. Büssing, Arndt. "Spirituality as a Resource to Rely on in Chronic Illness: The Spreuk Questionnaire." *Religions* 1 (2010): 9–17. [CrossRef]

MDPI

St. Alban-Anlage 66

4052 Basel

Switzerland

Tel. +41 61 683 77 34

Fax +41 61 302 89 18

www.mdpi.com

Religions Editorial Office

E-mail: religions@mdpi.com

www.mdpi.com/journal/religions

www.ingramcontent.com/pod-product-compliance
Lightning Source LLC
Chambersburg PA
CBHW041141120626
46547CB00020B/3069